Number System to Follow Mass

I. Before Mass Begins, read Explanation of the Sunday's Mass on page as listed on Calendar below.

II. When Mass Begins, turn to ❶ on page 35. Then read until directed to ❷ in the "Proper" of today's Mass. Then turn back to ❸ in the "Ordinary" and so on through ⑰

MASS CALENDAR

INDICATES PAGE for "PROPER" of TODAY'S MASS

1951	
Sep.	*Page*
2	273
9	277
16	280
23	284
30	288
Oct.	*Page*
7	292
14	296
21	300
28	317
Nov.	*Page*
1	321
2	325
4	112
11	115
18	119
25	304

1951	
Dec.	*Page*
2	67
8	309
9	71
16	75
23	78
25	81
30	85
1952	
Jan.	*Page*
1	89
2	92
6	96
13	100
20	104
27	108
Feb.	*Page*
3	112
10	123

1952	
Feb.	*Page*
17	127
24	132
Mar.	*Page*
2	136
9	141
16	145
23	150
30	155
Apr.	*Page*
6	159
13	174
20	178
27	182
May	*Page*
4	185
11	189
18	193
22	197

1952	
May	*Page*
25	201
June	*Page*
1	205
8	210
15	215
22	220
29	225
July	*Page*
6	229
13	233
20	237
27	241
Aug.	*Page*
3	245
10	249
15	313
17	253
24	257

1952	
Aug.	*Page*
31	261
Sep.	*Page*
7	265
14	269
21	273
28	277
Oct.	*Page*
5	280
12	284
19	288
26	317
Nov.	*Page*
1	321
2	296
3	325
9	300
16	119
23	304
30	67

1952	
Dec.	*Page*
7	71
8	309
14	75
21	78
25	81
28	85
1953	
Jan.	*Page*
1	89
4	92
6	96
11	100
18	104
25	108

Continued Next Page →

For Weekday Mass see page 325 ("Mass for the Dead") or use Mass of preceding Sunday.

MADE IN U. S. A.

MASS CALENDAR

(Continued from Page 1)

INDICATES PAGE for "PROPER" of TODAY'S MASS

1953	
Feb.	*Page*
1	123
8	127
15	132
22	136
Mar.	*Page*
1	141
8	145
15	150
22	155
29	159
Apr.	*Page*
5	174
12	178
19	182
26	185
May	*Page*
3	189
10	193
14	197
17	201
24	205
31	210
June	*Page*
7	215
14	220
21	225
28	229
July	*Page*
5	233
12	237
19	241
26	245
Aug.	*Page*
2	249
9	253
15	313
16	257
23	261
30	265
Sep.	*Page*
6	269
13	273

1953	
Sep.	*Page*
20	277
27	280
Oct.	*Page*
4	284
11	288
18	292
25	317
Nov.	*Page*
1	321
2	325
8	115
15	119
22	304
29	67
Dec.	*Page*
6	71
8	309
13	75
20	78
25	81
27	85
1954	
Jan.	*Page*
1	89
3	92
6	96
10	100
17	104
24	108
31	112
Feb.	*Page*
7	115
14	123
21	127
28	132
Mar.	*Page*
7	136
14	141
21	145
28	150

1954	
Apr.	*Page*
4	155
11	159
18	174
25	178
May	*Page*
2	182
9	185
16	189
23	193
27	197
30	201
June	*Page*
6	205
13	210
20	215
27	220
July	*Page*
4	225
11	229
18	233
25	237
Aug.	*Page*
1	241
8	245
15	313
22	253
29	257
Sep.	*Page*
5	261
12	265
19	269
26	273
Oct.	*Page*
3	277
10	280
17	284
24	288
31	317
Nov.	*Page*
1	321
2	325
7	296

1954	
Nov.	*Page*
14	300
21	304
28	67
Dec.	*Page*
5	71
8	309
12	75
19	78
25	81
26	85
1955	
Jan.	*Page*
1	89
2	92
6	96
9	100
16	104
23	108
30	112
Feb.	*Page*
6	123
13	127
20	132
27	136
Mar.	*Page*
6	141
13	145
20	150
27	155
Apr.	*Page*
3	159
10	174
17	178
24	182
May	*Page*
1	185
8	189
15	193
19	197
22	201

1955	
May	*Page*
29	205
June	*Page*
5	210
12	215
19	220
26	225
July	*Page*
3	229
10	233
17	237
24	241
31	245
Aug.	*Page*
7	249
14	253
15	313
21	257
28	261
Sep.	*Page*
4	265
11	269
18	273
25	277
Oct.	*Page*
2	280
9	284
16	288
23	292
30	317
Nov.	*Page*
1	321
2	325
6	300
13	119
20	304
27	67
Dec.	*Page*
4	71
8	309
11	75
18	78
25	81

1956	
Jan.	*Page*
1	89
6	96
8	100
15	104
22	108
29	123
Feb.	*Page*
5	127
12	132
19	136
26	141
Mar.	*Page*
4	145
11	150
18	155
25	159
Apr.	*Page*
1	174
8	178
15	182
22	185
29	189
May	*Page*
6	193
10	197
13	201
20	205
27	210
June	*Page*
3	215
10	220
17	225
24	229
July	*Page*
1	233
8	237
15	241
22	245
29	249

MASS CALENDAR

(Continued from Previous Page)

INDICATES PAGE for "PROPER" of TODAY'S MASS

1956

Aug.	Page
5	253
12	257
15	313
19	261
26	265

Sep.	Page
2	269
9	273
16	277
23	280
30	284

Oct.	Page
7	288
14	292
21	296
28	317

Nov.	Page
1	321
2	325
4	112
11	115
18	119
25	304

Dec.	Page
2	67
8	309
9	71
16	75
23	78
25	81
30	85

1957

Jan.	Page
1	89
6	96
13	100
20	104
27	108

1957

Feb.	Page
3	112
10	115
17	123
24	127

Mar.	Page
3	132
10	136
17	141
24	145
31	150

Apr.	Page
7	155
14	159
21	174
28	178

May	Page
5	182
12	185
19	189
26	193
30	197

June	Page
2	201
9	205
16	210
23	215
30	220

July	Page
7	225
14	229
21	233
28	237

Aug.	Page
4	241
11	245
15	313
18	249
25	253

Sep.	Page
1	257

1957

Sep.	Page
8	261
15	265
22	269
29	273

Oct.	Page
6	277
13	280
20	284
27	317

Nov.	Page
1	321
2	325
3	292
10	296
17	300
24	304

Dec.	Page
1	67
8	309
15	75
22	78
25	81
29	85

1958

Jan.	Page
1	89
5	92
6	96
12	100
19	104
26	108

Feb.	Page
2	123
9	127
16	132
23	136

Mar.	Page
2	141
9	145

1958

Mar.	Page
16	150
23	155
30	159

Apr.	Page
6	174
13	178
20	182
27	185

May	Page
4	189
11	193
15	197
18	201
25	205

June	Page
1	210
8	215
15	220
22	225
29	229

July	Page
6	233
13	237
20	241
27	245

Aug.	Page
3	249
10	253
15	313
17	257
24	261
31	265

Sep.	Page
7	269
14	273
21	277
28	280

Oct.	Page
5	284
12	288

1958

Oct.	Page
19	292
26	317

Nov.	Page
1	321
2	300
3	325
9	115
16	119
23	304
30	67

Dec.	Page
7	71
8	309
14	75
21	78
25	81
28	85

1959

Jan.	Page
1	89
4	92
6	96
11	100
18	104
25	123

Feb.	Page
1	127
8	132
15	136
22	141

Mar.	Page
1	145
8	150
15	155
22	159
29	174

Apr.	Page
5	178
12	182
19	185

1959

Apr.	Page
26	189

May	Page
3	193
7	197
10	201
17	205
24	210
31	215

June	Page
7	220
14	225
21	229
28	233

July	Page
5	237
12	241
19	245
26	249

Aug.	Page
2	253
9	257
15	313
16	261
23	265
30	269

Sep.	Page
6	273
13	277
20	280
27	284

Oct.	Page
4	288
11	292
18	296
25	317

Nov.	Page
1	321
2	325
8	115

MASS CALENDAR CONTINUED PAGE 352

OUR LIFE and OUR MASS

This diagram reveals the Mass as our guide for daily life in our search for Truth and Love. At Mass, Divine Truth enlightens our intellect; Divine Love unites our wills to God and neighbor. Thus, the Mass is also the forerunner of future life in Heaven with its eternal Vision of Divine Truth and its eternal Union with Divine Love.

MY SUNDAY MISSAL

USING NEW TRANSLATION
FROM NEW TESTAMENT

And a

SIMPLIFIED METHOD
OF FOLLOWING MASS

With an

EXPLANATION
BEFORE EACH
MASS OF ITS
THEME

LATIN-ENGLISH EDITION
ALSO DIALOGUE MASS

Page 34

Rt. Rev. Msgr. Joseph F. Stedman
Director of the
CONFRATERNITY of the PRECIOUS BLOOD
5300 Ft. Hamilton Parkway, Brooklyn, N. Y.

« Now there stood by the Cross of Jesus,

MARY, HIS MOTHER »

WHO, BY HER PERFECT ASSISTANCE AT

HIS FIRST MASS

ON CALVARY

BECAME OUR MODEL . . . TO WHOM

WE NOW OFFER THE PRAYER THAT SHE

MAY HELP US TO STAND MORE

WORTHILY BY THE

"CROSS OF JESUS" . . . OUR SUNDAY MASS

WHEN USING

"MY SUNDAY MISSAL."

Nihil obstat. James H. Griffiths, S.T.D., Censor Librorum
Imprimatur. ✠ Thomas E. Molloy, S.T.D., Bishop of Brooklyn
January 6, 1938

Scriptural Quotations from Revised Text of New Testament as copyrighted 1941 by Confraternity of Christian Doctrine

Contents

CALENDAR for locating today's Mass... Page 1

Using the Missal: the Mass, its requisites and Vestments. Mass Year with Christ.. 9 to 33

DIALOGUE MASS (Explained) 34

ORDINARY of the Mass (same each Sunday) (LATIN pages 35 to 65)...... 35 to 66

PROPER of the Mass (different each Sunday) .... 67 to 328

Masses of Christmas Season

Preparation in Advent .... 67 to 80

Celebration—Christmas to Epiphany... 81 to 99

Continuation—Sundays after Epiphany. 100 to 122

Masses of Easter Season

Preparation before and in Lent...... 123 to 173

Celebration—Easter 174

Continuation—Sundays after Easter .. 178 to 196

Masses of Pentecost Season

Preparation—Ascension to Pentecost .. 197 to 204

Celebration—Pentecost 205

Continuation—Sundays after Pentecost. 210 to 308

Other Masses for Holydays .... 309 to 324

† **Mass for the Dead** † 325

CATECHISM Brief review at end of each Mass.

PRAYERS selected from J. M. J. Manual.

Prayers to be memorized 329

Daily Prayers 330-334

Confession 337

Communion (Before or After Mass).. 340-342

Miscellaneous 343-352

USE THE MISSAL AS THE PRIEST DOES.

NINE FEATURES of "MY SUNDAY MISSAL"

1. AUTHORIZED NEW TRANSLATION

Of "My Sunday Missal", now using the New Translation of the New Testament with accurate, dignified, present-day idiomatic English, Bishop O'Hara, Chairman of the Episcopal Committee, writes as follows:

"Father Stedman's Sunday Missal is bringing to the millions a *fuller understanding* of their privilege, responsibility and consequent dignity in their participation at Holy Mass. It is rendering *magnificent service* in the cause of Christ. I am happy that the Confraternity of Christian Doctrine by its revision of the New Testament (*used in this Missal*) may claim a small part in opening the doors of the Christ-life to those who use My Sunday Missal."

✠ Edwin V. O'Hara
Bishop of Kansas City

II. NUMBER SYSTEM to FOLLOW MASS

WHILE instructing Week-End Retreatants in the use of what they termed *"complicated Missals"*, we marked them with *"guide numbers"* from ❶ to ⓱, such as now followed in "MY SUNDAY MISSAL". This Number System is *self-instructing*. It enables the user to turn from the "Proper" to the "Ordinary" and back again in correct sequence.

III. The MASS CALENDAR

BEFORE Mass, on Pages 1, 2, 3 and 352, *at a quick glance*, you will note the dates of all Sundays and Holydays for many years to come. For instance, look at December 8; it indicates page 309, Feast of the Immaculate Conception. This "Ordo" *saves valuable time;* it is not necessary to wait for the priest's announcement later on in the Mass, as to which Sunday it is.

IV. EXPLANATION of the "PROPER"

IT TAKES only a minute or so to read! Yet by it, you appreciate the *special message* of each Mass, with its ever changing, ever continuous story of Christ's Life and teachings. Does your Sunday Mass go by, year after year, leaving you much the same as before, *indifferent, irresponsive?* What is the reason? We fail to recognize or assimilate the special theme of each Mass. BEFORE MASS READ THIS EXPLANATION.

I also recommend arranging your time at home before Mass; or arriving at Church early enough to read the

EXPLANATION together with the "Proper" parts, namely numbers ②, ④, ⑤, ⑥, ⑧, ⑩, ⑫, ⑭, ⑯. This would be ideal.

V. ORDINARY in LATIN-ENGLISH WITH LITURGICAL EXPLANATIONS

THE "Ordinary" of the Mass (pages 35 to 65) is only *too often taken for granted.* Each prayer is full of Divine Beauty and Power; its revelation of Divine Truth for the human mind; its revelation of Divine Goodness for the human heart. *Each prayer is a sure guide* in offering Jesus and ourselves to the Eternal Father. Therefore, at the bottom of each page in the Ordinary, *each prayer* is briefly explained in the form of a *liturgical footnote,* to be read as a review two or three times each year.

VI. BRIEF REVIEW of the CATECHISM

THIS may be found at the end of each Mass ⑱. Our knowledge of God *fades,* little by little, *unless reviewed frequently.* This Sunday use of the Missal and review of the Catechism becomes our *everyday guide* of "what to pray and what to believe". Religious educators and experienced lay people welcome this feature as a most timely and necessary safeguard against collapse in adult Christian life.

VII. "DIALOGUE" or "COMMUNITY" MASS

(*page 34 for further details*)

"MY SUNDAY MISSAL" is now arranged for the "DIALOGUE" or "COMMUNITY" MASS; sometimes called "DIALOGUE" because the officiating priest does not recite the Mass alone in a "monologue" but the congregation recites aloud the server's responses and other parts of the Mass, uniting with the priest in a "DIALOGUE"; also called "COMMUNITY" MASS because the people also pray aloud, publicly and in common, together with the priest. Such a "COMMUNITY" MASS is the most practical means we have at hand for making the power and life of the Mass a vital force in private life. Moreover by publicly praying aloud and co-offering the Mass, in union with the priest, this unity of Social worship is the basis and guarantee of unity in Social Action.

VIII. ORDINARY of the MASS NEW STANDARD TRANSLATION

WE HAVE the honor herein of introducing a new arrangement of the "Ordinary," the Uniform Text of this Editorial Board: Rev. Gerald Ellard, S.J., Rev. Richard E. Powers, Rev. Godfrey Diekmann, O.S.B., Rev. Paul Bussard, and other scriptural and liturgical scholars. This new translation of the "Ordinary," now being widely accepted as a standard text, is a timely, necessary and useful complement to the revised Translation of the New Testament used in the Proper.

IX. PICTURES at BEGINNING of EACH MASS

AN ORIGINAL SERIES of Mass Theme illustrations! Executed in a lively two-color scheme, these reverent portrayals by Miss Nina Barr Wheeler are ideally suited for liturgical meditation before Holy Mass.

VEST-POCKET MISSAL

"MY SUNDAY MISSAL" has been arranged for the Sundays and Holydays of Obligation. This marks the first appearance of such a Missal in a size fitted to vest-pocket or pocketbook. We may be reluctant to agree with the modern dislike of large prayerbooks and Missals: but investigation amongst actual and prospective users indicates a decided preference for a book of smaller size, yet of readable type. Hence, *after taking authoritative counsel, we believed it more prudent to use only the essentials.* Otherwise the average person feels the Missal is too bulky to carry. With too many references, it becomes too intricate to use. The most general complaint is inability to keep up with the priest at Mass. This is partly due to the Latin text being shorter than the English, and partly because the priest can read the Mass Prayers with greater ease, since he is more familiar with the Missal. Discouraged, the user then abandons its use. *Hence at times you may omit certain prayers to keep up with the priest.* Nevertheless, only a few references have been omitted, as in the "Manual of Prayers," prepared in 1889 by order of the Third Plenary Council of Baltimore.

For ALL CHILDREN and ADULTS

"MY SUNDAY MISSAL" is intended for every Catholic. Its Number System adapts it for use even by those in the upper grades of elementary school. I recall one very active Catholic mentioning how *he regretted not to have grown up with the Missal;* how, on the other hand, he was happy to witness its ever increasing use amongst students, due to the liturgical teachings of recent Popes and the low costs of modern printing. The "Explanation of each Mass Theme" in "My Sunday Missal" is a two-minute outline (to be read before Mass) of the particular story contained in the "Proper" of this particular Mass. This makes the reading of these Scriptural references and prayers both interesting and understandable even to children, and yet we believe it is profound enough for the most erudite.

A BOOK for LIFE

The Missal is a book for life use. Its unchanging character makes for stability. Yet its rich variety can never be exhausted. It is the result of thousands of years of Divine revelation and human thought guided by the Holy Spirit.

For CONVERTS

For prospective or actual converts it is both ideal and practical. Formerly a prejudice existed that the Missal was suitable only to the well-trained Catholic. In these days of widespread Missal popularity, we have been brought to realize that it is both a form of prayer and *a method of instruction.* One of New York's frequently mentioned doctors became a Catholic through a layman's explanation of the Missal. The convert then realized that its *doctrinal teaching* is most complete; that it was selected not for mere intellectual study but for personal participation in the Drama of the Mass.

MISSAL is OFFICIAL

Certainly no other book of any individual author, however learned or saintly, can compare with the official book and method of the Church itself. *No one could offer, or even claim to offer,* a method of assisting at Mass better than the Missal, as arranged by Mother Church. Its contents are of genuine piety and solid doctrine taken from Scripture, Tradition and the Living Church.

At MASS USE the MISSAL ONLY

THE MASS, according to the saintly Pope Pius X, is the "PRIMARY and INDISPENSABLE source of the true Christian spirit, and the faithful will be filled with this spirit only in proportion as they participate in the Sacred Mysteries." Notice the words *"primary"* and *"indispensable."* All other exercises, private or public, are secondary. All honor to devotions such as the Rosary and other devotional prayers, but let them be recited at their proper time, *not during Mass.*

DAILY MASS? USE ANOTHER BOOK

TO "My Daily Reading from the New Testament" (640 pages) has been added the "Ordinary of the Mass." For those who find a Daily Missal too bulky, heavy or complicated, this new book (pocket size) can be used as a Daily Mass Book, with a different Epistle and Gospel for each day. The user can thus cover the entire life and teachings of Jesus from the New Testament twice in each year.

How to "PARTICIPATE ACTIVELY"

YOU "WILL BE FILLED with this spirit only in proportion" as you "actively participate" in the Mass, says Pope Pius X. How do you actively participate? As a lay person you actively participate: first, by *offering the Divine Victim* to the Eternal Father in union with the priest, your official representative; second, by *offering yourself* to the Eternal Father in union with the Divine Victim. To be a co-offerer with the priest, you must have a sacrificial will,so as to make this twofold oblation of Christ and yourself. Your most practical guide, "how to participate," is to recite the same prayers from the Missal as the priest.

You SHARE in the PRIESTHOOD

ALL DURING the Mass the Missal reminds you that you share in the Priesthood of Christ. You too, though a *lay person,* are a *"lay priest,"* to quote many of our liturgical theologians. "You are a royal priesthood," wrote St. Peter to the first Christian converts, both men and women. You have this sublime privilege by the grace of Baptism. You have not, indeed, the power of the ordained priest to change bread and wine into the Body and Blood of Christ, but you can offer the Holy Sacrifice in union with the priest at the altar. This, then, is the meaning of the plea of the priest at the altar when he turns to the faithful in the pews and says aloud, *"Pray, brethren, that my sacrifice and yours,* etc." Too long have people forgotten that they are not merely to assist at Mass but actually to participate in it; *not merely to hear* Mass but to *take a personal part* in it; that the Missal is not the private prayer of the priest at the altar, but the collective prayer of all present both in the pews as well as at the altar.

PREPARING to "RECEIVE"

SOME otherwise well-instructed people make the mistake of not using the Missal during a part or perhaps all of the Mass when they receive Holy Communion. They occupy their time by making acts of faith, hope, love, humility, contrition and desire, etc. They *ignore the Missal* prayers of the Sacrifice and *substitute* "private" or "devotional" prayers to prepare them for the Sacrament. Such a custom is unfortunate. It lays too much stress on the word "*receive*" and not enough on the word "*give.*" The use of the Missal is the best way to prepare. It features the gift that you are permitted to give unto the Eternal Father in the Divine Sacrifice, the gift of His own Son and of yourself, rather than the gift that you expect Him to give unto you. Remember, too, that all the above "Acts" of devotion are contained in the Missal. They may not be called "acts" of this or that virtue, but every sentiment necessary to receive worthily is found in your Sunday Mass.

THE MASS is like an *act of contrition* from the prayers at the foot of the altar to the "Lord, have mercy on us"; an *act of faith* from the Prayer to the Creed; an *act of hope* and *surrender* from the Offertory, through the Canon to the "Our Father," that our human offering will be acceptable for our salvation because it will be consecrated; an *act of petition* from the "Our Father" to the "Lamb of God," etc.; an *act of love* before and at Communion time; an *act of gratitude* and a plea for perseverance from the "Communion Verse" to the end of Mass. Your favorite "Before Communion" or "After Communion" prayers not found in the Mass itself should be recited before or after Mass.

Grateful acknowledgments are hereby rendered to the authors of the following recommended books:

THE SACRAMENTARY (5 Volumes), His Eminence Ildefonso Cardinal Schuster, O.S.B.; THE LITURGICAL YEAR (6 Volumes), Dom Prosper Gueranger, O.S.B.; CHRISTIAN LIFE AND WORSHIP, Rev. Gerald Ellard, S.J.; LITURGY OF THE ROMAN MISSAL, Dom Leduc, O.S.B.; MEANING OF THE MASS, Rev. John Kearney, C.S. SP.; EUCHARISTIA, Rev. Joseph Kramp, S.J.; LIFE OF THE SOUL IN THE LITURGY, Rev. Antoine De Serent, S.J.; IN MEMORY OF ME, Rev. John Forester, S.J.; THE HOLY SACRIFICE OF THE MASS, Rev. Nicholas Gihr, D.D.; CHRIST, LIFE OF THE SOUL; also CHRIST IN HIS MYSTERIES, Abbot Marmion, O.S.B.; also all the excellent brochures published by the Liturgical Press, Collegeville, Minnesota, viz.: SPIRIT OF THE LITURGY, Abbot Caronti, O.S.B.; LITURGY, THE LIFE OF THE CHURCH, Dom Beauduin, O.S.B.; MY SACRIFICE AND YOURS, Dom Virgil Michel, O.S.B.; IF I BE LIFTED UP, Rev. Paul Bussard; THE MASS DRAMA, Rev. William Busch.

I PRAY AND TRUST that you will always refer to this book as "My Sunday Missal." It is yours! May you always call it "My." By its various features, it will make your Sunday Mass acceptable to God, profitable for you in graces merited by the Precious Blood. Your Mass Hour will reveal God more and more; it will be a truly delightful spiritual experience. Your name has been written in this "book of life" in letters of indelible red by "the Lamb" of God, "ever living to make intercession for you."

(Rt. Rev. Msgr.) *JOSEPH F. STEDMAN*

Feast of Our Lady's Assumption, 1937.

AFTER ALL, WHAT is the MASS?

YOUR SUNDAY MASS is the climax on earth, of God's search for you and your search for God, beginning with interior prayer and leading to exterior sacrifice. Our personal prayers and sacrifices *are incomplete without* Jesus; hence the absolute necessity of your Sunday Mass.

PRAYER is NECESSARY

ONLY THE FOOL ignores God. Wisdom recognizes God, worships His infinite excellence and acknowledges our absolute dependence on Him, and all this is Prayer. To ADORE God is the first Commandment, since as Creator and Preserver of all things, He is supreme. To THANK God for all the gifts of nature that you have received as His creatures; for all the gifts of grace that you have received as His children. To IMPLORE PARDON from God, because sin is the evil responsible for all temporal and eternal punishment. To PETITION God for His graces and blessings, because not to ask is either to ignore or reject them.

SACRIFICE is NECESSARY

MOREOVER, MAN has always *expressed* his interior prayer by exterior acts. He selected victims from his possessions, living animals or the fruits of the earth and offered them in sacrifice to God. He has ever recognized that it would be a *perversion* of his dependence on God if he used created things for his own self-interest without recognizing whence they came and why they were given. The offering of a

victim to God symbolized man's offering of himself and showed his *reverence* for the rights of God, his *dependence* on the bounty of God and his desire to enter into *communion* with God.

OUR SACRIFICE INSUFFICIENT without JESUS

BECAUSE OF man's original and actual sin, both his prayer and sacrifice are unable to satisfy God or himself. Hence Jesus as Head of the human race offered the sacrifice of His own Life that the "world might know" of a Sacrifice *acceptable to the Father* and *one that fully atones for our sins.* From the crib to the cross His Life was a testimony that God is supreme, that man is dependent. His sacrifice was necessary before His Father that Divine Justice might be satisfied. It was necessary for us that we might be cleansed of sin and reconciled with our Heavenly Father. It restored the balance between God and man since sin is a double evil, a turning from God by refusing obedience to the Creator, a turning to a creature by preferring it to God Himself. His sacrifice by obedience was *more pleasing* to His Father than man's disobedience was displeasing.

THE MASS as a MEMORIAL

THE MASS is a living "Memorial," a perpetual memorial "bringing to mind" how I must approach the altar with reverence and awe, since it is Calvary itself. The words and actions of the Mass, interwoven with the Sign of the Cross, make it *impossible not to think of*

Calvary. The Host lying on the altar separated from the chalice reminds us of His white bloodless Body and the red *Blood shed* from It. His lowly state of subjection on the altar reminds us of the Agony of His Body scourged and crucified, warning us to hate sin and its occasions and to accept our crosses in reparation for sin. Again, the Savior of Mercy, entirely at the mercy of every soul that receives Him, reminds us of the anguish of His "soul sorrowful unto death." Finally, the Sunday Mass is a weekly *memorial* of what made His Sacrifice possible, namely LOVE. Love actually caused His Heart to break physically. He *loved us at the cost of His pain and death.* To love a person is to wish and to do him well and to make him happy, not in short-lived things to satisfy the five senses, but in eternal gifts to satisfy the immortal soul.

The MASS a REAL SACRIFICE

THE MASS is a real sacrifice, made by Jesus, as *real and actual* as the sacrifice of His Life unto death on Calvary. How? Why? Both on Calvary in His suffering Body, and on the altar in His Sacramental Body, *Jesus is ever offering, ever offered* as Priest and Victim before His Eternal Father. On Calvary Jesus suffered a physical death when His Blood was drained from His Body. In the Mass there are two separate consecrations; one for His Body, the other for His Blood. These words of consecration are like a sword, which *of themselves* would actually separate His Blood from His Body. However, in point of fact Jesus is entirely present, Body and Blood, Soul and Divin-

ity under each appearance of bread and wine. This mystical death of Jesus on the altar can express His willingness to die again just as much as His real death on Calvary. Moreover, on the altar, Jesus is present in the state of a victim, once immolated on Calvary and now offered again in the Mass. All this makes the Mass a real sacrifice.

WHY go to MASS?

BECAUSE YOUR Sunday Mass is your weekly *opportunity for Jesus* to make a real and living contact with your soul. On Calvary He achieved the work of redeeming us. At Mass He applies these graces to our soul. He prepares us for the mystery of our daily death-blow to sin by offering His Sacrifice. He prepares us for the mystery of daily life with God by giving us His Sacrament. On Calvary we were not actually present when He, the Priest, offered Himself as a substitute Victim for all. In the Mass He unites Himself to us when we become offerers to offer ourselves.

ACCEPTABLE to GOD, HELPFUL to US

POPE PIUS XI comments, "not they alone [referring to ordained priests] but the entire body of Christians" are, as St. Peter says, a "holy priesthood, to offer spiritual sacrifices acceptable to God through Jesus Christ" in the Mass. When we pray, therefore, and unite our sacrifices "through Jesus, with Jesus, in Jesus," *we may be absolutely sure that our worship is acceptable to God and profitable to us.* Your Sunday Mass is the most precious hour of the week,

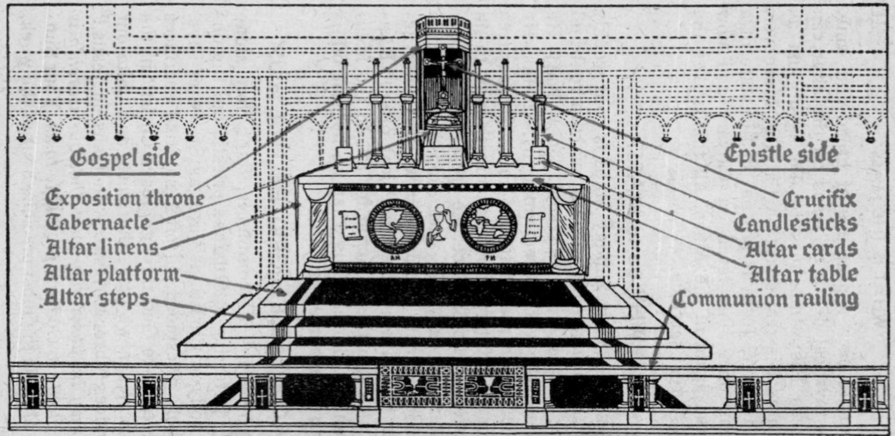

Altar and Sanctuary at the Monastery of the Precious Blood, Brooklyn, N. Y.
Maps show where Mass is being offered throughout world day and night.

because Jesus then *applies* the merits of His Calvary Sacrifice to you and because you then have an opportunity to *participate* actively with Him in co-offering to the Father His Sacrifice and yours.

The CHALICE

THE CHALICE recalls the same type of cup used by Jesus at the Last Supper, for the wine to be consecrated into His Blood. It is made of gold or silver, usually silver. If not gold, the interior of the cup, at least, must be gold plated. The Chalice and Paten receive no ordinary blessing but are anointed with holy chrism by a Bishop.

CHALICE with PURIFICATOR

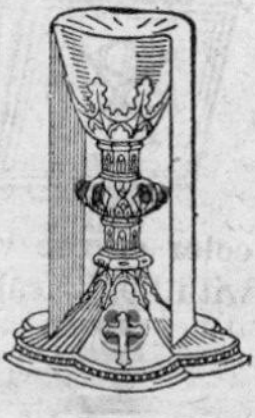

THE PURIFICATOR, as the name implies, is used for cleansing and drying the Chalice, fingers and mouth of the priest after his communion. It is a linen cloth, about 14 inches long. Its width of about 9 inches is folded three times, becoming approximately 14 by 3 inches.

CHALICE and PATEN with HOST

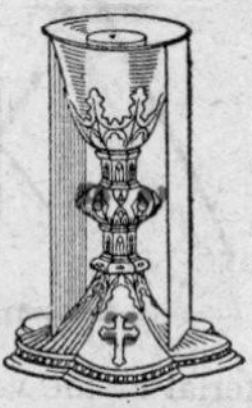

THE PATEN is a small round plate, made of the same material as the Chalice. If silver, the upper side must be gold-plated. On it rests the bread or host to be consecrated into the Body of Christ.

CHALICE with PALL COVERING HOST

THE PALL or cover is a double piece of linen, about 5 to 7 inches square, with a cardboard inserted to stiffen it. It is placed on the top of the Chalice to prevent dust or anything else from dropping into it.

The CORPORAL

THE CORPORAL is a piece of plain linen, usually about 15 inches square. It resembles a napkin. The Chalice and Hosts are placed on the Corporal. It is called Corporal, from the Latin word "corpus," meaning "body," since the "Body" of Christ rests on it.

The BURSE

THE BURSE is a square bag or container, like a flat pocketbook. It is designed to hold the Corporal when it is carried to and from the altar. It is made of the same material and color as the vestments, but is strongly reinforced with heavy cardboard.

CHALICE VEILED

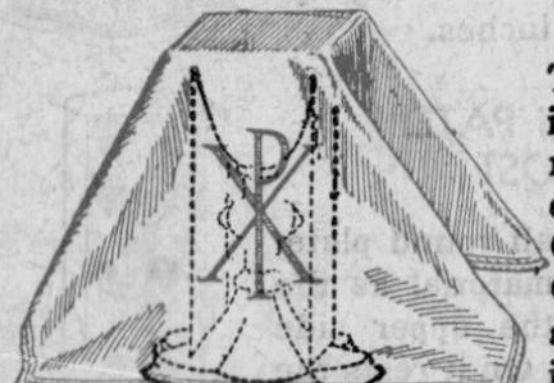

THE CHALICE VEIL is just what the name signifies; a cloth to cover the Chalice until the Offertory and again after the Communion. It is made of the same color and material as the vestments worn by the priest.

WHY MASS VESTMENTS?

Holy Mother Church speaks with her Vestments both to priests and people. They are her "sign language," more powerful than mere words.

THESE MASS Vestments have a *history.* In the first centuries of Christianity these garments, now worn by the priest, were much the same as those worn by laymen in their homes and on the street. Since that time, as we all know, fashions have changed century by century. Yet the Church still uses her first vestments as precious heirlooms; *carrying us through the ages, back to Christ at the Last Supper;* providing a vivid historical *witness* to the antiquity of the Mass, ever old, yet ever new; not behind the times, but for all times; a strong historical testimony to the unchanging character of the sameness of Calvary with the Mass in your own parish church.

THESE MASS Vestments are *the garments of Sacrifice.* The priest is reminded that each vestment has a relation to Christ, awaiting His Sacrifice of the Cross. You see the priest clothed from head to foot with garments symbolical of Christ's Sacred Passion, bearing a message for you, too, how you must vest your spiritual self, by "putting on Christ"; divest your entire self of anti-Christ! Life has *many* departments, physical, marital, spiritual, mental, social, commercial. But only *one* principle, that you must be clothed with Christ. Sacrifice everything for that!

SYMBOLS of SERVICE

THESE MASS vestments are SYMBOLS of Christian Service; symbols of virtues and duties. They symbolize *"how to prepare for Mass"*; *"how to live after Mass."* These vestments of the priest are not mere pretty things. They stand for tremendous reality, for vital truth. Each vestment contains a lesson and provides a motive. The priest is required to put each one on with a prayer and to wear it with a thought of what it stands for. Even as ordinary clothes, worn in the home or at business, at funerals or weddings, indicate minds and moods; even as soldier or police uniforms stand for service, so much more is this true of Mass vestments. They stand for service to God and neighbor!

MASS VESTMENTS a SYMBOL

of

what you wear to Mass

"DO NOT BE ANXIOUS for your body, what you shall put on" (Luke 12-*22*) when you come to Sunday Mass, "for after all these things the Gentiles seek" (Matt. 6-*32*). Realize that "clothes do not make the man". The "well-dressed" Christian is he who prepares for Mass. "Yet I say to you that not even Solomon in all his glory was arrayed like one" (Luke 12-*27*) who clothes his soul and wears to Mass the spiritual vestments of Sacrifice and Service.

The AMICE

MAKE-UP AND PRESENT USE. A piece of linen about the size of a small shawl. Priest touches it to his head, drops it over shoulders, tucks it around neck, ties it around waist. HISTORY OF FORMER USE. A covering or hood for head out-of-doors. Indoors it was lowered over shoulders.

RELATION TO CHRIST. Recalls cloth when He was blindfolded, mocked and asked who struck Him. MEANING FOR US. A symbol of our "Helmet of Salvation" (Eph. 6-*17*); touched to the head to protect us against idle or evil thoughts at Mass; tucked around neck to restrain use of tongue before and after Mass. PRAYER WHILE VESTING. *"Place, O Lord, the helmet of salvation on my head to resist the attacks of the devil."*

The ALB

MAKE-UP AND PRESENT USE. A full flowing robe of white linen reaching to the feet, covering entire body and worn over the Amice. HISTORY OF FORMER USE. Alb is the Latin word for "white." An ordinary outer garment worn in warm climates, even today in the Near-East. A full-sleeved white tunic worn by those having any dignity or authority in Ancient Rome.

RELATION TO CHRIST. Herod placed the garment of a fool around Jesus, making Him the sport of his indecent court. MEANING FOR US. Purity of body and soul required of God's priest and of those worthily assisting at Mass. Symbolizes our darkness being changed into the Light of Jesus. PRAYER WHILE VESTING. *"Make me white, O Lord, and purify my heart, so that being made white in the Blood of the Lamb, I may deserve an eternal reward."*

The CINCTURE or CORD

MAKE-UP AND PRESENT USE. **A thick cord of silk, linen or cotton with tassel ends. Secures Alb around the waist.** HISTORY OF FORMER USE. **Used to gird up the long, loose flowing Alb, so as not to interfere with walking or working.** RELATION TO CHRIST. **At Last Supper, Jesus washed feet of disciples, then dried them, using the towel girded around His waist. Also symbolizes cord that bound Jesus to pillar when being scourged.** MEANING FOR US. **A symbol of girding ourselves for hard service, keeping the passions in check; to be pure and strong spiritually so as to fight evil and do good.** PRAYER WHILE VESTING. ***"Gird me, O Lord, with the cincture of purity and extinguish in my heart the fire of concupiscence so that, the virtue of continence and chastity always abiding in my heart, I may the better serve Thee."***

The MANIPLE

MAKE-UP AND PRESENT USE. **A band of cloth, of same material and color as Stole and Chasuble, worn on left arm, about 4 inches wide by 30 inches long.** HISTORY OF FORMER USE. **Customary in hot climates to wear such a cloth on the arm to wipe away both dust and perspiration; also its folds were used as a purse.**

RELATION TO CHRIST. **Recalls the manacles with which the Hands of Jesus were bound; also the rope by which He was led to death.** MEANING FOR US. **Maniple comes from two Latin words, "manus plena," meaning "the hand is full." Hence symbolizes hand full of patient work and service, which are precious things to earn the reward of salvation. Suggests wiping off the mind and heart, of all sloth or fear of labor.** PRAYER WHILE VEST-

ING. *"May I deserve, O Lord, to carry this maniple of sorrow and penance so that I may one day enjoy the reward of all my labors."*

The STOLE

MAKE-UP AND PRESENT USE. A long strip of cloth about 3 to 4 inches wide and from 7 to 8 feet long; of same material and color as the Chasuble; worn around neck, across shoulders, crossed over the breast, and fastened in place with the ends of the cincture. HISTORY OF FORMER USE. A scarf or neck-piece; later a badge of honor for those enjoying any dignity; or a distinctive mark of duty for those exercising any authority.

RELATION TO CHRIST. It reminds us of the cross of Christ resting and carried on His Shoulders.

MEANING FOR US. Covering the neck, shoulders and breast, naturally it reminds us of the daiiy dignity and duty of working joyously, zealously for the cause of Christ while keeping in mind the eternal state of immortality. PRAYER WHILE VESTING. *"Restore unto me, O Lord, the Stole of immortality which I lost through the sin of my first parents and, although unworthy to approach Thy sacred Mystery, may I nevertheless attain to joy eternal."*

The CHASUBLE

MAKE-UP AND PRESENT USE. The outer vestment, covering nearly all the other vestments from the priest's shoulders to his knees, back and front; hence, with large cross on its back, it becomes the most familiar of all vestments. HISTORY OF FORMER USE. Used as a circular cape, without sleeves; with a hole in the middle for the head to pass through; this garment completely enveloped the body; a practical outdoor garment of protection against

the weather. Called "chasuble" from Latin word "casula" meaning a little house.
RELATION TO CHRIST. Recalls the seamless garment of Christ, traditionally believed to have been woven by Mary. On Calvary, the soldiers, not wishing to divide it into parts, cast dice for it. MEANING FOR US. Symbolizes the all-enveloping yoke of Christ's service made sweet by His all-embracing love; and of His commandments made possible by the same ever-present love. PRAYER WHILE VESTING. *"O Lord, Who hast said, 'My yoke is sweet and My burden light,' grant that I may so carry it as to merit Thy grace."*

COLORS of VESTMENTS

THE AMICE, ALB AND CINCTURE are usually made of white linen. The Maniple, Stole and Chasuble are of different or more precious material. They vary in six liturgical colors according to the feast or Church Season. GOLD may be used in place of White, Red or Green.

WHITE IS the symbol of light, of joy, of purity, used on all feasts of Jesus, except those of His Sufferings; on all feasts of Our Lady; on feasts of saints not martyred. RED is the symbol of blood, of fire; worn in Masses of the Holy Ghost and on feasts of martyrs. GREEN is the symbol of hope; used on Sundays after Epiphany to Septuagesima Sunday and on Sundays after Pentecost to Advent. VIOLET, sometimes called purple, is the symbol of penance, worn during Advent and Lent. ROSE, substituted as a symbol of joy (during penitential seasons) is worn on third Sunday of Advent and fourth Sunday of Lent. BLACK is the symbol of mourning, worn only on Good Friday and in Masses for the Dead.

PRAYER BEFORE MASS

ETERNAL FATHER, I unite myself with the intentions and affections of our Lady of Sorrows on Calvary and I offer Thee the Sacrifice which Thy Beloved Son Jesus made of Himself on the Cross, and now renews on this holy altar:

First. To adore Thee and give Thee the honor which is due to Thee, confessing Thy supreme dominion over all things, and the absolute dependence of everything upon Thee, Thou Who art our one and last end.

Second. To thank Thee for countless benefits received.

Third. To appease Thy Justice provoked by so many sins, and to make satisfaction for them.

Fourth. To implore grace and mercy for myself, for (*name*), for all afflicted and sorrowing, for all poor sinners, and for the holy souls in Purgatory. ***300 days Indulgence.***

Ordinary of the Mass

O IN NOMINE Patris, ✠ et Fílii, et Spíritus Sancti. Amen. Introíbo ad altáre Dei. [R] *Ad Deum qui lætíficat juventútem meam.*

In Mass for Dead, omit all paragraphs marked with Cross †

† [P] Júdica me, Deus, et discérne causam meam de gente non sancta: ab hómine iníquo et dolóso érue me. [R] *Quia tu es, Deus, fortitúdo mea: * quare me repulísti, et quare tristis incédo, ' dum afflígit me inimícus?*

† [P] Emítte lucem tuam et veritátem tuam: ipsa me deduxérunt, et adduxérunt in montem sanctum tuum, et in tabernácula tua. [R] *Et introíbo ad altáre*

MASS OF THE CATECHUMENS[1]

(Mass of the Learners)

NUMBER SYSTEM EXPLAINED ON PAGE 1

At foot of altar, priest begins with Sign of Cross

IN THE NAME of the Father, ✠ and of the Son, and of the Holy Ghost. Amen. 1

[P] † I will go to the altar of God.

[R] ‡ *To God, the joy of my youth.*[2]

In Mass for Dead, omit paragraphs marked with †

[P] Give judgment for me, O God, and decide my cause against an unholy people, from unjust and deceitful men deliver me. †

[R] *For Thou, O God, art my strength, * why hast Thou forsaken me? And why do I go about in sadness, | while the enemy afflicts me?*[3] †

[P] Send forth Thy light and Thy truth; they have led me and brought me to Thy holy hill and Thy dwelling-place. †

NOTE 1. Mass of the Catechumens (converts preparing for Baptism) is a prayer service up to the Epistle, then an instruction service to the Creed. Catechumens were not admitted to Mass of the Faithful (page 42) until after their Baptism on Holy Saturday. NOTE 2. Indicates joy of those to be "born again" in Baptism. NOTE 3. Yet fear is experienced because of sins.

† [P] *Words of priest.* ‡ [R] *Response. At DIALOGUE MASS, congregation responds aloud with half-pauses marked by a bar* | *and full pauses by an asterisk* *.

Dei: ¹ *ad Deum qui lætíficat juventútem meam.*

✝ [P] Confitébor tibi in cíthara, Deus, Deus meus: ¹ quare tristis es, ánima mea, et quare contúrbas me? [R] *Spera in Deo, quóniam adhuc confitébor illi:* ¹ *salutáre vultus mei,* ¹ *et Deus meus.**

✝ [P] Glória Patri, et Fílio, et Spirítui Sancto. [R] *Sicut erat in princípio, et nunc, et semper:* ¹ *et in sæcula sæculórum. Amen.*

✝ [P] Introíbo ad altáre Dei. [R] *Ad Deum qui lætíficat juventútem meam.*

[P] Adjutórium nostrum ✠ in nómine Dómini. [R] *Qui fecit cælum et terram.*

[P] Confíteor Deo . . . [R] *Misereátur tui omnípotens Deus,* et dimíssis peccátis tuis,* ¹ *perdúcat te ad vitam ætérnam.*

[P] Amen.

[R] *And I will go to the altar of God,* ¹ *to God, the joy of my youth.* †

[P] I shall yet praise Thee on the harp, O God, my God. Why art thou sorrowful, my soul, and why dost thou trouble me? †

[R] *Trust in God, for I shall yet praise Him,* ¹ *the salvation of my countenance* ¹ *and my God.**[4] †

[P] Glory be to the Father, and to the Son, and to the Holy Ghost. †

[R] *As it was in the beginning, is now, and ever shall be,* ¹ *world without end. Amen.* †

[P] I will go to the altar of God. †

[R] *To God, the joy of my youth.*[5] †

[P] Our help ✠ is in the name of the Lord.

[R] *Who made heaven and earth.*[6]

[P] I confess to almighty God, etc.

[R] *May almighty God have mercy upon thee,* forgive thee thy sins,* ¹ *and bring thee to life everlasting.* [P] Amen.

The CONFITEOR

[R] ***I*** *confess to almighty God,* to blessed Mary, ever virgin,* ¹ *to blessed Michael the*

NOTES 4 and 6. God, as Redeemer and Creator, is the source of present hope and final victory. NOTE 5. Even the baptized faithful express joy in offering Mass as "lay priests" (see page 15). Therefore always use the missal as priest does.

[R] *Confíteor Deo omnipoténti, * beátæ Maríæ semper Vírgini, ׀ beáto Michaéli Archángelo, * beáto Joánni Baptístæ, ׀ sanctis Apóstolis Petro et Paulo, * omnibus sanctis, ׀ et tibi, pater, * quia peccávi nimis cogitatióne, verbo et ópere: mea culpa, ׀ mea culpa, ׀ mea máxima culpa.* Ideo precor beátam Maríam semper Vírginem, ׀ beátum Michaélem Archángelum, * beátum Joánnem Baptístam, ׀ sanctos Apóstolos Petrum et Paulum, * omnes Sanctos, ׀ et te, pater, * oráre pro me ad Dóminum Deum nostrum.**

[P] Misereátur vestri omnípotens Deus, et dimíssis peccátis vestris, perdúcat vos ad vitam ætérnam. [R] *Amen.* [P] Indulgéntiam, ✠ absolutiónem, et remissiónem peccatórum nostrórum tríbuat nobis omnípotens et miséricors Dóminus.
[R] *Amen.*

[P] Deus, tu convérsus vivificábis nos. [R] *Et plebs tua lætábitur in te.* [P] Osténde nobis, Dómine, misericórdiam tuam. [R] *Et salutáre tuum da nobis.* [P] Dómine, exáudi oratiónem meam. [R] *Et clamor meus ad te véniat.* [P] Dóminus vobíscum. [R] *Et cum spíritu tuo.* [P] Orémus.

archangel, to blessed John the Baptist, ꜝ to the holy apostles, Peter and Paul,* to all the saints, ꜝ and to you, father,* that I have sinned exceedingly in thought, word and deed, through my fault, ꜝ through my fault, ꜝ through my most grievous fault.*[7] Therefore I beseech blessed Mary, ever virgin, ꜝ blessed Michael the archangel,* blessed John the Baptist, ꜝ the holy apostles, Peter and Paul,* all the saints, ꜝ and you, father,* to pray to the Lord our God for me.**

[P] May almighty God have mercy upon you, forgive you your sins, and bring you to life everlasting. [R] *Amen.* [P] May the almighty and merciful God grant us pardon, ✠ absolution and full remission of our sins. [R] *Amen.* [P] Thou wilt turn, O God, and bring us to life. [R] *And Thy people shall rejoice in Thee.* [P] Show us, O Lord, Thy mercy. [R] *And grant us Thy salvation.* [P] O Lord, hear my prayer. [R] *And let my cry come unto Thee.* [P] The Lord be with you. [R] *And with thy spirit.* [P] Let us pray.

NOTE 7. A dramatic picture indeed! humbly striking our breast, symbol of stirring up conscience, of disciplining body and soul; first confessing our sins publicly, then beseeching grace and help from God, the Church in heaven and on earth.

AUFER a nobis, quæsumus, Dómine, iniquitátes nostras: ut ad Sancta sanctórum puris mereámur méntibus introíre. Per Christum Dóminum nostrum. Amen.

ORAMUS te, Dómine, per mérita Sanctorum tuorum, quorum relíquiæ hic sunt, et ómnium Sanctórum: ut indulgére dignéris ómnia peccáta mea. Amen.

TURN TO ❷ INTROIT IN Today's Mass

❸ KYRIE

KÝRIE, eléison. [R] *Kýrie, eléison.* [P] Kýrie, eléison. [R] *Christe, eléison.* [P] Christe, eléison. [R] *Christe, eléison.* [P] Kýrie, eléison. [R] *Kýrie, eléison.* [P] Kýrie, eléison.

Priest goes up to the altar, saying privately:

TAKE FROM US our sins, O Lord, that we may enter with pure minds into the holy of holies. Through Christ our Lord. Amen.

As he kisses altar stone: 8

WE BESEECH THEE, O Lord, by the merits of Thy saints whose relics lie here, and of all the saints: deign in Thy mercy to pardon me all my sins. Amen.

Priest goes to Epistle side

TURN TO 2 INTROIT 9 IN Today's Mass

After Introit priest returns to middle of altar

The KYRIE 10 3

LORD, have mercy on us. [R] *Lord, have mercy on us.* [P] Lord, have mercy on us. [R] *Christ, have mercy on us.* [P] Christ, have mercy on us. [R] *Christ, have mercy on us.* [P] Lord, have mercy on us. [R] *Lord, have mercy on us.* [P] Lord, have mercy on us.

The GLORIA 11 †

Omitted when black or violet vestments are worn

NOTE 8. Priest ascends to altar, Calvary itself (see page 19), kisses martyrs' relics in altar stone. NOTE 9. Keynote to theme of each Mass. NOTE 10. Each divine person implored three times. NOTE 11. All now declare with Christmas angels that peace only comes when God is recognized.

† LORIA IN EXCELSIS DEO. *Et in terra pax | homínibus bonæ voluntátis. * Laudámus te. Benedícimus te. | Adorámus te. Glorificámus te.**

† *Grátias ágimus tibi propter magnam glóriam tuam. * Dómine Deus, Rex cæléstis, | Deus Pater omnípotens.**

† *Dómine Fili unigénite, | Jesu Christe.* Dómine Deus, Agnus Dei, Fílius Patris.* Qui tollis peccáta mundi, | miserére nobis.**

† *Qui tollis peccáta mundi, | súscipe deprecatiónem nostram.**

† *Qui sedes ad déxteram Patris, | miserére nobis.**

† *Quóniam tu solus Sanctus. Tu solus Dóminus. | Tu solus Altíssimus, Jesu Christe.* Cum Sancto Spíritu ✠ | in glória Dei Patris. Amen.*

[P] Dóminus vobíscum. [R] *Et cum spíritu tuo.* [P] Orémus.

TURN TO ④ PRAYER W Today's Mass

After Prayer: [R] *Amen.*

After Epistle ⑤: [R] *Deo grátias.*

GLORY TO GOD *in the highest. And on earth peace* ¹ *to men of good will.* We praise Thee. We bless Thee.* ¹ *We adore Thee. We glorify Thee.* We give Thee thanks for Thy great glory.* O Lord God, heavenly King,* ¹ *God the Father almighty.**[12] *O Lord Jesus Christ,* ¹ *the only-begotten Son.* Lord God, Lamb of God. Son of the Father.* Who takest away the sins of the world,* ¹ *have mercy on us.**

Who takest away the sins of the world, ¹ *receive our prayer.* Who sittest at the right hand of the Father,* ¹ *have mercy on us.* For Thou alone art holy. Thou alone art Lord.* ¹ *Thou alone, O Jesus Christ, art most high.* Together with the Holy Ghost,* ✠ ¹ *in the glory of God the Father. Amen.*[13]

Priest kisses altar stone, turns to people, says:

[P] The Lord be with you.[14] [R] *And with thy spirit.* *Priest now goes to Epistle side*

[P] Let us pray.

TURN TO 4 PRAYER 15 IN Today's Mass

See page 66 for various Prayer endings

NOTE 12. Adoration to God, our Father and Creator. NOTE 13. Petition to Jesus, our Brother and Redeemer; concludes with homage to entire Trinity. NOTE 14. Christians formerly greeted each other in this way. NOTE 15. Always an invocation or thanksgiving for graces through Jesus.

7 MUNDA cor meum, ac lábia mea, omnípotens Deus, qui lábia Isaíæ Prophétæ cálculo mundásti ignito: ita me tua grata miseratióne dignáre mundáre, ut sanctum Evangélium tuum digne váleam nuntiáre. Per Christum Dóminum nostrum. Amen.

† Jube, Dómine, benedícere.
Dóminus sit in corde meo et in lábiis meis: ut digne et competénter annúntiem Evangélium suum. Amen.

[P] Dóminus vobíscum.

[R] *Et cum spíritu tuo.*

[P] ✠ Sequéntia sancti Evangélii secúndum N.

[R] ***Glória tibi, Dómine.***

Having read ⑤ Epistle 16 and ⑥ Gradual (or Alleluia), priest, with bowed head, recites before the tabernacle, the following while boy carries missal to Gospel side:

CLEANSE MY HEART and my lips, O almighty God, who didst cleanse the lips of the prophet Isaias with a burning coal; deign of Thy gracious mercy, so to purify me that I may worthily proclaim Thy holy Gospel. Through Christ our Lord. Amen. ⑦

Lord, grant Thy blessing. The Lord be in my heart and on my lips, that I may worthily and fittingly proclaim His holy Gospel. Amen. †

The GOSPEL 17 *[Stand]*

[P] The Lord be with you. *At Gospel side*

[R] *And with thy spirit.*

[P] ✠ The continuation of the holy Gospel according to *Matthew, Mark, Luke or John* *(as Today's Mass indicates.)*

[R] *Glory be to Thee, O Lord.*

NOTE 16. Epistle written by God's messengers, prepares us for worthy participation in Mass; how to live before and after Mass. The Gradual is named after "gradus," Latin for "step," from where it was formerly sung. NOTE 17. After reciting prayers for purity of heart and lips (top of page), we read the Gospel message of Jesus; signing our forehead to understand it, our lips to declare it publicly, our heart to love it interiorly.

TURN TO 8 TODAY'S GOSPEL IN Today's Mass

9 [R] *Laus tibi, Christe.* [P] Per evangélica dicta deleántur nostra delícta.

† CREDO IN UNUM DEUM, *Patrem omnipoténtem, factórem cæli et terræ,* | *visibílium ómnium, et invisibílium.* * *Et in unum Dóminum Jesum Christum,* | *Fílium Dei unigénitum.* | *Et ex Patre natum ante ómnia sæcula.* * *Deum de Deo,* | *lumen de lúmine,* | *Deum verum de Deo vero.* * *Génitum, non factum,* | *consubstantiálem Patri:* | *per quem ómnia facta sunt.* * *Qui propter nos hómines, et propter nostram salútem* | *descéndit de cælis.* * *Genuflect*

† ET INCARNATUS EST
DE SPIRITU SANCTO EX MARIA VIRGINE: |
ET HOMO FACTUS EST.*

† *Crucifíxus étiam pro nobis:* | *sub Póntio Piláto passus, et sepúltus est.* * *Et resurréxit*

TURN TO 8 TODAY'S GOSPEL IN Today's Mass

At end of Gospel:

[R] ***Praise be to Thee, O Christ.*** 9

Priest kisses the sacred page, prays:[18]

[P] By the words of the holy Gospel may our sins be blotted out.

Priest returns to middle of altar and says:

The CREED[19]

I BELIEVE IN ONE GOD, *the Father almighty, Maker of heaven and earth, | and of all things visible and invisible.* And in one Lord, Jesus Christ, | the only-begotten Son of God. | Born of the Father before all ages.* God of God, | light of light, | true God of true God.* Begotten, not made; | of one being with the Father: | by whom all things were made.* Who for us men, and for our salvation | came down from heaven.**

[Genuflect]

AND WAS MADE FLESH
BY THE HOLY GHOST, OF THE VIRGIN
MARY: | AND WAS MADE MAN.*

He was also crucified for us, | suffered under

NOTE 18. Formerly, Gospel book was passed around, each kissing it. NOTE 19. Nicene Creed (composed A.D. 325) stresses divinity of Christ, recalls truths revealed by God, beyond power of reason to discover. This act of faith, first heard at our Baptism, now prepares mind and heart to appreciate what will be revealed on altars of time and eternity. The Creed is recited only on Sundays and certain feasts.

✝ *tertia die, secúndum Scriptúras.* Et ascéndit in cælum: sedet ad déxteram Patris. ˡ Et íterum ventúrus est cum glória judicáre vivos et mórtuos:ˡ cujus regni non erit finis.* Et in Spíritum Sanctum, Dóminum, et vivificántem: ˡ Qui ex Patre, Filióque procédit.* Qui cum Patre, et Fílio simul adorátur,ˡ et conglorificátur:ˡ qui locútus est per Prophétas.* Et unam, sanctam, cathólicam et apostólicam Ecclésiam.* Confíteor unum baptísma in remissiónem peccatórum. * Et exspécto resurrectiónem mortuórum.ˡ Et vitam* ✠ *ventúri sǽculi. Amen.*

[P] Dóminus vobíscum.

[R] *Et cum spíritu tuo.*

[P] Orémus.

TURN TO ⑩ OFFERTORY IN Today's Mass

Pontius Pilate, and was buried. And on the third day He arose again, according to the Scriptures.* And ascending into heaven, He sitteth at the right hand of the Father. ' And He shall come again with glory to judge the living and the dead: ' and of His kingdom there shall be no end.* And in the Holy Ghost, the Lord and Giver of life, ' who proceedeth from the Father and the Son.* Who together with the Father and the Son is no less adored ' and glorified: ' who spoke by the prophets.* And in one, holy, catholic and apostolic Church.* I confess one baptism for the remission of sins.* And I look for the resurrection of the dead. ' And the life ✠ of the world to come. Amen.*

MASS OF THE FAITHFUL[20]

(Mass of the Offerers)

[P] *Faces people* The Lord be with you. [*Sit*]
[R] ***And with thy spirit.*** [P] Let us pray.

TURN TO ⑩ OFFERTORY IN Today's Mass

The priest removes veil from chalice[21]

NOTE 20. Mass of the Faithful (only baptized Christians formerly allowed to participate) is a Sacrifice-Offering to bottom of page 56; a Sacrifice-Banquet from page 57 to end of Mass. NOTE 21. At the Budapest Eucharistic Congress, each Hungarian child offered a grain of wheat for the bread, a grape for the wine, at the Mass celebrated by Pope Pius XII. Offertory collection, now necessary for religious works, replaces these offerings of bread and wine; it is the same outward token of our inward desire to consecrate our life to God.

11 SUSCIPE, sancte Pater, omnípotens ætérne Deus, hanc immaculátam hóstiam, quam ego indígnus fámulus tuus óffero tibi, Deo meo vivo et vero, pro innumerabílibus peccátis, et offensiónibus, et negligéntiis meis, et pro ómnibus circumstántibus, sed et pro ómnibus fidélibus christiánis vivis atque defúnctis: ut mihi et illis profíciat ad salútem in vitam ætérnam. Amen. ✠

DEUS, ✠ qui humánæ substántiæ dignitátem mirabíliter condidísti, et mirabílius reformásti: da nobis per hujus aquæ et vini mystérium, ejus divinitátis esse consórtes, qui humanitátis nostræ fíeri dignátus est párticeps, Jesus Christus Fílius tuus, Dóminus noster: Qui tecum vivit et regnat in unitáte Spíritus Sancti Deus: per ómnia sǽcula sæculórum. Amen.

Priest, lifting host on the paten, says:

ACCEPT, O holy Father, almighty and eternal God, this spotless host, which I, Thy unworthy servant, offer unto Thee, my living and true God, to atone for my numberless sins, offenses and negligences; on behalf of all here present and likewise for all faithful Christians living and dead, that it may profit me and them as a means of salvation unto life everlasting. Amen. ✠[22] (11)

At Epistle side, priest pours wine into chalice

O GOD, ✠ who hast established the nature of man in wondrous dignity and even more wondrously hast renewed it, grant *(priest adds water to wine)* that through the mystery of this water and wine, we may be made partakers of His divinity, who has deigned to become partaker of our humanity, Jesus Christ, Thy Son, our Lord, who liveth and reigneth with Thee, in the union of the Holy Ghost, God world without end. Amen.[23]

NOTE 22. We, too, should spiritually place ourselves on corporal, as small hosts near the large. Let us not withdraw from Christ during the day. NOTE 23. Water added to wine symbolizes: 1) the human and divine in Christ; 2) our redemption by Blood and Water from Side of Christ; 3) our share in divine life even as He shared our human life. Jesus and we are both offered to the Father.

OFFERIMUS tibi, Dómine, cálicem salutáris, tuam deprecántes cleméntiam: ut in conspéctu divínæ majestátis tuæ, pro nostra et totíus mundi salúte, cum odóre suavitátis ascéndat. Amen. ✠

IN SPIRITU humilitátis, et in ánimo contríto suscipiámur a te, Dómine: et sic fiat sacrifícium nostrum in conspéctu tuo hódie, ut pláceat tibi, Dómine Deus.

VENI, sanctificátor omnípotens, ætérne Deus: et béne ✠ dic hoc sacrifícium, tuo sancto nómini præparátum.

Priest returns to middle of altar, offers chalice:

WE OFFER unto Thee, O Lord, the chalice of salvation, humbly begging of Thy mercy that it may arise before Thy divine majesty with a pleasing fragrance, for our salvation and that of all the world. Amen. ✠[24]

Priest bows down and says:

IN A HUMBLE SPIRIT and a contrite heart, may we be accepted by Thee, O Lord, and may our sacrifice so be offered in Thy sight this day as to please Thee, O Lord God.[25]

Priest raises eyes, blesses bread and wine, saying:

COME, Thou Sanctifier, almighty and eternal God, and bless ✠ this sacrifice prepared for the glory of Thy holy name.[26]

NOTE 24. Priest places chalice on corporal with Sign of Cross, indicating that Jesus and we are now ready for Christian sacrifice. Here we must realize that "Catholic" means universal. Only the Mystical Body of Christ, the Church, makes for true solidarity. We pray "for our salvation," yes, "and that of all the world." NOTE 25. Prays to Father that our "sacrifice so be offered as to please," like unto that of Jesus. NOTE 26. Prays to Holy Ghost that He will bless the great sacrifice that we are together offering to the Father.

LAVABO inter innocéntes manus meas et circúmdabo altáre tuum, Dómine: Ut áudiam vocem laudis, et enárrem univérsa mirabília tua.
Dómine, diléxi decórem domus tuæ, et locum habitatiónis glóriæ tuæ.
Ne perdas cum ímpiis, Deus, ánimam meam, et cum viris sánguinum vitam meam:
In quorum mánibus iniquitátes sunt: déxtera eórum repléta est munéribus.
Ego autem in innocéntia mea ingréssus sum: rédime me, et miserére mei.
Pes meus stetit in diréсto: in ecclésiis benedícam te, Dómine.
✝ Glória Patri, et Fílio, et Spirítui Sancto. Sicut erat in princípio, et nunc, et semper: et in sǽcula sæculórum. Amen.

SUSCIPE, sancta Trínitas, hanc oblatiónem, quam tibi offérimus ob memóriam Passiónis, Resurrectiónis et Ascensiónis Jesu Christi Dómini nostri: et in honórem beátæ Maríæ semper Vírginis, et beáti Joánnis Baptístæ, et sanctórum Apostolórum Petri et Pauli,

WASHING OF FINGERS

Priest washes fingers at Epistle side[27]

I WILL WASH my hands among the innocent, and will walk 'round Thy altar, O God. To hear the voice of Thy praise and to tell all Thy wondrous deeds. O Lord, I love the beauty of Thy house, and the place where Thy glory dwells. Destroy not my soul with the impious, O God, nor my life with men of blood.
In whose hands there is iniquity, whose right hand is full of bribes. But as for me, I will walk in my innocence, rescue me and be gracious to me. My foot is on the straight way, in assemblies will I bless Thee, O Lord.
Glory be to the Father, and to the Son, ✝ and to the Holy Ghost: as it was in the beginning, is now, and ever shall be, world without end. Amen.

Priest returns to middle, bows and says:

ACCEPT, most holy Trinity, this offering which we are making to Thee in remembrance of the passion, resurrec-

---

NOTE 27. Washing of fingers formerly necessary after handling and incensing the offerings; now a symbol of soul washed pure of sin, so necessary for Mass. "If I do not wash thee, thou shalt have no part with Me," said Jesus to Peter at the first Mass.

et istórum, et ómnium Sanctórum: ut illis profíciat ad honórem, nobis autem ad salútem: et illi pro nobis intercédere dignéntur in cælis, quorum memóriam ágimus in terris. Per eúmdem Christum Dóminum nostrum. Amen.

ORATE, fratres: ut meum ac vestrum sacrifícium acceptábile fiat apud Deum Patrem omnipoténtem.

[R] *Suscípiat Dóminus sacrifícium de mánibus tuis,| ad laudem et glóriam nóminis sui,| ad utilitátem quoque nostram,| totiúsque Ecclésiæ suæ sanctæ.**

[P] Amen.

TURN TO ⑫ SECRET IN Today's Mass

tion, and ascension of Jesus Christ, our Lord; and in honor of blessed Mary, ever virgin, blessed John the Baptist, the holy apostles, Peter and Paul, and of these, and of all the saints; that it may add to their honor and aid our salvation; and may they deign to intercede in heaven for us who cherish their memory here on earth. Through the same Christ our Lord. Amen.[28]

Priest kisses altar, turns to people, raises voice:[29]

PRAY, brethren, that my sacrifice and yours may become acceptable to God the Father almighty.

[R] *May the Lord accept the sacrifice at thy hands, | unto the praise and glory of His name, | for our advantage | and that of all His holy Church.**

[P] Amen.

TURN TO 12 SECRET 30 IN Today's Mass

NOTE 28. We plead with saints to intercede, that we offer Mass worthily, since it is a memorial of Jesus. NOTE 29. We must actively unite with priest and not be idle spectators. NOTE 30. Secret (from Latin word for "separated") is usually a petition for acceptance of gifts now "separated" from secular use.

⑬ [P] Per ómnia sǽcula sæculórum. [R] *Amen.* [P] Dóminus vobíscum. [R] *Et cum spíritu tuo.* [P] Sursum corda. [R] *Habémus ad Dóminum.* [P] Grátias agámus Dómino Deo nostro. [R] *Dignum et justum est.*

VERE dignum et justum est, æquum et salutáre, nos tibi semper, et ubíque grátias ágere: Dómine sancte, Pater omnípotens, ætérne Deus: Qui cum unigénito Fílio tuo, et Spíritu Sancto, unus es Deus, unus es Dóminus: non in uníus singularitáte persónæ, sed in uníus Trinitáte substántiæ. Quod enim de tua glória, revelánte te, crédimus, hoc de Fílio tuo, hoc de Spíritu Sancto, sine differéntia discretiónis sentímus. Ut in confessióne veræ sempiternǽque Dei-

[P] World without end. [R] *Amen.* 13

The PREFACE[31]

[P] The Lord be with you. [R] *And with thy spirit.* [P] Lift up your hearts. [R] *We have them lifted up to the Lord.*
[P] Let us give thanks to the Lord our God. [R] *It is meet and just.*

IT IS MEET INDEED and just, right and helpful unto salvation, always and everywhere to give thanks to Thee, holy Lord, Father almighty, eternal God, who with Thine only-begotten Son and the Holy Ghost art one God, one Lord; not in the unity of a single person, but in the trinity of a single nature. For that which we believe from Thy revelation concerning Thy glory, that same we believe of Thy Son, that same of the Holy Ghost, without difference or discrimination. So that in confessing the true and everlasting Godhead, we shall adore distinction in persons, oneness in being, and equality in majesty. This the angels and archan-

NOTE 31. A majestic hymn of praise and thanksgiving well fitted to exalt the mind and heart for the sacred actions about to come. Jesus Himself "gave thanks" to His Father before offering the first Mass at the Last Supper.

tátis, et in persónis propríetas, et in esséntia únitas, et in majestáte adorétur æquálitas. Quam laudant Angeli atque Archángeli, Chérubim quoque ac Séraphim: qui non cessant clamáre quotídie, una voce dicéntes:

Sanctus, Sanctus, Sanctus, Dóminus Deus Sábaoth. Pleni sunt cæli et terra glória tua. Hosánna in excélsis.* Benedíctus ✠ qui venit in nómine Dómini.* Hosánna in excélsis.*

clementíssime Pater, per Jesum Christum Fílium tuum Dóminum nostrum, súpplices rogámus, ac pétimus, uti accépta hábeas, et benedícas, hæc ✠ dona, hæc ✠ múnera, hæc ✠ sancta sacrifícia illibáta, in primis, quæ tibi offérimus pro Ecclésia tua sancta cathólica: quam pacificáre, custodíre, adunáre, et régere dignéris toto orbe terrárum: una cum fámulo tuo Papa nostro N., et Antístite nostro N., et ómnibus orthodóxis, atque cathólicæ, et apostólicæ fídei cultóribus.

gels, the cherubim, too, and the seraphim do praise; day by day they cease not to cry out, saying as with one voice:

Bell rings thrice  *[Kneel]*

HOLY, HOLY, HOLY, Lord God of hosts! Heaven and earth are filled with Thy glory. Hosanna in the highest!* ✠ Blessed is He that comes in the name of the Lord.* Hosanna in the highest!*

The CANON[32]

Priest bows low; asks God to accept offerings

FIRST REMEMBRANCE—Clergy and All Believers

THEREFORE, most gracious Father, we humbly beg of Thee and entreat Thee, through Jesus Christ, Thy Son, our Lord *(priest kisses altar)*, to deem acceptable and bless these ✠ gifts, these ✠ offerings, these ✠ holy and unspotted oblations, which we offer unto Thee in first instance for Thy holy and Catholic Church, that Thou wouldst deign to give her peace and

---

NOTE 32. In the Canon, pages 48 to 56 (Greek word for rule or standard; always the same, except for a few words changed on great feasts), there are six Prayers of Remembrance, also five Prayers of Offering; arranged dramatically, half before, half after the Consecration. Everyone, everything is remembered. It is punctuated with faith, full of power and action.

MEMENTO, Dómine, famulórum, famularúmque tuárum N. et N. et ómnium circumstántium, quorum tibi fides cógnita est, et nota devótio, pro quibus tibi offérimus: vel qui tibi ófferunt hoc sacrifícium laudis, pro se, suísque ómnibus: pro redemptióne animárum suárum, pro spe salútis et incolumitátis suæ: tibíque reddunt vota sua ætérno Deo, vivo et vero.

COMMUNICANTES et memóriam venerántes, in primis gloriósæ semper Vírginis Maríæ, Genitrícis Dei et Dómini nostri Jesu Christi: sed et beatórum Apostolórum ac Mártyrum tuórum, Petri et Pauli, Andréæ, Jacóbi, Joánnis, Thomæ, Jacóbi, Philíppi, Bartholomæi, Matthæi, Simónis et Thaddæi, Lini, Cleti,

protection, to unite and guide her the whole world over; together with Thy servant N., our Pope, and N., our bishop, and all true believers, who cherish the catholic and apostolic faith.

SECOND REMEMBRANCE—Friends and Parishioners[33]

BE MINDFUL, O Lord, of Thy servants and handmaids *(priest pauses and includes certain names and intentions)* and of all here present, whose faith is known to Thee, and likewise their devotion, on whose behalf we offer unto Thee, or who themselves offer unto Thee, this sacrifice of praise for themselves and all their own, for the good of their souls, for their hope of salvation and deliverance from all harm, and who pay Thee the homage which they owe Thee, eternal God, living and true.

THIRD REMEMBRANCE—all the Saints[34]

IN THE UNITY of holy fellowship we observe the memory first of the glorious and ever virgin Mary, mother of our Lord and God, Jesus Christ; next that of Thy blessed apostles and martyrs, Peter

---

NOTE 33. The primary fruit of the Mass is for "all here present"; the secondary is for the absent; to both, we have a duty above the egoism of our personal needs. NOTE 34. Church militant on earth pleads with Church triumphant in heaven to intercede for us.

Cleméntis, Xysti, Cornélii, Cypriáni, Lauréntii, Chrysógoni, Joánnis et Pauli, Cosmæ et Damiáni, et ómnium Sanctórum tuórum; quorum méritis precibúsque concédas, ut in ómnibus protectiónis tuæ muniámur auxílio. Per eúmdem Christum Dóminum nostrum. Amen.

HANC ígitur oblatiónem servitútis nostræ, sed et cunctæ famíliæ tuæ, quæsumus, Dómine, ut placátus accípias: diésque nostros in tua pace dispónas, atque ab ætérna damnatióne nos éripi, et in electórum tuórum júbeas grege numerári. Per Christum Dóminum nostrum. Amen.

and Paul, Andrew, James, John, Thomas, James, Philip, Bartholomew, Matthew, Simon and Thaddeus; of Linus, Cletus, Clement, Sixtus, Cornelius, Cyprian, Lawrence, Chrysogonus, John and Paul, Cosmas and Damian, and of all Thy saints, by whose merits and prayers grant that we may be always fortified by the help of Thy protection. Through the same Christ our Lord. Amen.[35]

PRAYERS of OFFERING— Before Consecration[36]

Priest spreads hands over the offerings

The bell  *is rung once*

GRACIOUSLY ACCEPT, then, we beseech Thee, O Lord, this service of our worship and that of all Thy household. Provide that our days be spent in Thy peace, save us from everlasting damnation, and cause us to be numbered in the flock Thou hast chosen. Through Christ our Lord. Amen.

NOTE 35. The word "canonize" means that a new saint's name is included in the Canon and mentioned in this prayer on the day of canonization. NOTE 36. Symbolizes Old Law custom of placing one's sins upon a scapegoat, then exiling him into desert to die. Now we place our sins on the head of Jesus, Victim for our sins, to save us.

QUAM oblatiónem tu, Deus, in ómnibus, quæsumus, bene ✠ díctam, ad ✠ scríptam, ra ✠ tam, rationábilem, acceptabilémque fácere dignéris: ut nobis Cor ✠ pus, et San ✠ guis fiat dilectíssimi Fílii tui Dómini nostri Jesu Christi.

QUI prídie quam paterétur, accépit panem in sanctas ac venerábiles manus suas: et elevátis óculis in cælum ad te Deum Patrem suum omnipoténtem, tibi grátias agens, bene ✠ díxit, fregit, dedítque discípulis suis, dicens: Accípite, et manducáte ex hoc omnes.

HOC EST ENIM CORPUS MEUM.

Do Thou, O God, deign to ✠ bless what we offer, and make it ✠ approved, ✠ effective, right and wholly pleasing in every way, that it may be for our good, the ✠ Body and the ✠ Blood of Thy dearly beloved Son, Jesus Christ our Lord.[37]

CONSECRATION of the BREAD

Who, the day before He suffered, took bread into His holy and venerable hands, and having raised His eyes to heaven, unto Thee, O God, His Father almighty, giving thanks to Thee, ✠ blessed, broke it, and gave it to His disciples, saying: Take ye all and eat of this:

FOR THIS IS MY BODY![38]

Priest genuflects, elevates Host
Bell rings thrice

Look at the sacred Host and devoutly say: "My Lord and my God" *(7 years indul.)*

NOTE 37. A final plea that our self-offering be accepted when united with the Offering of our Victim-Redeemer. NOTE 38. Instantly the substance of bread is gone; it is changed into Jesus Christ, true God, true Man. The person of the priest recedes. It is Christ who speaks through the lips of the priest and offers Himself in the hands of the priest to His Father for our sakes.

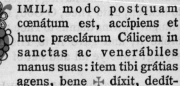

SIMILI modo postquam cœnátum est, accípiens et hunc præclárum Cálicem in sanctas ac venerábiles manus suas: item tibi grátias agens, bene ✠ díxit, dedítque discípulis suis, dicens: Accípite, et bíbite ex eo omnes.

HIC EST ENIM CALIX SANGUINIS MEI,
NOVI ET AETERNI TESTAMENTI:
MYSTERIUM FIDEI:
QUI PRO VOBIS ET PRO MULTIS
EFFUNDETUR
IN REMISSIONEM PECCATORUM.

Hæc quotiescúmque fecéritis, in mei memóriam faciétis.

CONSECRATION of the WINE

IN LIKE MANNER, when the supper was done, taking also this goodly chalice into His holy and venerable hands, again giving thanks to Thee, He ✠ blessed it and gave it to His disciples, saying: Take ye all, and drink of this:[39]

FOR THIS IS THE CHALICE OF MY BLOOD OF THE NEW AND ETERNAL COVENANT: THE MYSTERY OF FAITH,[40] WHICH SHALL BE SHED FOR YOU AND FOR MANY UNTO THE FORGIVENESS OF SINS.

As often as you shall do these things, in memory of Me shall you do them.[41]

Priest genuflects, elevates chalice
Bell rings thrice

Look at the chalice and devoutly say:

"We beseech Thee, therefore, help Thy servants, whom Thou hast redeemed with Thy Precious Blood." *(300 days indul.)*

NOTE 39. How does Jesus die again and renew His Sacrifice? On Calvary He died "physically" by the separation of His Body from His Blood. On the altar He dies "mystically," since the words of Consecration are like a sword, "mystically" separating the Body from the Blood by two separate Consecrations. NOTE 40. A mystery! yes, but by faith, we believe and adore. NOTE 41. Words of our Lord when instituting the priesthood and empowering priests to offer Mass as a memorial, yes, and a renewal of His love, "obedient to death."

UNDE et mémores, Dómine, nos servi tui, sed et plebs tua sancta, ejúsdem Christi Fílii tui Dómini nostri tam beátæ Passiónis, nec non et ab ínferis Resurrectiónis, sed et in cælos gloriósæ Ascensiónis: offérimus præcláræ majestáti tuæ de tuis donis ac datis, Hóstiam ✠ puram, Hóstiam ✠ sanctam, Hóstiam ✠ immaculátam, Panem ✠ sanctum vitæ ætérnæ et Cálicem ✠ salútis perpétuæ.

SUPRA quæ propítio ac seréno vultu respícere dignéris: et accépta habére, sícuti accépta habére dignátus es múnera púeri tui justi Abel, et sacrifícium Patriárchæ nostri Abrahæ: et quod tibi óbtulit summus sacérdos tuus Melchísedech, sanctum sacrifícium, immaculátam hóstiam.

PRAYERS of OFFERING — After Consecration

Priest extends hands and continues

MINDFUL, therefore, O Lord, not only of the blessed passion of the same Christ, Thy Son, our Lord, but also of His resurrection from the dead, and finally His glorious ascension into heaven, we, Thy ministers, as also Thy holy people, offer unto Thy supreme majesty, of Thy gifts bestowed upon us, the pure ✠ Victim, the holy ✠ Victim, the all-perfect ✠ Victim: the holy Bread ✠ of life eternal and the Chalice ✠ of unending salvation.[42]

AND THIS do Thou deign to regard with gracious and kindly attention and hold acceptable, as Thou didst deign to accept the offerings of Abel, Thy just servant, and the sacrifice of Abraham our patriarch, and that which Thy chief priest Melchisedech, offered unto Thee, a holy sacrifice of thanks, and a spotless Victim.[43]

NOTE 42. Priest makes Sign of Cross 5 times: (a) indicating Christ is on the Cross; (b) blessing the faithful on the altar with Christ. NOTE 43. Spans all history: refers to Old Testament figures of Christ, then to the Reality Himself.

SUPPLICES te rogámus, omnípotens Deus: jube hæc perférri per manus sancti Angeli tui in sublíme altáre tuum, in conspéctu divínæ majestátis tuæ: ut quotquot, ex hac altáris participatióne sacrosánctum Fílii tui, Cor ✠ pus et Sán ✠ guinem sumpsérimus, omni benedictióne cæléesti et grátia repleámur. Per eúmdem Christum Dóminum nostrum. Amen.

MEMENTO étiam, Dómine, famulórum, famularúmque tuárum N. et N. qui nos præcessérunt cum signo fídei et dórmiunt in somno pacis.

Ipsis, Dómine, et ómnibus in Christo quiescéntibus, locum refrigérii, lucis et pacis, ut indúlgeas, deprecámur. Per eúmdem Christum Dóminum nostrum. Amen.

Priest bows profoundly, hands joined on altar

MOST HUMBLY we implore Thee, almighty God, bid these our mystic offerings to be brought by the hands of Thy holy Angel unto Thy altar above, before the face of Thy divine majesty; that *(priest kisses altar)* those of us who, by sharing in the Sacrifice of this altar, shall receive the most sacred ✠ Body and ✠ Blood of Thy Son, may be filled with every grace and heavenly blessing. Through the same Christ our Lord. Amen.[44]

FOURTH REMEMBRANCE—Souls in Purgatory

BE MINDFUL, O Lord, also of Thy servants and handmaids, N. and N., who have gone before us with the sign of faith, and rest in the sleep of peace.

Priest prays for the dead mentioned above[45]

To these, O Lord, and to all who sleep in Christ, we beseech Thee to grant, of Thy goodness, a place of comfort, light, and peace. Through the same Christ our Lord. Amen.

NOTE 44. "Bid these our mystic offerings to be brought" indicates the infinite merits of Christ, also our humble offerings. NOTE 45. Before the Consecration, we remembered the Church militant, invoked the Church triumphant; now we offer the Precious Blood for the Church suffering, our known and forgotten dead.

NOBIS QUOQUE PECCATORIBUS fámulis tuis, de multitúdine miseratiónum tuárum sperántibus, partem áliquam et societátem donáre dignéris, cum tuis sanctis Apóstolis et Martýribus: cum Joánne, Stéphano, Matthía, Bárnaba, Ignátio, Alexándro, Marcellíno, Petro, Felicitáte, Perpétua, Agatha, Lúcia, Agnéte, Cæcília, Anastásia, et ómnibus Sanctis tuis: intra quorum nos consórtium, non æstimátor mériti, sed véniæ, quæsumus, largítor admítte. Per Christum Dóminum nostrum.

FIFTH REMEMBRANCE — Sinners

Priest strikes breast, says first three words aloud: [46]

TO US ALSO, sinners, yet Thy servants, trusting in the greatness of Thy mercy, deign to grant some part and fellowship with Thy holy apostles and martyrs: with John, Stephen, Matthias, Barnabas, Ignatius, Alexander, Marcellinus, Peter, Felicitas, Perpetua, Agatha, Lucy, Agnes, Cecilia, Anastasia, and all Thy saints; into whose company we implore Thee to admit us, not weighing our merits, but freely granting us pardon. Through Christ our Lord.

SIXTH REMEMBRANCE — All Nature[47]

NOTE 46. Priest invites all to acknowledge their sins; the good "fellowship" and "company" mentioned here (the saints) are drawn from all states of life, apostles, priests, laymen, virgins, married women, as an encouragement to us. NOTE 47. Nowadays blessings of food are given outside of Mass; formerly, given here, emphasizing that the Mass is the center of all worship, the source of all grace.

Per quem hæc ómnia, Dómine, semper bona creas, sanctí✠ficas, viví✠ficas, bene✠dícis et præstas nobis.

PER ✠ IPSUM, ET CUM ✠ IPSO, ET IN ✠ IPSO, est tibi Deo Patri ✠ omnipoténti, in unitáte Spíritus ✠ Sancti, omnis honor et glória. [P] Per ómnia sǽcula sæculórum. [R] *Amen.*

THROUGH WHOM, Lord, Thou dost ever create, ✠ hallow, ✠ fill with life, ✠ bless and bestow upon us all good things.[48]

THROUGH ✠ HIM,
AND WITH ✠ HIM,
AND IN ✠ HIM,[49]

IS TO THEE, GOD THE FATHER ✠ ALMIGHTY,
IN THE UNION OF THE HOLY ✠ GHOST,
ALL HONOR AND GLORY[50]
(P) WORLD WITHOUT END. (R) AMEN.

NOTE 48. "Good things" refer to bread and wine now become Body and Blood of Christ; also all things of nature, created, sanctified, vivified as source of divine life for us. NOTE 49. "Through Him," because Christ is our Mediator; "with Him," we unite in homage to the Father, source of all good; "in Him," since we are incorporated, "in-bodied" in Him through Baptism. NOTE 50. The six Remembrances are now all offered to the Father, made acceptable to Him through His Son, who also enriches us with every blessing and grace for our eternal victory. This offering sums up the entire purpose of the Mass.

[P] OREMUS. Præcéptis salutáribus móniti, et divína institutióne formáti, audémus dícere:

PATER NOSTER, qui es in cælis: Sanctificétur nomen tuum: Advéniat regnum tuum: Fiat volúntas tua, sicut in cælo, et in terra. Panem nostrum quotidiánum da nobis hódie: Et dimítte nobis débita nostra, sicut et nos dimíttimus debitóribus nostris. Et ne nos indúcas in tentatiónem.

[R] *Sed líbera nos a malo.* [P] Amen.

LIBERA NOS, quæsumus, Dómine, ab ómnibus malis, prætéritis, præséntibus et futúris: et intercedénte beáta et gloriósa semper Vírgine Dei Genitríce María, cum beátis Apóstolis tuis Petro et Paulo, atque Andréa, et ómnibus

LORD'S METHOD of PRAYER 51

[P] LET US PRAY: Directed by saving precepts and schooled in divine teaching, we make bold to say:

OUR FATHER, who art in heaven, hallowed be Thy name; Thy kingdom come; Thy will be done on earth as it is in heaven. Give us this day our daily bread; and forgive us our trespasses as we forgive those who trespass against us. And lead us not into temptation.

[R] *But deliver us from evil.* [P] Amen.

Holding paten, priest says:

DELIVER US, O Lord, we beseech Thee, from all evils, past, present, and to come; and through the intercession of the glorious and blessed Mary, ever virgin, mother of God, together with Thy blessed apostles, Peter and Paul and Andrew, and all the saints *(makes Sign of Cross on himself with paten, kisses it)* ✠, grant of Thy goodness, peace in our days,

---

NOTE 51. Having offered to the Father the acceptable Sacrifice of His own Son, he now invites us to the Lord's Supper at which our Victim, Jesus, will give Himself as Food. We prepare by praying according to His method: "hallowing" His name, spreading His "kingdom," doing His "will." Then will He give "bread" sufficient for our body, forgive the "trespasses" of our soul and save us "from the evil" of hell.

Sanctis, ✠ da propítius pacem in diébus nostris: ut ope misericórdiæ tuæ adjúti, et a peccáto simus semper líberi, et ab omni perturbatióne secúri. Per eúmdem Dóminum nostrum Jesum Christum Fílium tuum, qui tecum vivit et regnat in unitáte Spíritus Sancti Deus, per ómnia sǽcula sæculórum. [R] *Amen.*

[P] Pax ✠ Dómini sit ✠ semper ✠ vobíscum. [R] *Et cum spíritu tuo.*

Hæc commíxtio, et consecrátio Córporis et Sánguinis Dómini nostri Jesu Christi, fiat accipiéntibus nobis in vitam ætérnam. Amen.

Agnus Dei, * *qui tollis peccáta mundi: ׀ miserére nobis.* *Said twice*

Agnus Dei, qui tollis peccáta mundi: ׀ dona nobis pacem. *In Masses for Dead say:*

«Dona eis réquiem» instead of *« miserére nobis»* and *« dona eis réquiem sempitérnam »* instead of *« dona nobis pacem.»*

that aided by the riches of Thy mercy, we may be always free from sin and safe from all disquiet.[52]

He genuflects, divides Host in half, breaks off particle, then says last words aloud

Through the same Jesus Christ, Thy Son, our Lord, who liveth and reigneth with Thee in the union of the Holy Ghost, God world without end. [R] *Amen.*

[P] May the peace ✠ of the Lord be ✠ always ✠ with you. [R] *And with thy spirit.*

Drops small particle into chalice

[P] May this mingling and hallowing of the Body and Blood of our Lord Jesus Christ help us who receive it unto life everlasting. Amen.[54]

He genuflects, bows down, strikes breast 3 times

LAMB OF GOD,* *who takest away the sins of the world,* | *have mercy on us.* Said twice *Lamb of God, who takest away the sins of the world,* | *grant us peace.* In Masses for Dead: « *Grant them rest* » *instead of* « *have mercy on us* » *and* « *grant them eternal rest* » *instead of* « *grant us peace.* »

NOTE 52. Sin causes war, class disturbance. NOTE 53. Necessary in early ages to break large Loaf into small pieces for those receiving. Eating of same Bread at same Table made for true social charity and justice. NOTE 54. Separated at the Consecration unto His death (see page 52); now united because He is risen from the dead.

✝ DOMINE JESU CHRISTE, qui dixísti Apóstolis tuis: Pacem relínquo vobis, pacem meam do vobis: ne respícias peccáta mea, sed fidem Ecclésiæ tuæ: eámque secúndum voluntátem tuam pacificáre et coadunáre dignéris: Qui vivis et regnas Deus per ómnia sǽcula sæculórum. Amen.

DOMINE JESU CHRISTE, Fili Dei vivi, qui ex voluntáte Patris, cooperánte Spíritu Sancto, per mortem tuam mundum vivificásti: líbera me per hoc sacrosánctum Corpus et Sánguinem tuum ab ómnibus iniquitátibus meis, et univérsis malis: et fac me tuis semper inhærére mandátis, et a te nunquam separári permíttas: Qui cum eódem Deo Patre, et Spíritu Sancto vivis et regnas Deus in sǽcula sæculórum. Amen.

The Three COMMUNION PRAYERS

Priest inclines, hands joined, eyes intent on Christ

O LORD JESUS CHRIST, who hast said ✝ to Thy apostles: Peace I leave with you, My peace I give to you, regard not my sins but the faith of Thy Church, and deign to give her peace and unity according to Thy will. Who livest and reignest, God world without end. Amen.55

LORD JESUS CHRIST, Son of the living God, who by the will of the Father, with the co-operation of the Holy Ghost, hast by Thy death given life to the world, deliver me by this Thy most sacred Body and Blood from all my sins and from every evil. Make me always cling to Thy commands, and never permit me to be separated from Thee. Who with the same God the Father and the Holy Ghost, livest and reignest, God world without end. Amen.56

NOTE 55. Social graces, unity and peace, in human society can only come through the Church. To commune with neighbor, we must first commune with God. NOTE 56. Interior graces, deliverance from evil, followed by union with God, come most fully to human soul only in Holy Communion.

PERCEPTIO Córporis tui, Dómine Jesu Christe, quod ego indígnus súmere præsúmo, non mihi provéniat in judícium et condemnatiónem: sed pro tua pietáte prosit mihi ad tutaméntum mentis et córporis, et ad medélam percipiéndam: Qui vivis et regnas cum Deo Patre in unitáte Spíritus Sancti Deus, per ómnia sǽcula sæculórum. Amen.

Panem cæléstem accípiam, et nomen Dómini invocábo.

Dómine, non sum dignus, ut intres sub tectum meum: sed tantum dic verbo et sanábitur ánima mea. *Said 3 times*

Corpus Dómini nostri Jesu Christi custódiat ánimam meam in vitam ætérnam. Amen.

Quid retríbuam Dómino pro ómnibus quæ retríbuit mihi? Cálicem salutáris accípiam, et nomen Dómini invocábo.

LET NOT the partaking of Thy Body, O Lord Jesus Christ, which I, all unworthy, make bold to receive, turn to my judgment and condemnation, but by reason of Thy lovingkindness, may it be to me a safeguard of both soul and body, and an effective remedy. Who livest and reignest with God the Father in the union of the Holy Ghost, God world without end. Amen.[57] *Priest genuflects, takes Host and says:* I will take the Bread of Heaven, and call upon the name of the Lord.[58]

Priest strikes breast and says 3 times:

Lord, I am not worthy that Thou shouldst come under my roof; but only say the word and my soul will be healed.[59]

Bell rings  *thrice*

May the Body of our Lord Jesus Christ keep my soul unto life everlasting. Amen.

Priest receives sacred Host

WHAT RETURN shall I make to the Lord for all He hath given me? I will take the chalice of salvation, and I will call upon the name of the Lord.[60]

NOTE 57. Lack of preparation or thanksgiving may gradually lead to unworthy, sacrilegious Communion. NOTE 58. Expresses ardent desire to receive. NOTE 59. Humility, sorrow for sin, yes, but hope of pardon, too. NOTE 60. Prepares soul to receive the Precious Blood by pledging to make a grateful return.

Laudans invocábo Dóminum, et ab inimícis meis salvus ero. Sanguis Dómini nostri Jesu Christi custódiat ánimam meam in vitam ætérnam. Amen.

Confiteor (page 37 LATIN) is said by server and people if Holy Communion is distributed.

[P] Misereátur vestri omnípotens Deus, et dimíssis peccátis vestris, perdúcat vos ad vitam ætérnam. [R] *Amen.*

[P] Indulgéntiam, ✠ absolutiónem, et remissiónem peccatórum vestrórum tríbuat vobis omnípotens et miséricors Dóminus. [R] *Amen.*

[P] Ecce Agnus Dei: ecce qui tollit peccáta mundi.

[P] *and* [R] ***Dómine, non sum dignus, ut intres sub tectum meum: * sed tantum dic verbo, et sanábitur ánima mea.*** *Said 3 times*

[P] Corpus Dómini nostri Jesu Christi custódiat ánimam tuam in vitam ætérnam. Amen.

Praising I will call upon the Lord and I shall be saved from my enemies.
May the Blood of our Lord Jesus Christ keep my soul unto life everlasting. Amen.

Priest receives the Precious Blood.

When faithful receive, all say Confiteor (page 36). If no one receives, omit Confiteor and prayers below.

[P] May almighty God have mercy upon you, forgive you your sins, and bring you to life everlasting. [R] *Amen.*

[P] May the almighty and merciful God grant you pardon, ✠ absolution and full remission of your sins. [R] *Amen.*

Priest lifts up a sacred Host, turns and says:

BEHOLD the Lamb of God, behold Him who taketh away the sins of the world. *Say the following 3 times:*

Lord, I am not worthy that Thou shouldst come under my roof;* but only say the word and my soul will be healed.

Bell rings  *thrice*

Placing Host on communicant's tongue, priest says:[61]

May the Body of our Lord Jesus Christ keep thy soul unto life everlasting. Amen.

NOTE 61. Since laity unite with priest in offering this Sacrifice, they should, like him also, partake of its Fruit; if you cannot or do not receive sacramentally, then make Act of Contrition (page 316) and a Spiritual Communion (page 65), uniting with the divine Victim on the altar.

QUOD ore súmpsimus, Dómine, pura mente capiámus: et de múnere temporáli fiat nobis remédium sempitérnum.

CORPUS tuum, Dómine, quod sumpsi, et Sanguis, quem potávi, adhæreat viscéribus meis: et præsta; ut in me non remáneat scélerum mácula, quem pura et sancta refecérunt sacraménta: Qui vivis et regnas in sæcula sæculórum. Amen.

TURN TO ⑭ COMMUNION VERSE IN Today's Mass

⑮ [P] Dóminus vobíscum. [R] *Et cum spíritu tuo.*

[P] Orémus.

TURN TO ⑯ POSTCOMMUNION IN Today's Mass

At end of Postcommunion: [R] *Amen.*

Priest closes tabernacle and rinses chalice with wine

WHAT HAS PASSED our lips as food, O Lord, may we possess in purity of heart, that what is given us in time be our healing for eternity. [*Sit*]

After consuming wine, priest goes to Epistle side, where wine and water are poured over fingers, while he says:

MAY THY BODY, O Lord, which I have eaten, and Thy Blood, which I have drunk, cleave unto my very soul, and grant that no trace of sin be found in me, whom these pure and holy mysteries have renewed. Who livest and reignest world without end. Amen.

Priest drinks from and dries chalice, then veils it and goes to Epistle side

TURN TO ⑭ COMMUNION VERSE 62 IN Today's Mass →

[P] *At the middle, facing people* The Lord be with you. ⑮

[R] ***And with thy spirit.***

[P] *At the Epistle side* Let us pray.

TURN TO ⑯ POSTCOMMUNION 63 IN Today's Mass →

At end of Postcommunion, the response is: [R] ***Amen.***

NOTE 62. Formerly a long psalm sung during Communion-time. NOTE 63. Prayer for abundant share and abiding possession of the fruits of both Sacrifice and Sacrament.

⑰ [P] Dóminus vobíscum. [R] *Et cum spíritu tuo.*

† [P] Ite, Missa est. [R] *Deo grátias.*

During Advent, also from Septuagesima to end of Lent, say:

† [P] Benedicámus Dómino. [R] *Deo grátias.*

In Masses for Dead: [P] Requiéscant in pace. [R] *Amen.*

PLACEAT tibi, sancta Trínitas, obséquium servitútis meæ: et præsta; ut sacrifícium, quod óculis tuæ majestátis indígnus óbtuli, tibi sit acceptábile, mihíque, et ómnibus pro quibus illud óbtuli, sit, te miseránte, propitiábile. Per Christum Dóminum nostrum. Amen.

† BENEDICAT vos omnípotens Deus, Pater, et Fílius, ✠ et Spíritus Sanctus. [R] *Amen.*

[P] Dóminus vobíscum. [R] *Et cum spíritu tuo.* [P] ✠ Inítium sancti Evangélii secúndum Joánnem. [R] *Glória tibi, Dómine.*

Priest returns to middle, faces people:

[P] The Lord be with you. [R] *And with thy spirit.* 17

[P][64] Go, you are sent forth. †
[R] *Thanks be to God.*

Priest turns to altar, bows, says:

MAY the tribute of my worship be pleasing to Thee, most holy Trinity, and grant that the sacrifice which I, all unworthy, have offered in the presence of Thy majesty, may be acceptable to Thee, and through Thy mercy obtain forgiveness for me and all for whom I have offered it. Through Christ our Lord. Amen.[65] [*Kneel*]

Priest turns to people to impart

The FINAL BLESSING

MAY God almighty bless you: The Father, the Son, ✠ and the Holy Ghost. [R] *Amen.*[66] †

NOTE 64. During Advent, also from Septuagesima to end of Lent, "Go, you are," etc. is replaced by [P] Let us bless the Lord. [R] *Thanks be to God.* In Mass for Dead it is [P] May they rest in peace. [R] *Amen.* NOTE 65. A final summary of the Offering Prayers before and after the Consecration. Public thanksgiving after Communion is brief, but communicants are expected to realize necessity of remaining in private prayer after Mass. NOTE 66. Last Gospel sums up final message: "to as many as received him he gave the power of becoming sons of God."

IN PRINCIPIO erat Verbum, et Verbum erat apud Deum, et Deus erat Verbum. Hoc erat in princípio apud Deum. Omnia per ipsum facta sunt: et sine ipso factum est nihil, quod factum est: in ipso vita erat, et vita erat lux hóminum: et lux in ténebris lucet, et ténebræ eam non comprehendérunt. Fuit homo missus a Deo, cui nomen erat Joánnes. Hic venit in testimónium, ut testimónium perhibéret de lumine, ut omnes créderent per illum. Non erat ille lux, sed ut testimónium perhibéret de lúmine. Erat lux vera, quæ illúminat omnem hóminem veniéntem in hunc mundum. In mundo erat, et mundus per ipsum factus est, et mundus eum non cognóvit. In própria venit, et sui eum non recepérunt. Quotquot autem recepérunt eum, dedit eis potestátem fílios Dei fíeri,

The LAST GOSPEL [*Stand*]

[P] The Lord be with you. [R] *And with thy spirit.* [P] ✠ The beginning of the holy Gospel according to St. John. [R] *Glory be to Thee, O Lord.*

IN THE BEGINNING was the Word, and the Word was with God; and the Word was God. He was in the beginning with God. All things were made through him, and without him was made nothing that has been made. In him was life, and the life was the light of men. And the *light shines* in the darkness; and the *darkness grasped it not.*

There was a man, one sent from God, whose name was John. This man came as a witness, to bear witness concerning the light, that all might believe through him. He was not himself the light, but was to bear witness to the light. It was the true light that *enlightens every man* who comes into the world. He was in the world, and the world was made through him, and the world knew him not. He came unto his own, and his own received him not.

But to *as many as received him* he gave

his, qui credunt in nómine ejus: qui non ex sanguínibus, neque ex voluntáte carnis, neque ex voluntáte viri, sed ex Deo nati sunt. ET VERBUM CARO FACTUM EST, et habitávit in nobis: et vídimus glóriam ejus, glóriam quasi Unigéniti a Patre, plenum grátiæ et veritátis. [R] *Deo grátias.*

SPIRITUAL COMMUNION

At Mass, page 61.

Ask Jesus to come into your soul with an increase of His own divine life since you do not now receive Him sacramentally. Commune with Him. No formal prayers are required. Any simple aspiration is sufficient, such as,

O JESUS, I look to the holy tabernacle in adoration, where Thou art really present for love of me. I, too, love Thee, O my God. I cannot, at this moment, receive Thee in Holy Communion. But come, Jesus, come to visit me by Thy grace; come in a spiritual way into my heart; come to cleanse it and make it like to Thine. Amen.

GO, MY DEAR ANGEL, I beg of thee, to where my Jesus lies; say to my divine Redeemer that I adore Him and that I love Him with all my heart. Invite the adorable Prisoner of love to come into my heart and make it His fixed abode. My heart is too small to afford a lodging for so great a King, but I purpose to enlarge it by faith and love. *«300 days Indul.»*

Return to page 61.

the *power of becoming sons of God;* to those who believe in his name: who were born not of blood, nor of the will of the flesh, nor of the will of man, but of God. *(Genuflect)* AND THE WORD WAS MADE FLESH, AND DWELT AMONG US. And we saw his glory—glory as of the only-begotten of the Father—full of grace and of truth. [R] *Thanks be to God.*

PRAYERS AFTER MASS

Prayers for Russia. His Holiness Pope Pius XI decreed and requested this to be the chief intention for these "Prayers after Mass." Realizing its importance to Russia and the rest of the world, will make for devout recitation.

« Hail Mary,» *three times. Then:*

HAIL, HOLY QUEEN Mother of mercy,| our life, our sweetness, and our hope!* To thee do we cry, poor banished children of Eve, | to thee do we send up our sighs,| mourning and weeping in this valley of tears.* Turn then, most gracious advocate,| thine eyes of mercy towards us;| and after this our exile show unto us the blessed fruit of thy womb| Jesus.* O clement, O loving, O sweet Virgin Mary.*

[P] Pray for us, O holy Mother of God. [R] *That we may be made worthy * of the promises of Christ.*

[P] Let us pray

O GOD, our refuge and our strength, look down with favor upon Thy people who cry unto Thee; and through the intercession of the glorious and immaculate Virgin Mary, Mother of God, of her spouse, blessed Joseph, of Thy holy apostles, Peter and Paul, and all the Saints, mercifully and graciously hear the prayers which we pour forth to Thee for the conversion of sinners and for the liberty and exaltation of holy mother Church. Through the same Christ our Lord. [R] *Amen.*

ST. MICHAEL, the archangel, defend us in battle, | be our protection against the malice and snares of the devil.*We humbly beseech God to command him, | and do thou, O prince of the heavenly host, | by the divine power thrust into hell Satan and the other evil spirits | who roam through the world seeking the ruin of souls. * [R] *Amen.*

Indulgence of 10 years.—S. C. Penit., May 30, 1934.

[P] Most Sacred Heart of Jesus,
[R] *Have mercy on us!* } *3 times*

7 years indulgence.

TURN TO 18 *CATECHISM REVIEW* IN Today's Mass

PRAYER CONCLUSIONS

Each Prayer, Secret and Postcommunion ends differently with one of the following conclusions. THESE SHOULD BE MEMORIZED, since only the first words appear at the end of each Prayer 4, *Secret* 12 *and Postcommunion* 16.

Through our Lord Jesus Christ, Thy Son, who liveth and reigneth with Thee in the union of the Holy Ghost, God world without end. [R] *Amen.*

Through the same Lord Jesus Christ, Thy Son, who liveth and reigneth with Thee in the union of the Holy Ghost, God world without end. [R] *Amen.*

Through Jesus Christ, Thy Son, our Lord, who liveth and reigneth with Thee *in the union of the same Holy Ghost*, God world without end. [R] *Amen.*

Who with Thee liveth and reigneth in the union of the Holy Ghost, God world without end. [R] *Amen.*

Who livest and reignest, with God the Father in the union of the Holy Ghost, God world without end. [R] *Amen.*

PICTURE AND MASS THEME EXPLAINED

"There will be signs in the . . . (heavens) . . . and upon the earth, distress of nations . . . they will see the Son of Man coming . . . lift up your heads, because your redemption is at hand" (GOSPEL).

On His second Advent at the end of the world Jesus will come in the fullness of Divine Power. Then will we be obliged to accept Him as King of Justice. So today let us begin to prepare for this year's anniversary of His first Advent as King of Mercy.

Because His coming is *"nearer"* we are warned to *"rise from sleep, . . . lay aside the works of darkness . . . and put on the Lord Jesus Christ"* (EPISTLE). For this we implore Him to *"show . . . Thy ways"* (INTROIT) where we may meet Him.

Aware of the dangers ahead during this preparation, we call upon His *"power"* to protect us (PRAYER) and to *"cleanse us"* (SECRET). Finally, we promise to *"prepare with due reverence for the coming festival"* (POSTCOMMUNION.)

NOW BEGIN MASS AT 1 ON PAGE 35.

INTROIT *Ps. 24* ❷

To Thee, O Lord, have I lifted up my soul: in Thee, O my God, I put my trust; let me not be ashamed. Neither let my enemies laugh at me; for none of them that wait on Thee shall be confounded.* *Show, O Lord, Thy ways* to me, and teach me Thy paths. Glory be, etc.

« The Introit is always repeated as far as the asterisk—which signifies "Psalm" »*

« The "GLORIA," page 39, is not said in Advent »

Turn to ❸ *on page 38.*

PRAYER ❹

Stir up Thy power, we beseech thee, O Lord, and come: that from the threatening dangers of our sins we may be rescued by Thy protection, and saved by Thy deliverance. Who livest, etc.
Continue below.

EPISTLE *Rom. 13* ❺

Brethren, understanding the time, for it is now the hour for us to *rise from sleep,* because now our salvation is nearer than when we came to believe. *The night is far advanced; the day is at hand.* Let us therefore *lay aside the works of darkness,* and put on the armor of light. Let us walk becomingly as in the day, not in revelry and drunkenness, not in debauchery and wantonness, not in strife and jealousy. But put on *the Lord Jesus Christ.* Thanks be to God.
Continue on next page.

GRADUAL *Ps. 24-84* ⑥

NONE OF THEM that wait on Thee shall be confounded, O Lord. Show, O Lord, Thy ways to me, and teach me Thy paths. Alleluia, alleluia. Show us, O Lord, Thy mercy: and grant us Thy salvation. Alleluia. *Turn to ⑦ on page 40.*

GOSPEL *Luke 21* ⑧

AT THAT TIME, Jesus said to His disciples: "There will be signs in the sun and moon and stars, and upon the earth distress of nations bewildered by the roaring of sea and waves; men fainting for fear and for expectation of the things that are coming on the world; for the powers of heaven will be shaken. And then they will see the Son of Man coming upon a cloud with great power and majesty. But when these things begin to come to pass, *look up, and lift up your heads, because your redemption is at hand.*" And He spoke to them a parable. "Behold the fig tree, and all the trees. When they now put forth their buds, you know that summer is near. Even so, when you see these things coming to pass, know that *the kingdom of God is near.* Amen I say to you, this generation will not pass away till all things have been accomplished. Heaven and earth will pass away, but My words will not pass away." *Turn to ⑨ on page 41.*

OFFERTORY *Ps. 24* ⑩

TO THEE have I lifted up my soul: in Thee, O my God, I put my trust; let me not be ashamed: neither let my enemies laugh at me: for none of them that wait on Thee shall be confounded. *Turn to ⑪ on page 43.*

SECRET ⑫

May these holy offerings, O Almighty God, cleanse us by their mighty power, and make us more pure to approach Him Who is their Author. Through, etc. *Turn to ⑬ on page 47.*

COMMUNION VERSE ⑭

The Lord will give goodness: and our earth shall yield her fruit. *Turn to ⑮ on page 62.*

POST-COMMUNION ⑯

May we receive Thy mercy, O Lord, in the midst of Thy temple, that we may prepare with due reverence for the coming festival of our redemption. Through, etc. *Turn to ⑰ on page 63.*

⑱ *AFTER MASS, REVIEW YOUR CATECHISM.*

I believe that there is one God Who created heaven and earth.

I believe that there are *three Persons* in God: the Father, the Son, and the Holy Ghost; that all three Persons are *distinct* from one another and *equal* in all things; that God has a deep concern for *my* welfare.

I believe that the Father Almighty *out of nothing* created both spiritual and corporeal creatures, namely, the Angels, then the world and finally man.

I believe that God *takes care of all* created things; preserves them, upholds them and governs them, so that there neither is nor can be anything that happens without God's will or permission.

I believe that it is *most helpful to make the Sign of the cross* often and devoutly, because as a three-in-one sign it signifies the *Unity* of God in *Three* Divine Persons and as a sign of the cross it is a reminder of Jesus dying on it to redeem us from sin.

PICTURE AND MASS THEME EXPLAINED

John the Baptist *"had heard in prison of the works of Christ. He sent two of his disciples to say to Him, 'Art Thou He Who is to come, or shall we look for another?'"* (GOSPEL).

Jesus referred to John as *"My messenger"* who prepared the *"way."* John now wanted his disciples to realize that they, too, must follow Christ in this *"way."* Only through the same Jesus Christ, the long expected Savior, will the *"blind"* of soul *"see;"* the *"lame"* of character *"walk;"* the *"lepers"* of sin become *"cleansed;"* the *"poor"* become rich with a new Gospel. (Red figures in picture indicate the blind the lame, the leper.)

The EPISTLE points to these interior and social aspects of the "Christ" way: interiorly, by prayer, to *"glorify"* the Fatherhood of God; socially, by our actions, to *"receive one another"* in the Brotherhood of Man, *"even as Christ has received you."*

Observe how the entire Mass, from INTROIT to POSTCOMMUNION, repeats the same pre-Christmas reminder of the need of serving Christ and neighbor. Why *"look for another"* way?

NOW BEGIN MASS AT 1 ON PAGE 35.

INTROIT *Is. 30* ❷

PEOPLE OF SION, behold the Lord shall come *to save the nations;* and the Lord shall make the glory of His voice to be heard in the joy of your heart.* Give ear, O Thou that rulest Israel: Thou that leadest Joseph *like a sheep.* Glory be, etc. *Turn to* ❸ *on page 38.*

PRAYER ❹

STIR UP OUR HEARTS, O Lord, to *prepare* the ways of Thine only-begotten Son, that through His coming we may be worthy to serve Thee with purified minds. Who with Thee liveth, etc. *Continue below.*

EPISTLE *Rom. 15* ❺

BRETHREN, whatever things have been written have been written for our instruction, that through the patience and the consolation afforded by the Scriptures we may have hope. May then the God of patience and of comfort grant you to be of one mind towards one another according to Jesus Christ; that, one in spirit, you may with one mouth glorify the God and Father of our Lord Jesus Christ. Wherefore *receive one another, even as Christ has received you* to the honor of God. For I say that Christ Jesus has been a minister of the circumcision in order to show God's fidelity in confirming the promises made to our fathers, but that the Gentiles glorify God because of His mercy, as it is written, "Therefore will I praise Thee among the Gentiles, and will sing to Thy Name." And again he says, "Rejoice, you Gentiles, with His people." And again, "Praise the Lord, all you Gentiles; and sing His praises, all you peoples." And again Isaias says, "There shall be the root of Jesse, and *He*

Who shall arise to rule the Gentiles . . . in Him the Gentiles shall hope." Now may the God of hope fill you with all joy and peace in believing, that you may abound in hope and in the power of the Holy Spirit. THANKS BE TO GOD. *Continue below.*

GRADUAL *Ps. 49* ⑥

OUT OF SION the loveliness of His beauty: God shall come manifestly. Gather ye together His saints to Him; who have set His covenant before sacrifices. Alleluia, alleluia. I rejoiced at the things that were said to me: we shall go into the house of the Lord. Alleluia. *Turn to* ⑦ *on page 40.*

GOSPEL Matt. 11 ⑧

AT THAT TIME, when *John* had heard in prison of the *works of Christ*, he *sent two of his disciples* to say to Him, *"Art Thou He Who is to come, or shall we look for another?"* And Jesus answering said to them, "Go and report to John *what you have heard and seen:* the blind see, the lame walk, the lepers are cleansed, the deaf hear, the dead rise, the poor have the gospel preached to them. And blessed is he who is not scandalized in Me." But as these were going, Jesus began to say to the crowds concerning John, "What did you go out to the desert to see? A reed shaken by the wind? But what did you go out to see? A man clothed in soft garments? Behold, those who wear soft garments are in the houses of kings. But what did you go out to see? A prophet? Yes, I tell you, and more than a prophet. This is he of whom it is written, 'Behold, I send My messenger before Thy face, who shall make ready Thy way before Thee.' "
Turn to ⑨ *on page 41.*

OFFERTORY *Ps. 84* ⑩

THOU WILT TURN, O God, and bring us to life; and Thy people shall rejoice in Thee: show us, O Lord, Thy mercy, and grant us Thy salvation. *Turn to ⑪ on page 43.*

SECRET ⑫

BE APPEASED, we beseech Thee, O Lord, by our humble prayers and offerings, and, since we cannot plead any merits of our own, grant us the aid of Thy protection. Through, etc. *Turn to ⑬ on page 47.*

COMMUNION VERSE ⑭

ARISE, O JERUSALEM, and stand on high: and *behold the joy* that cometh to thee from thy God. *Turn to ⑮ on page 62.*

POST-COMMUNION ⑯

HAVING BEEN FILLED with Thy food of spiritual nourishment, we humbly beseech Thee, O Lord, through our reception of this Sacrament to teach us how to spurn earthly goods and to love those of heaven. Through Our Lord, etc. *Turn to ⑰ on page 63.*

⑱ ***AFTER MASS, REVIEW YOUR CATECHISM.***

I believe that Jesus Christ is the Second Person of the Blessed Trinity, equal to God the Father and God the Holy Ghost.

I believe that Jesus Christ came down from heaven and *took human form* while remaining God.

I believe that the one Person, Jesus Christ, is both God and man.

Review "Winter", page 31.

PICTURE AND MASS THEME EXPLAINED

"I (John) *am the voice of one crying in the desert,... but* (pointing to Christ) *in the midst of you there has stood One Whom you do not know"* (GOSPEL).

This is known as *"Rejoice"* Sunday, from the opening word of the INTROIT. Despite our self-praised progress, real joy is missing from modern life. In such a "desert" we must look to Christ. Only He can *"bring light to the darkness of our minds"* (PRAYER). Only He can bless, deliver and forgive (OFFERTORY). Only He can "say to the faint-hearted, 'Take courage'" (COMMUNION VERSE).

During these days before Christmas *"have no anxiety"* about selecting or receiving mere tinsel gifts, but prepare *"in... prayer... with thanksgiving"* and *"guard... your minds in Christ,"* the true source of our joy (EPISTLE).

NOW BEGIN MASS AT 1 ON PAGE 35.

INTROIT 2
Philip. 4

REJOICE IN THE LORD always; again I say, rejoice. Let your moderation be known to all men. The Lord is near. Have no anxiety, but in every prayer and supplication with thanksgiving let your petitions be made known to God.* Lord, Thou hast blest Thy land; Thou hast turned away the captivity of Jacob. Glory be, etc.

Turn to 3 on page 38.

PRAYER ④

WE BESEECH THEE, O Lord, incline Thine ear to our petitions and *bring light to the darkness of our minds* by the grace of Thy visitation. Who livest, etc. *Continue below.*

EPISTLE *Philip. 4* ⑤

BRETHREN: rejoice in the Lord always; again I say, rejoice. Let your moderation be known to all men. *The Lord is near. Have no anxiety,* but in every *prayer* and supplication *with thanksgiving* let your petitions be made known to God. And may the peace of God which surpasses all understanding *guard your hearts and your minds in Christ Jesus,* Our Lord. THANKS BE TO GOD. *Continue below.*

GRADUAL *Ps. 79* ⑥

THOU, O LORD, that sittest upon the Cherubim, stir up Thy might, *and come.* Give ear, O Thou that rulest Israel: Thou that leadest Joseph like a sheep. Alleluia, alleluia. Stir up Thy might, O Lord, *and come:* that Thou mayest save us. Alleluia. *Turn to* ⑦ *on page 40.*

GOSPEL *John 1* ⑧

AT THAT TIME, the Jews sent to John from Jerusalem priests and Levites to ask him, "Who art thou?" And he acknowledged and did not deny; and he acknowledged, "I am not the Christ." And they asked him, "What then? Art thou Elias?" And he said, "I am not." "Art thou the Prophet?" And he answered, "No." They therefore said to him, "Who art thou? that we may give an answer to those who sent us. What has thou to say of thyself?" He said, "I am the voice of one crying in the desert, 'Make straight the way of the Lord,' as said Isaias the prophet." And they who had been sent were from among the Pharisees. And they asked him, and said to him, "Why, then, dost thou baptize, if thou art not the Christ, nor Elias, nor the Prophet?" John said to them in answer, "I baptize with water; *but in the midst of you there has stood One Whom you do not know.* He it is Who is to come after me, Who has been set above me, the strap of Whose sandal I am not worthy to loose." These things took place at Bethany, beyond the Jordan, where John was baptizing. *Turn to* 9 *on page 41.*

OFFERTORY *Ps. 84* 10

LORD, Thou hast blest Thy land: Thou hast turned away the captivity of Jacob: Thou hast forgiven the iniquity of Thy people. *Turn to* 11 *on page 43.*

SECRET 12

MAY THIS SACRIFICE of our devotion, we pray Thee, O Lord, be continually offered to Thee, both to fulfill Thy purpose in these holy mysteries and to work in us the wonders of Thy salvation. Through Our Lord, etc. *Turn to* 13 *on page 47.*

COMMUNION VERSE 14

SAY TO THE *faint-hearted, "Take courage,* and fear not: behold our God will come and will save us." *Turn to* 15 *on page 62.*

POST-COMMUNION 16

WE IMPLORE Thy mercy, O Lord, that these Divine aids may help us to atone for sin and prepare for the coming Feast. Through, etc. *Turn to* 17 *on page 63.*

18 ***Review "Share in Priesthood", page 15.***

Fourth Sunday of Advent

PICTURE AND MASS THEME EXPLAINED

"John, the son of Zachary," to a world now awaiting its God, pleads for our final pre-Christmas "make-ready." *"Make ready the way of the Lord, make straight His paths"* (GOSPEL).

Heroically, in the desert, he warns against the softness of life in the city, pictured in the background. Alive to the danger of a "soft-garments" life, he is seen in a rough "garment of camel's hair," carrying a baptismal shell, *"preaching a baptism of repentance."*

NOW BEGIN MASS AT ❶ ON PAGE 35.

INTROIT *Is. 45* ❷

DROP DOWN DEW, ye heavens, from above, and let the clouds rain the just; let the earth be opened and bud forth a Savior.* The heavens show forth the glory of God, and the firmament declareth the work of His hands. Glory be, etc. *Turn to ❸ on page 38.*

PRAYER ❹

STIR UP THY MIGHT, we beseech Thee, O Lord, and come; accompany us with great power, so that by the help of Thy grace, we may be mercifully hastened along when our sins weigh us down, Who livest, etc. *Continue below.*

EPISTLE
1 Cor. 4 ❺

BRETHREN, let a man so account us, as servants of Christ and *stewards of the mysteries of God.* Now here it is required in stewards that a man be found trustworthy. But with me it is a very small matter to be judged by you or by man's tribunal. Nay I do not even judge my own self. For I have nothing on my conscience, yet I am not thereby justified; but He Who judges me is the Lord. Therefore, pass no judgment before the time, *until the Lord comes,* Who will both bring to light the things hidden in darkness and make manifest the counsels of hearts; and then everyone will have his praise from God. THANKS BE TO GOD. *Continue below.*

GRADUAL
Ps. 144 ❻

THE LORD is nigh unto all them that call upon Him, to all that call upon Him in truth. My mouth shall speak the praise of the Lord: and let all flesh bless His Holy Name. Alleluia, alleluia. Come, O Lord, and do not delay; forgive the sins of Thy people Israel. Alleluia. *Turn to* ❼ *on page 40.*

GOSPEL
Luke 3 ❽

NOW IN THE FIFTEENTH YEAR of the reign of Tiberius Cæsar, when Pontius Pilate was procurator of Judea, and Herod tetrarch of Galilee, and Philip his brother tetrarch of the district of Iturea and Trachonitis, and Lysanias tetrarch of

Abilina, during the high priesthood of Annas and Caiphas, the word of God came to John, the son of Zachary, in the desert. And he went into all the region about the Jordan, *preaching a baptism of repentance* for the forgiveness of sins, as it is written in the book of the words of Isaias the prophet, "The voice of one *crying in the desert, 'Make ready the way of the Lord, make straight His paths.* Every valley shall be filled, and every mountain and hill shall be brought low, and the crooked shall be made straight, and the rough ways smooth; *and all mankind shall see the salvation of God.'"* *Turn to ⑨ on page 41.*

OFFERTORY *Luke 1* ⑩

HAIL, MARY, full of grace, the Lord is with thee. Blessed art thou among women and *blessed is the fruit of thy womb!* *Turn to ⑪ on page 43.*

SECRET ⑫

LOOK DOWN favorably upon these sacrifices, we beseech Thee, O Lord, that they may be profitable both to our devotion and salvation. Through Our Lord, etc. *Turn to ⑬ on page 47.*

COMMUNION VERSE ⑭

BEHOLD A VIRGIN shall conceive, and *bring forth a son;* and His name shall be called Emmanuel. *Turn to ⑮ on page 62.*

POST-COMMUNION ⑯

HAVING RECEIVED Thy gifts, we pray Thee, O Lord, that the frequent reception of this Sacrament may advance the work of our salvation. Through Our Lord, etc. *Turn to ⑰ on page 63.*

⑱ **Review *"Preparing to Receive"*, page 16.**

PICTURE AND MASS THEME EXPLAINED

"And she brought forth her firstborn Son, and wrapped Him in swaddling clothes, and laid Him in a manger, because there was no room for them in the inn" (GOSPEL). This picture recalls the *triple* Birth of Jesus. (In homage, each priest is privileged to offer three Masses today.)

Our first duty is to adore Jesus as true God in His *eternal* birth as "Son of the Father;" to ignore Him would be our everlasting folly (INTROIT, GRADUAL, COMMUNION VERSE).

Our second duty is to recognize Jesus as true Man in His *earthly* or temporal birth as "Son of Mary."

Our third duty is to realize more and more the *spiritual* birth of Jesus in our souls at the time of our Baptism. Then were we "Christened," *reborn* as members of His Mystical Body.

We must grow with Him during the coming year, by *"rejecting ungodliness,"* by *"pursuing good works"* (EPISTLE). Before the crib today, in union with Mary, contemplate this *threefold* Birth of Jesus.

NOW BEGIN MASS AT ❶ ON PAGE 35.

INTROIT *Ps. 2* ❷

THE LORD hath said to me: Thou art My Son, this day have I begotten Thee.* Why have the Gentiles raged, and the people devised vain things? Glory be, etc. *Turn to* ❸ *on page 38.*

PRAYER ❹

O GOD, Who hast made this most sacred night to shine forth with the brightness of the True Light, grant, we beseech Thee, that we, who *have known* the mysteries of His Light *on earth,* may also enjoy His happiness in heaven. Who with Thee, etc. *Continue below.*

EPISTLE *Titus 2* ❺

DEARLY BELOVED, the grace of God our Savior *has appeared to all men,* instructing us, in order that, rejecting ungodliness and worldly lusts, we may live temperately and justly and piously in this world; looking for the blessed hope and glorious coming of our great God and Savior, Jesus Christ, Who *gave Himself for us* that He might redeem us from all iniquity and cleanse for Himself an acceptable people, pursuing good works. Thus speak, and exhort: in Christ Jesus Our Lord. THANKS BE TO GOD. *Continue below.*

GRADUAL *Ps. 109* ❻

WITH THEE is the principality in the day of Thy strength; in the brightness of the saints, from the womb before the day-star I begot Thee. The Lord said to my Lord: Sit Thou at My right hand, until I make Thy enemies Thy footstool. Alleluia, alleluia. The Lord hath said to Me: Thou art My Son, this day have I begotten Thee. Alleluia. *Turn to* ❼ *on page 40.*

GOSPEL
Luke 2 8

AT THAT TIME, there went forth a decree from Cæsar Augustus that a census of the whole world should be taken. This first census took place while Cyrinus was governor of Syria. And all were going, each to his own town, to register. And Joseph also went from Galilee out of the town of Nazareth into Judea to the town of David, which is called Bethlehem—because he was of the house and family of David—to register, together with Mary his espoused wife, who was with child. And it came to pass while they were there, that the days for her to be delivered were fulfilled. And *she brought forth her firstborn Son, and wrapped Him in swaddling clothes, and laid Him in a manger, because there was no room for them in the inn.* And there were shepherds in the same district living in the fields and keeping watch over their flock by night. And behold, an angel of the Lord stood by them and the glory of God shone round about them, and they feared exceedingly. And the angel said to them, "Do not be afraid, for behold, I bring you good news of great joy which shall be to all the people; for there has been born to you today in the town of David a Savior, Who is Christ the Lord. And this shall be a sign to you: you will find an infant wrapped in swaddling clothes and lying in a manger." And suddenly there was with the angel a multitude of the heavenly host praising God and saying, *"Glory to God* in the highest, and *peace on earth among men* of good will." *Turn to* 9 *on page 41.*

OFFERTORY *Ps. 95* ⑩

LET THE HEAVENS rejoice, and let the earth be glad before the face of the Lord, because He cometh. *Turn to* ⑪ *on page 43.*

SECRET ⑫

MAY OUR OFFERING on this feast day be acceptable to Thee, O Lord, and through this holy interchange of gifts, may we be found like unto Him, Who has *united* our human nature with the Divine. Who with Thee, etc. *Turn to* ⑬ *on page 47.*

COMMUNION VERSE ⑭

IN THE BRIGHTNESS of the saints, from the womb before the day-star I begot Thee. *Turn to* ⑮ *on page 62.*

POST COMMUNION ⑯

GRANT, we beseech Thee, O Lord, our God, that we who rejoice in celebrating the birth of our Lord Jesus Christ, may deserve by worthy conduct to be *admitted* into His company. Who with Thee, etc. *Turn to* ⑰ *on page 63.*

⑱ *AFTER MASS, REVIEW YOUR CATECHISM.*

I believe that Jesus Christ lived, suffered, and died to *redeem me from my sins,* and opened the gates of heaven which had been closed to me by the sin of my first parents, Adam and Eve.

I believe that Jesus Christ *rose from the dead* by His own power; reunited His Soul to His Body to live again in His human nature, immortal and glorious as the *promise and guarantee of our resurrection.*

I believe that Jesus Christ *ascended* from this earth into heaven.

Sunday between Christmas and New Year's

PICTURE AND MASS THEME EXPLAINED

"Behold, this Child is destined for the fall and for the rise of many in Israel" (GOSPEL).

This prophecy that Jesus is also *"a sign that shall be contradicted,"* indicates what we, too, may expect as "sons of God"; yet it strengthens our hope, if we but place ourselves daily under Mary's care; then the last words of the GOSPEL may also be applied to us: *"the Child grew and became strong ... full of wisdom."*

Yes, we are the *"sons"* and *"heirs"* of God, Whom we can call *"Father,"* because of *"His Son, born of a woman,"* Mary (EPISTLE). Hence, Jesus, our Brother, actually *"leapt down from heaven ... with beauty, ... with strength"* (INTROIT), to *"direct our actions"* in His *"Name"* (PRAYER).

In the GRADUAL we offer our *"good word"* of gratitude for the final victory. Then we will realize that Antichrists *"who sought the Child's life are dead"* (COMMUNION VERSE).

NOW BEGIN MASS AT ❶ ON PAGE 35.

INTROIT *Wis. 18* ❷

WHILE ALL THINGS were in quiet silence, and the night was in the midst of her course, Thy almighty Word, O Lord, *leapt down from heaven,* from Thy royal throne.* The Lord hath reigned, He is clothed with *beauty:* the Lord is clothed with *strength,* and hath girded Himself. Glory be, etc. *Turn to* ❸ *on page 38.*

PRAYER ❹

O ALMIGHTY and Eternal God, do Thou *direct our actions* according to Thy good pleasure, that we may deserve to abound in good works in the Name of Thy beloved Son, Who with Thee, etc. *Continue below.*

EPISTLE *Gal. 4* ❺

BRETHREN, as long as the heir is a child, he differs in no way from a slave, though he is the master of all; but he is under guardians and stewards until the time set by his father. So we too, when we were children, were enslaved under the elements of the world. But when the fullness of time came, *God sent His Son, born of a woman,* born under the Law, that He might redeem those who were under the Law, that we might receive the *adoption of sons.* And because *you are sons,* God has sent the Spirit of His Son into our hearts, crying, *"Abba, Father."* So that he is *no longer a slave, but a son;* and *if a son, an heir also* through God. THANKS BE TO GOD. *Continue below.*

GRADUAL *Ps. 44-92* ❻

THOU ART BEAUTIFUL above the sons of men: grace is poured abroad in Thy lips. My heart hath uttered *a good word,* I speak my works to the King: my tongue is the pen of a scrivener that writeth swiftly. Alleluia, alleluia. The Lord hath reigned, He is clothed with beauty: the Lord is clothed with strength, and hath girded Himself with power. Alleluia. *Turn to* 7 *on page 40.*

GOSPEL *Luke 2* 8

AT THAT TIME, Joseph and Mary, the mother of Jesus, were marvelling at the things spoken concerning Him. And Simeon blessed them, and said to Mary His mother, *"Behold, this Child is destined for the fall and for the rise of many in Israel, and for a sign that shall be contradicted.* And thy own soul a sword shall pierce, that the thoughts of many hearts may be revealed." And there was Anna, a prophetess, daughter of Phanuel, of the tribe of Aser. She was of a great age, having lived with her husband seven years from her maidenhood, and by herself as a widow to eighty-four years. She never left the temple, worshipping with fastings and prayers night and day. And coming up at that very hour, she began to give praise to the Lord, and spoke of Him to all who were awaiting the redemption of Jerusalem. And when they had fulfilled all things as prescribed in the Law of the Lord, they returned into Galilee, to their own town of *Nazareth.* And *the Child grew and became strong. He was full of wisdom* and the grace of God was upon Him. *Turn to* 9 *on page 41.*

OFFERTORY *Ps. 92* 10

GOD HATH ESTABLISHED the world, which shall not be moved: Thy throne, O God, is prepared from of old; Thou art from everlasting. *Turn to* ⑪ *on page 43.*

SECRET ⑫

GRANT, we beseech Thee, O Almighty God, that this gift now offered in the sight of Thy Majesty, may obtain for us both the grace of a tender devotion and the reward of a happy eternity. Through Our Lord, etc. *Turn to* ⑬ *on page 47.*

COMMUNION VERSE ⑭

"TAKE the Child and His mother, and go into the land of Israel, for those who sought the Child's life are dead." *Turn to* ⑮ *on page 62.*

POST-COMMUNION ⑯

BY THE ACTION of this Sacrament within us, O Lord, may our vices be purged, and our just desires be satisfied. Through Our Lord, etc. *Turn to* ⑰ *on page 63.*

⑱ *AFTER MASS, REVIEW YOUR CATECHISM.*

I believe that the Holy Ghost is the Third Person of the Blessed Trinity equal in all things to the Father and to the Son.

I believe that the Holy Ghost came down *visibly* upon the Apostles on Pentecost Day; that He *confirmed* them in their faith and filled them with the fulness of all gifts so that they might *preach* the Gospel and *spread the Church* throughout the whole world.

I believe that the Holy Ghost will guide my Church *infallibly without error* in the way of truth and charity until the end of time.

New Year's Day
« Feast of Circumcision of Christ »

PICTURE AND MASS THEME EXPLAINED

"When eight days were fulfilled for His circumcision, His name was called Jesus" (GOSPEL). Thus does a New Year begin! Jesus immediately sheds a few drops of His Precious Blood as a pledge of His complete Bloodshedding later on.

Our new year began at our Baptism (pictured in background). Then were we *reborn;* then were we given a Christian name. Today, Jesus is marked as a victim for sacrifice. He will take our *"government . . . upon His shoulder"* (INTROIT). Now it can be said: *"All the ends of the earth have seen . . . salvation"* (GRADUAL, COMMUNION VERSE). Why He *"gave Himself"* is explained in the EPISTLE, namely, to *"redeem us."* Moreover, it is through Mary *"we have deserved to receive the Author of Life, Jesus Christ"* (PRAYER). We implore her aid that our sacrificial *"offerings"* (SECRET) and Communion may *"wash away our guilt"* (POSTCOMMUNION).

NOW BEGIN MASS AT ❶ ON PAGE 35.

INTROIT *Is. 9* ❷

A CHILD IS BORN to us, and a Son is given to us: Whose *government is upon His shoulder:* and His name shall be called the Angel of great counsel.* Sing ye to the Lord a new canticle:

because He hath done wonderful things. Glory be, etc. *Turn to* ❸ *on page 38.*

PRAYER ❹

O God, Who, by the fruitful virginity of Blessed Mary, hast bestowed upon mankind the rewards of eternal salvation, grant, we beseech Thee, that we may always feel the *benefit of her intercession,* through whom we have deserved to receive the Author of Life, Jesus Christ, Thy Son and Our Lord, Who with Thee, etc. *Continue below.*

EPISTLE ❺
Titus 2

Dearly beloved, the grace of God our Savior has appeared to all men, instructing us, in order that, rejecting ungodliness and worldly lusts, we may live temperately and justly and piously in this world; looking for the blessed hope and glorious coming of our great God and Savior, Jesus Christ, *Who gave Himself* for us that He might *redeem us* from all iniquity and *cleanse* for Himself an acceptable people, pursuing good works. Thus speak, and exhort: in Christ Jesus our Lord. Thanks be to God. *Continue below.*

GRADUAL ❻
Ps. 97

All the ends *of the earth have seen the salvation* of our God: sing joyfully to God, all the earth. The Lord hath made known His salvation: He hath revealed His justice in the sight of the Gentiles. Alleluia, alleluia. God, Who diversely spoke in times past to the fathers by the prophets, last of all in these days hath spoken to us by His Son. Alleluia. *Turn to* ❼ *on page 40.*

GOSPEL *Luke 2* ⑧

AT THAT TIME, when eight days were fulfilled for His circumcision, His name was called Jesus, the Name given Him by the angel before He was conceived in the womb. *Turn to* ⑨ *on page 41.*

OFFERTORY *Ps. 88* ⑩

THINE ARE THE HEAVENS and Thine is the earth: the world and the fulness thereof Thou hast founded; justice and judgment are the preparation of Thy throne. *Turn to* ⑪ *on page 43.*

SECRET ⑫

RECEIVE OUR OFFERINGS and prayers, we beseech Thee, O Lord; and through these heavenly mysteries, cleanse us and graciously hear us. Through Our Lord, etc. *Turn to* ⑬ *on page 47.*

COMMUNION VERSE ⑭

ALL THE ends of the earth have seen the salvation of our God. *Turn to* ⑮ *on page 62.*

POST-COMMUNION ⑯

MAY THIS COMMUNION, O Lord, *wash away our guilt* and make us ready, through the intercession of the Blessed Virgin Mary, Mother of God, to share in this heavenly remedy. Through the same, etc. *Turn to* ⑰ *on page 63.*

⑱ *AFTER MASS, REVIEW YOUR CATECHISM.*

I believe that Jesus Christ will come again at the end of the world, *for a Last Judgment,* to reward me or punish me, according as I have done good or evil in this life.

Sunday between New Year's and Epiphany

« Feast of the Holy Name — If no Sunday occurs it is celebrated on January 2nd »

PICTURE AND MASS THEME EXPLAINED

"All the nations . . . shall come and adore before Thee, O Lord; and they shall glorify Thy Name" (COMMUNION VERSE). In this picture the Church Militant on earth, represented by a human family, unites with the Church Triumphant in heaven, represented by Mary and Joseph.

What is in a name? Salvation, if it be the Holy Name of Jesus ! Reverence for this *"Name"* is urged in the INTROIT. *"Heaven"* is promised to those who *"venerate"* It *"on earth"* (PRAYER). Miracles have been wrought by invoking His *"Name"* (EPISTLE). The call to Christian action is found in this *"Name"* (GRADUAL).

The Eternal Father bestowed this *"name"* through *"the angel,"* thereby indicating the work *"Jesus"* was to do (GOSPEL). Each Christian must glorify this *"Name"* of Mercy in his own private life (OFFERTORY). Our Mass today is a *"sacrifice of praise"* to the majesty of this "*Name*" (SECRET), written in letters of indelible red on the parchment of His Flesh, that our "*names*" might be "*written in heaven*" (POSTCOMMUNION).

NOW BEGIN MASS AT 1 ON PAGE 35.

INTROIT *Philip. 2* 2

AT the *Name of Jesus every knee should bend* of those in heaven, on earth and under the earth, and every tongue should confess that the Lord Jesus Christ is in the glory of God the Father.* O Lord, our Lord, how wonderful is Thy Name in the whole earth! Glory be, etc. *Turn to* 3 *on page 38.*

PRAYER 4

O GOD, Who didst appoint Thine only-begotten Son to be the Savior of the human race, and didst command that He be called Jesus, mercifully grant that we may enjoy in heaven the vision of Him *Whose Holy Name we venerate on earth.* Through the same Lord, etc. *Continue below.*

EPISTLE *Acts 4* 5

IN THOSE DAYS, Peter, filled with the Holy Spirit, said to them, "Rulers of the people and elders, if we are on trial today about a good work done to a cripple, as to how this man has been made whole, be it known to all of you and to all the people of Israel that *in the Name of Jesus* Christ of Nazareth, Whom you crucified, Whom God has raised from the dead, even in this Name does he stand here before you, sound. This is 'the stone that was rejected by you, the builders, which has become the corner stone.' Neither is there salvation in any other. For there is *no other name* under heaven given to men by which we must be saved." THANKS BE TO GOD. *Continue below.*

GRADUAL *Ps. 105* ⑥

SAVE US, O Lord, our God, and gather us from among the nations: that *we may give thanks to Thy Holy Name,* and may glory in Thy praise. Thou, O Lord, art our Father and Redeemer. Thy Name is from eternity. Alleluia, alleluia. My mouth shall speak the praise of the Lord, and let all flesh bless His Holy Name. Alleluia. *Turn to* ⑦ *on page 40.*

GOSPEL *Luke 2* ⑧

AT THAT TIME, when eight days were fulfilled for His circumcision, *His name was called Jesus,* the name given Him by the angel before He was conceived in the womb. *Turn to* ⑨ *on page 41.*

OFFERTORY *Ps. 85* ⑩

I WILL PRAISE THEE, O Lord my God, with my whole heart, and *I will glorify Thy Name forever;* for Thou, O Lord, art sweet and mild, and plenteous in mercy to all that call upon Thee. Alleluia. *Turn to* ⑪ *on page 43.*

SECRET ⑫

MAY THY BLESSING, O most merciful God, by which every creature lives, sanctify this our sacrifice, which we offer unto Thee for the glory of the Name of Thy Son, Our Lord Jesus Christ; that it may please Thy Majesty as an act of praise and help us as a means of salvation. Through the same, etc. *Turn to* ⑬ *on page 47.*

COMMUNION VERSE (14)

ALL THE *nations* Thou hast made shall come and adore before Thee, O Lord; and they shall glorify Thy Name: for Thou art great and dost wonderful things. Thou art God alone. Alleluia. *Turn to* (15) *on page 62.*

POST-COMMUNION (16)

O ALMIGHTY and eternal God, Who hast created and redeemed us, graciously look upon our petitions, and with a favorable and kind regard, please receive the sacrifice of the Saving Victim, which we have offered to Thy Majesty, in honor of the Name of Thy Son, Our Lord Jesus Christ; that by Thy grace, we may rejoice to see our *names written in heaven,* under the glorious Name of Jesus, the pledge of our eternal predestination. Through the same Lord, etc. *Turn to* (17) *on page 63.*

(18) *AFTER MASS, REVIEW YOUR CATECHISM.*

I believe that the Holy Ghost begins the work of saving and sanctifying my soul by *incorporating me into Christ* through sanctifying grace; by infusing His virtues, His gifts and actual graces of every kind, enlightening my mind, moving my will; that *I must cooperate* with Him to gain everlasting life.

I believe that the chief purpose of my life is to give *glory to God* and to *save my immortal soul.*

I believe that a Christian is a person *baptized* into the Mystical Body of Christ; that henceforth, he becomes a *follower of Christ* by *professing* the true and entire faith of Christ and by striving to *keep the law* of Christ according to his state of life before God and neighbor.

PICTURE AND MASS THEME EXPLAINED

"There came Magi from the East to Jerusalem, saying, 'Where is the newly born King of the Jews? . . . We have seen His star in the East and have come to worship Him'" (GOSPEL).

Epiphany means "an apparition, or manifestation" of God becoming visible to the Gentile world. Today Jesus manifests a new *"kingdom"* (INTROIT), to which the star-light of *"faith"* guides all wise men (PRAYER).

The EPISTLE is a revealing picture of the *"darkness"* of the Jewish Old Testament; a prophecy also of the *"brightness"* of Christ shining in a world where men may now *"see."*

The GOSPEL tells of the faith of the *"Magi"* divinely guided by the *"star"*; how this faith manifested itself in action by their seeking instruction from God's priests, by prostrating their very beings and offering their best treasures before the frail Babe in Mary's arms: *GOLD* in homage to His new Kingship, symbol of their *hearts* offering love; *INCENSE* in homage to His Divinity, symbol of their *minds* offering adoration; *MYRRH* in homage to His Humanity, symbol of their *bodies* offering to do penance.

A truly great Feast ! *"Arise, be enlightened"* (EPISTLE).

NOW BEGIN MASS AT ❶ ON PAGE 35.

INTROIT *Mal. 3* ❷

BEHOLD THE *Lord the Ruler is come:* and a kingdom is in His hand, and power and dominion.* Give to the king Thy judgment, O God: and to the king's Son Thy justice. Glory be, etc. *Turn to* ❸ *on page 38.*

PRAYER ❹

O GOD, Who didst manifest Thine only-begotten Son to the Gentiles by the guidance of a star, mercifully grant that we, who know Thee now by faith, may be led even further to gaze on the beauty of Thy Majesty. Through the same, etc. *Continue below.*

EPISTLE *Is. 60* ❺

ARISE, *be enlightened, O* Jerusalem; for *thy light is come,* and the glory of the Lord is risen upon thee. For behold *darkness shall cover the earth,* and a mist the people; but the *Lord shall arise upon thee,* and His glory shall be seen upon thee. And the Gentiles shall *walk in thy light,* and kings in the brightness of thy rising. Lift up thy eyes round about, and see; all these are gathered together, they are come to thee: thy sons shall come from afar, and thy daughters shall rise up at thy side. Then shalt thou see and abound and thy heart shall wonder and be enlarged, when the multitude of the sea shall be converted to thee, the strength of the Gentiles shall come to thee. The multitude of camels shall cover thee, the dromedaries of Madian and Epha; all they from Saba shall come, bringing *gold and frankincense,* and showing forth praise to the Lord. THANKS BE TO GOD. *Continue on next page.*

GRADUAL *Is. 60* 6

ALL THEY from Saba shall come, bringing gold and frankincense, and showing forth praise to the Lord. Arise and be enlightened, O Jerusalem, for the glory of the Lord is risen upon thee. Alleluia, alleluia. We have seen His star in the east: and are come with gifts to adore the Lord. Alleluia. *Turn to* 7 *on page 40.*

GOSPEL *Matt. 2* 8

WHEN JESUS was born in Bethlehem of Judea, in the days of King Herod, behold, there came Magi from the East to Jerusalem, saying, "Where is the newly born King of the Jews? For *we have seen His star in the East and have come to worship Him."* But when King Herod heard this, he was troubled, and so was all Jerusalem with him. And gathering together all the chief priests and Scribes of the people, he inquired of them where the Christ was to be born. And they said to him, "In Bethlehem of Judea; for thus it is written through the prophet, 'And thou, Bethlehem, of the land of Juda, art by no means least among the princes of Juda; for from thee shall come forth a leader Who shall rule My people Israel.' " Then Herod summoned the Magi secretly, and carefully ascertained from them the time when the star had appeared to them. And sending them to Bethlehem, he said, *"Go and make careful inquiry concerning the Child,* and when you have found Him, bring me word, that I too may go and worship Him." Now they, having heard the king, went their way. And behold, the star that they had seen in the East went before them, until it came and stood over the place where the Child was. And *when they saw the star they rejoiced exceedingly.* And entering the house, they *found the Child with Mary His mother* (*here all kneel down*) and falling down *they worshipped Him.* And opening their treasures they offered Him gifts of *gold, frankincense* and *myrrh.* And being warned in a dream not to return to Herod, they went back to their own country by another way. *Turn to* ⑨ *on page 41.*

OFFERTORY *Ps. 71* ⑩

THE KINGS of Tharsis and the islands shall offer presents: the kings of the Arabians and of Saba shall bring gifts: and all kings of the earth shall adore Him; all nations shall serve Him. *Turn to* ⑪ *on page 43.*

SECRET ⑫

O LORD, look down in Thy mercy upon these gifts of Thy Church in which gold, frankincense and myrrh are no longer offered; but rather He is sacrificed and received Who is signified by these gifts, namely, Jesus Christ, Thy Son, Our Lord. Who with Thee, etc. *Turn to* ⑬ *on page 47.*

COMMUNION VERSE ⑭

"WE HAVE SEEN His star in the East, and have come to worship Him." *Turn to* ⑮ *on page 62.*

POST-COMMUNION ⑯

GRANT, we beseech Thee, O Almighty God, that we may obtain by the understanding of a purified mind what we have just celebrated in solemn rite. Through Our Lord, etc. *Turn to* ⑰ *on page 63.*

⑱ *Review "Prayer is Necessary", page 18.*

First Sunday After Epiphany

« *Feast of the Holy Family* »

PICTURE AND MASS THEME EXPLAINED

"(Jesus) *came to Nazareth, and was subject to them*" (GOSPEL).

"Subject to them" is the awe-inspiring phrase which sums up His Life. Humbly did He abide by the decrees of human law! Obedience to *"My Father's business"* must come first, as a guide to all other business, if heaven is to find our family unbroken (PRAYER).

If Jesus withdraws from us as a test of our love, or if we lose Him by the commission of sin, we will not regain the joy of His Presence amid the distractions of *"relatives and acquaintances;"* but we will find Him *"in the temple"* at Confession and Communion.

So-called "modern" ideas and practices are evicting Christ from the home. As an antidote, at the family meal let us read aloud "My Daily Reading from the New Testament" (dated 3-minute readings for each day of the year). *"Let the word of Christ dwell"* in your home (EPISTLE). Then will your family, even though living in "obscurity" as did the Holy Family, advance *"in wisdom and . . . grace before God and men"* (GOSPEL). (*See page 342, Consecration of Family.*)

NOW BEGIN MASS AT 1 ON PAGE 35.

INTROIT *Prov. 23* ❷

LET THE FATHER of the Just rejoice greatly; let Thy father and Thy mother be joyful, *and let her rejoice that bore Thee.** How lovely are Thy tabernacles, O Lord of hosts; my soul longeth and fainteth for the courts of the Lord. Glory be, etc. *Turn to* ❸ *on page 38.*

PRAYER ❹

O LORD JESUS Christ, Who didst consecrate family life with sublime virtues, in Thy obedience to Mary and Joseph; by their help, grant that we may be *instructed in this example* of Thy Holy Family and thus *obtain a share* in their eternal happiness. Who livest, etc. *Continue below.*

EPISTLE *Col. 3* ❺

BRETHREN, put on therefore, as God's chosen ones, holy and beloved, a heart of mercy, kindness, humility, meekness, patience. Bear with one another and forgive one another, if anyone has a grievance against any other; even as the Lord has forgiven you, so also do you forgive. But above all these things have *charity,* which is the bond of perfection. And may the peace of Christ reign in your hearts; unto that peace, indeed, you were called *in one body*. Show yourselves thankful. Let the word of Christ dwell in you abundantly: in all wisdom teach and admonish one another by psalms, hymns and spiritual songs, singing in your hearts to God by His grace. Whatever you do in word or in work, do all in the Name of the Lord Jesus, giving thanks to God the Father through Jesus Christ Our Lord. THANKS BE TO GOD. *Continue on next page.*

GRADUAL *Ps. 26* 6

ONE THING I have asked of the Lord: this will I seek after: that *I may dwell* in the *house of the Lord all the days of my life.* Blessed are they who dwell in Thy house, O Lord; they shall praise Thee forever and ever. Alleluia, alleluia. Truly Thou art a hidden King, the God of Israel, the Savior. Alleluia. *Turn to* 7 *on page 40.*

GOSPEL *Luke 2* 8

AND WHEN JESUS was twelve years old, they went up to Jerusalem according to the custom of the feast. And after they had fulfilled the days, when they were returning, the boy Jesus remained in Jerusalem, and His parents did not know it. But thinking that He was in the caravan, they had come a day's journey before it occurred to them to look for Him among their relatives and acquaintances. And not finding Him, they returned to Jerusalem in search of Him. And it came to pass after three days, that they found Him in the temple, sitting in the midst of the teachers, both listening to them and asking them questions. And all who were listening to Him were amazed at His understanding and His answers. And when they saw Him, they were astonished. And His mother said to Him, "Son, why hast Thou done so to us? Behold, Thy father and I have been seeking Thee sorrowing." And He said to them, "How is it that you sought Me? Did you not know that *I must be about My Father's business*?" and they did not understand the word that He spoke to them. And He went down with them and *came to Nazareth, and was subject to them;* and His mother kept all these things carefully in her heart. And Jesus advanced in wisdom and age and grace before God and men. *Turn to* ⑨ *on page 41.*

OFFERTORY ⑩
Luke 2

THE PARENTS of Jesus took Him up to Jerusalem to present Him to the Lord. *Turn to* ⑪ *on page 43.*

SECRET ⑫

WE OFFER THEE, O Lord, this Victim of our ransom, and by the intercession of the God-bearing Virgin, together with blessed Joseph, we fervently implore Thee firmly to *establish our families in Thy peace and grace.* Through the same Lord, etc. *Turn to* ⑬ *on page 47.*

COMMUNION VERSE ⑭

JESUS WENT down with them, and came to Nazareth and was *subject to them.* *Turn to* ⑮ *on page 62.*

POST-COMMUNION ⑯

O LORD JESUS, do Thou bring us, after being refreshed with Thy heavenly Sacrament, to *follow in the footsteps of Thy Holy Family* and, after being welcomed at the hour of our death by the glorious Virgin Mary with St. Joseph, may we be found worthy to be *received by Thee into our eternal home.* Who livest, etc. *Turn to* ⑰ *on page 63.*

⑱ *AFTER MASS, REVIEW YOUR CATECHISM.*

I believe that our first parents, Adam and Eve, *lost their original state of union with God,* together with other marvelous gifts of grace and nature because of pride and disobedience; that they became *subject to concupiscence and death,* and that, through original sin, we have *inherited* the effects of their sin.

PICTURE AND MASS THEME EXPLAINED

"A wedding took place . . . (Mary) *said to Jesus, 'They have no wine.' . . . Jesus said to* (the attendants), *'Fill the jars with water . . . Draw out now' . . . When the chief steward had tasted the water . . . become wine . . .* (he said to the bridegroom), *'Thou hast kept the good wine until now'"* (GOSPEL).

A lesson to our young married couples of today! Believe and trust in Him to keep your family if you keep His Word! A spiritual change also took place, since *"His disciples believed in Him"* (GOSPEL).

Consider the daily miracle of God's *"grace that has been given us"* (EPISTLE), to change from evil to good in both single and married life. Jesus *"kept the good wine"* of Divine Life for us (symbolized by Chalice at left in the picture). We must *"fill the jars . . .* (of our good will) *to the brim"* (GOSPEL).

Let us recognize the *"great things"* (OFFERTORY) done for our soul through Mary's prayers to Jesus. Like the disciples, let us *"believe"* and *"do whatever He tells"* us (GOSPEL).

NOW BEGIN MASS AT 1 ON PAGE 35.

INTROIT
Ps. 65 ❷

LET ALL THE EARTH adore Thee, O God, and sing to Thee: let it sing a psalm to Thy Name, O Thou Most High.* Shout with joy to God, all the earth, sing ye a psalm to His Name: give glory to His praise. Glory be, etc. *Turn to* ❸ *on page 38.*

PRAYER ❹

ALMIGHTY and Everlasting God, Who dost preside over all things in heaven and on earth, graciously hear the prayers of Thy people and grant us Thy peace all the days of our life. Through Our Lord, etc. *Continue below.*

EPISTLE
Rom. 12 ❺

BRETHREN, we have gifts differing according to *the grace that has been given us,* such as prophecy to be used according to the proportion of faith; or ministry, in ministering; or he who teaches, in teaching; he who exhorts, in exhorting; he who gives, in simplicity; he who presides, with carefulness; he who shows mercy, with cheerfulness. Let love be without pretense. *Hate what is evil, hold to what is good. Love one another with fraternal charity,* anticipating one another with honor. Be not slothful in zeal; be fervent in spirit, serving the Lord, rejoicing in hope. Be patient in tribulation, persevering in prayer. Share the needs of the saints, practising hospitality. Bless those who persecute you; bless and do not curse. Rejoice with those who rejoice; weep with those who weep. Be *of one mind towards one another.* Do not set your mind on high things but condescend to the lowly. THANKS BE TO GOD. *Continue on next page.*

GRADUAL
Ps. 106
6

THE LORD sent His word, and healed them; and delivered them *out of their distress*. Let the mercies of the Lord give glory to Him; and His wonderful works to the children of men. Alleluia, alleluia. Praise ye the Lord, all His angels: praise ye Him, all His hosts. Alleluia. *Turn to* 7 *on page 40.*

GOSPEL
John 2
8

AT THAT TIME, a wedding took place at Cana of Galilee, and the mother of Jesus was there. Now Jesus too was invited to the marriage, and also His disciples. And the wine having run short, the mother of Jesus said to Him, "They have no wine." And Jesus said to her, "What wouldst thou have Me do, woman? My hour has not yet come." His mother said to the attendants, *"Do whatever He tells you."* Now six stone water-jars were placed there, after the Jewish manner of purification, each holding two or three measures. Jesus said to them, "Fill the jars with water." And they filled them to the brim. And Jesus said to them, "Draw out now, and take to the chief steward." And they took it to him. Now when the chief steward had tasted the water after it had become wine, not knowing whence it was (though the attendants who had drawn the water knew), the chief steward called the bridegroom, and said to him, "Every man at first sets forth the good wine, and when they have drunk freely, then that which is poorer. But thou hast kept the good wine until now." This first of His signs Jesus worked at Cana of Galilee; and He manifested His glory, and *His disciples believed in Him.* *Turn to* 9 *on page 41.*

OFFERTORY *Ps. 65* ⑩

SHOUT WITH JOY to God, all the earth: sing ye a psalm to His name: come and hear, and I will tell you, all ye that fear God, what *great things the Lord hath done for my soul.* Alleluia. *Turn to ⑪ on page 43.*

SECRET ⑫

SANCTIFY, O LORD, the gifts we offer, and cleanse us from the stains of our sins. Through Our Lord, etc. *Turn to ⑬ on page 47.*

COMMUNION VERSE ⑭

THE LORD SAID: "Fill the jars with water, and take to the chief steward of the feast." When the chief steward had tasted the water after it had become wine, he said to the bridegroom: "Thou hast kept the good wine until now." This first of His signs Jesus worked before His disciples. *Turn to ⑮ on page 62.*

POST-COMMUNION ⑯

INCREASE WITHIN US, we implore Thee, O Lord, the *exercise of Thy power;* so that, being nourished by *Thy Divine Sacraments,* we may be prepared to obtain out of Thy bounty that which they promise. Through Our Lord, etc. *Turn to ⑰ on page 63.*

⑱ *AFTER MASS, REVIEW YOUR CATECHISM.*

I believe that God created me to *know* Him, to *love* Him and *serve* Him, so that after death, I might possess God in the *Beatific Vision* and *Union* and thus be happy with Him forever.

I believe that my success in life depends not on amassing wealth or on winning honors but on my *serving God and neighbor.*

Third Sunday After Epiphany

[Sometimes used on Last Sundays after Pentecost]

PICTURE AND MASS THEME EXPLAINED

"Only say the word, and my servant will be healed" (GOSPEL).

By a twofold display of His Mercy Jesus first confirmed His Divinity before the Jewish priests when He cleansed the despised leper (pictured in background), then before the Gentiles by curing the centurion's paralyzed servant. We, too, publicly profess faith in His Divinity by our mercy in taking *"the words of grace"* to leprous, paralyzed sinners (COMMUNION VERSE).

What kind of mercy? St. Paul outlines certain practices in the EPISTLE: refrain from rendering *"evil for evil;" "provide good things"* to *"all men;"* peace to our enemy, leaving *"vengeance"* to God Who knows how to *"repay."*

NOW BEGIN MASS AT 1 ON PAGE 35.

INTROIT *Ps. 96* 2

ADORE GOD, all you His angels: Sion heard, and was glad; and the daughters of Juda rejoiced.* The Lord hath reigned; let the earth rejoice: let many islands be glad. Glory be, etc. *Turn to* 3 *on page 38.*

PRAYER ④

O Almighty and Eternal God, look forgivingly upon our weakness and *stretch forth the right hand* of Thy Majesty to protect us. Through Our Lord, etc. *Continue below.*

EPISTLE *Rom. 12* ⑤

Brethren, be not wise in your own conceits. *To no man render evil for evil,* but provide good things not only in the sight of God, but also in the sight of all men. If it be possible, as far as in you lies, be at peace with all men. Do not avenge yourselves, beloved, but give place to the wrath, for it is written, "Vengeance is mine; I will repay, says the Lord." But "If thy enemy is hungry, give him food; if he is thirsty, give him drink; for by so doing thou wilt heap coals of fire upon his head." *Be not overcome by evil, but overcome evil with good.* Thanks be to God. *Continue below.*

GRADUAL *Ps. 101* ⑥

The Gentiles shall fear Thy Name, O Lord, and all the kings of the earth Thy glory. For the Lord hath built up Sion, and He shall be seen in His majesty. Alleluia, alleluia. The Lord hath reigned, let the earth rejoice: let many islands be glad. Alleluia. *Turn to ⑦ on page 40.*

GOSPEL *Matt. 8* ⑧

At that time, when Jesus had come down from the mountain, great crowds followed Him. And behold, a leper came and worshipped Him, saying, "Lord, if Thou wilt, Thou canst make me clean." And *stretching forth His hand Jesus touched him,* saying, "I will; be thou made clean." And immediately his leprosy was cleansed. And Jesus said to him, "See thou tell no one; but go, show thyself to the priest, and offer the gift that Moses commanded, for a witness to them." Now when He had entered Capharnaum, there came to Him a centurion who entreated Him, saying, "Lord, my servant is lying sick in the house, paralyzed, and is grievously afflicted." Jesus said to him, "I will come and cure him." But in answer the centurion said, *"Lord, I am not worthy that Thou shouldst come under my roof; but only say the word, and my servant will be healed.* For I too am a man subject to authority, and have soldiers subject to me; and I say to one, 'Go,' and he goes; and to another, 'Come,' and he comes; and to my servant, 'Do this,' and he does it." And when Jesus heard this, He marvelled, and said to those who were following Him, "Amen I say to you, I have not found so great a faith in Israel. And I tell you that many will come from the east and from the west, and will feast with Abraham and Isaac and Jacob in the kingdom of heaven, but the *children of the kingdom will be put forth into the darkness outside;* there will be the weeping, and the gnashing of teeth." Then Jesus said to the centurion, "Go thy way; as thou hast believed, so be it done to thee." And the servant was healed in that hour. *Turn to* 9 *on page 41.*

OFFERTORY *Ps. 117* 10

THE RIGHT HAND of the Lord hath wrought strength, the right hand of the Lord hath exalted me: I shall not die, but live, and shall declare the works of the Lord. *Turn to* 11 *on page 43.*

SECRET ⑫

MAY THIS VICTIM, we pray Thee, O Lord, *take away our sins,* and sanctify the bodies and minds of Thy servants for the celebration of this sacrifice. Through Our Lord, etc. *Turn to* ⑬ *on page 47.*

COMMUNION VERSE ⑭

THEY ALL *marvelled at* the words of grace that came from the mouth of Jesus. *Turn to* ⑮ *on page 62.*

POST-COMMUNION ⑯

O LORD, since Thou hast permitted us to receive so great a Sacrament, we entreat Thee to make us more worthy to receive its effects. Through Our Lord, etc. *Turn to* ⑰ *on page 63.*

⑱ *AFTER MASS, REVIEW YOUR CATECHISM.*

I believe that it will *avail me nothing* "to gain the whole world if I suffer the loss of my own soul."

I believe that I am put in this life to *live at peace* with God and my fellow men, and to perform my *duties* to the best of my ability.

I believe that I must *rise above* the evils of the world to God, for Whom I was created.

I believe that I have a revealed *CREED* to believe, a Christian *CODE* to live, and a *CULT* to worship God.

I believe that the *Sunday use* of the Missal is a *review* of my Christian *belief and practice* and the most practical way to worship God at Mass.

Fourth Sunday After Epiphany

[*Sometimes used on Last Sundays after Pentecost*]

PICTURE AND MASS THEME EXPLAINED

"'Why are you fearful, O you of little faith?' Then He arose and rebuked the wind and the sea, and there came a great calm" (GOSPEL).

This is a picture of both the human and the Divine in Jesus and in His Church (symbolized by the dome of St. Peter's at the right). Jesus, a *tired* Man, fell off to sleep during *"a great storm."* Jesus, the *tireless*, wide-awake God, *"arose,"* as it were from the tomb of a dead sleep, to restore *"a great calm."*

Enemies of the Church are ever ready to gloat over our human *"weakness"* (PRAYER, SECRET), tossed about by the *"waves"* of human passion, by the *"winds"* of inhuman evil spirits.

The Divine Presence is within our baptized, absolved souls. Let us rise up *"from the fascination of earthly things"* (POSTCOMMUNION).

NOW BEGIN MASS AT 1 ON PAGE 35.

INTROIT *Ps. 96* ❷

ADORE God, all you His angels: Sion heard, and was glad; and the daughters of Juda rejoiced.* The Lord hath reigned; let the earth rejoice: let many islands be glad. Glory be, etc. *Turn to* ❸ *on page 38.*

PRAYER ❹

O GOD, Who dost realize how difficult it is for us to stand up against dangers *too great for our weak nature,* grant us health of mind and body, so that, by Thy help, we may be *victorious* over the sufferings caused by our sins. Through Our Lord, etc. *Continue below.*

EPISTLE *Rom. 13* ❺

BRETHREN, owe no man anything except to love one another; for he who loves his neighbor has fulfilled the Law. For "Thou shalt not commit adultery; thou shalt not kill; thou shalt not steal; *thou shalt not bear false witness;* thou shalt not covet"; and if there is any other commandment, it is summed up in this saying, "Thou shalt love thy neighbor as thyself." *Love does no evil to a neighbor.* Love therefore is the fulfillment of the Law. THANKS BE TO GOD. *Continue below.*

GRADUAL *Ps. 101* ❻

THE GENTILES shall fear Thy Name, O Lord, and all the kings of the earth Thy glory. For the Lord hath built up Sion, and He shall be seen in His majesty. Alleluia, alleluia. The Lord hath reigned, let the earth rejoice: let many islands be glad. Alleluia. *Turn to* ❼ *on page 40.*

GOSPEL
Matt. 8
8

AT THAT TIME, Jesus got into a boat, and His disciples followed Him. And behold, there arose a great storm on the sea, so that the boat was covered by the waves; but He was asleep. So they came and woke Him, saying, "Lord, save us! we are perishing!" But He said to them, "Why are you fearful, O you of little faith?" *Then He arose* and rebuked the wind and the sea, and there came a great calm. And the men marvelled, saying, "What manner of man is this, that even the wind and the sea obey Him?"
Turn to 9 *on page 41.*

OFFERTORY
Ps. 117
10

THE RIGHT HAND of the Lord hath wrought strength, the right hand of the Lord hath exalted me: I shall not die, but live, and shall declare the works of the Lord. *Turn to* 11 *on page 43.*

SECRET
12

GRANT, we beseech Thee, O Almighty God, that the offering of this Sacrifice may ever cleanse and *protect our weakness* from all evil. Through Our Lord, etc. *Turn to* 13 *on page 47.*

COMMUNION VERSE
14

THEY ALL *marvelled at the words of grace that came* from the mouth of Jesus. *Turn to* 15 *on page 62.*

POST-COMMUNION
16

MAY THY GIFTS, O God, free us from the *fascination of earthly things* and ever give us new strength by their heavenly nourishment. Through Our Lord, etc. *Turn to* 17 *on page 63.*

18 ***Review** Last Paragraph, page 17.*

Fifth Sunday After Epiphany

[Sometimes used on Last Sundays after Pentecost]

PICTURE AND MASS THEME EXPLAINED

"'Sir, didst thou not sow good seed in thy field? How then does it have weeds?' He said to them, 'An enemy has done this'" (GOSPEL).

The problem of evil is indeed a mystery. But the problem of good would indeed be a greater mystery, did not the good seed of *"the word of Christ dwell"* amongst us unto a *"harvest"* of *"mercy, kindness, humility, meekness, patience"* (EPISTLE); did not Jesus offer up today's *"sacrifice of reparation"* (SECRET) and give us a Sacrament *"of salvation"* (POSTCOMMUNION).

During the week, the *"enemy"* will try to *"sow weeds"* in the *"field"* of our daily life; but in our Mass today, the Divine Sower *"sows"* His *"good seed,"* that it may *"grow"* and ripen until *"gathered"* by the Divine *"Reaper"* into the heavenly *"barns."*

NOW BEGIN MASS AT 1 ON PAGE 35.

INTROIT *Ps. 96* **2**

ADORE GOD, all you His angels: Sion heard, and was glad; and the daughters of Juda rejoiced.* The Lord hath reigned; let the earth rejoice: let many islands be glad. Glory be, etc.

Turn to 3 *on page 38.*

PRAYER ❹

O Lord, we beg Thee in Thy never-failing *goodness, to guard Thy family,* and since it depends entirely on the hope of Thy heavenly grace, defend it always by Thy protection. Through Our Lord, etc. *Continue below.*

EPISTLE *Col. 3* ❺

Brethren, put on therefore, as God's chosen ones, holy and beloved, a heart of *mercy,* kindness, *humility,* meekness, *patience.* Bear with one another and forgive one another, if anyone has a grievance against any other; even as the Lord has forgiven you, so also do you forgive. But above all these things have charity, which is the bond of perfection. And may the peace of Christ reign in your hearts; unto that peace, indeed, you were called in one body. Show yourselves thankful. *Let the word of Christ dwell in you abundantly:* in all wisdom teach and admonish one another by psalms, hymns and spiritual songs, singing in your hearts to God by His grace. Whatever you do in word or in work, do all in the name of the Lord Jesus, giving thanks to God the Father through Him. Thanks be to God. *Continue below.*

GRADUAL *Ps. 101* ❻

The Gentiles shall fear Thy Name, O Lord, and all the kings of the earth Thy glory. For the Lord hath built up Sion, and He shall be seen in His majesty. Alleluia, alleluia. The Lord hath reigned, let the earth rejoice: let many islands be glad. Alleluia. *Turn to* ❼ *on page 40.*

GOSPEL *Matt. 13* ⑧

AT THAT TIME, Jesus spoke this parable to the crowds: "The kingdom of heaven is like a man who sowed good seed in his field; but *while* men were *asleep, his enemy* came and *sowed weeds* among the wheat, and went away. And when the blade sprang up and brought forth fruit, then the weeds appeared as well. And the servants of the householder came and said to him, *'Sir, didst thou not sow good seed in thy field? How then does it have weeds?'* He said to them, *'An enemy has done this.'* And the servants said to him, 'Wilt thou have us go and gather them up?' 'No,' he said, 'lest in gathering the weeds you root up the wheat along with them. Let both grow together until the harvest; and at harvest time I will say to the reapers, Gather up first the weeds, and bind them in bundles to burn; but the wheat gather into my barn.' " *Turn to* ⑨ *on page 41.*

OFFERTORY *Ps. 117* ⑩

THE RIGHT HAND of the Lord hath wrought strength, the right hand of the Lord hath exalted me: I shall not die, but live, and shall declare the works of the Lord. *Turn to* ⑪ *on page 43.*

SECRET ⑫

WE OFFER THEE, O Lord, this *sacrifice of reparation*, so that, taking pity on us, Thou wilt forgive our sins and direct our fickle hearts. Through Our Lord, etc. *Turn to* ⑬ *on page 47.*

COMMUNION VERSE ⑭

THEY ALL marvelled at the words of grace that came from the mouth of Jesus. *Turn to* ⑮ *on page 62.*

POST-COMMUNION ⑯

WE PLEAD with Thee, O Almighty God, that we may receive the *grace of salvation*, the pledge of which we have received in Thy Sacrament. Through Our Lord, etc. *Turn to* ⑰ *on page 63.*

⑱ *AFTER MASS, REVIEW YOUR CATECHISM.*

I believe that Jesus always has "*compassion on the multitude.*"

I believe that *spiritual depression* is the root of all our temporal misery; that social envy, discontent, greed, lack of social justice and charity become widespread in private and public life when men *fail to* "*seek first* the Kingdom of God and His justice."

I believe that only Jesus, by the *example of His Human Life* and the *strength of His Divine Grace* can supply the ideals and incentive necessary to realize the principles of social justice and social charity.

I believe that emphasis should be placed, both by *prayer and action,* on keeping respect for the *dignity of labor* by a decent living wage; on *protecting family life* from divorce and sins against nature; on upholding *religious and political liberty;* on restoring *God to our schools* of learning.

I believe that the encyclical letters of recent Popes, who are the Vicars of Christ Himself, should be given *more publicity and translated into modern social activities* of labor, government, education and home life.

Sixth Sunday After Epiphany

[*Sometimes used on Last Sundays after Pentecost*]

PICTURE AND MASS THEME EXPLAINED

"The kingdom of heaven is like a grain of mustard seed, . . . smallest of all the seeds, but when it grows up it . . . becomes a tree, so that the birds . . . dwell in its branches" (GOSPEL).

So the Church from humble beginnings in underground Catacombs, has stretched out to the remotest ends of foreign missions . . . a living shelter for man as he flees upward from the earth; a miraculous *"leaven"* transforming fallen human into the Divine.

Yes, the Life of Christ is a *"leaven"* hiding, as it were, from the time of our Baptism in the *"three measures"* of faith, hope and charity until *"all"* of our humanity is *"leavened."* Like the first Christians, we, too, are to become *"a pattern to all,"* so that our neighbors *"in Macedonia and Achaia"* (EPISTLE), like *"birds of the air,"* will *"come and dwell"* in the *"branches"* of the Church.

NOW BEGIN MASS AT 1 ON PAGE 35.

INTROIT
Ps. 96 ❷

ADORE GOD, all you His angels: Sion heard, and was glad; and the daughters of Juda rejoiced.* The Lord hath reigned; let the earth rejoice: let many islands be glad. Glory be, etc. *Turn to* ❸ *on page 38.*

PRAYER ❹

GRANT US, we beseech Thee, O Almighty God, ever to fix our thoughts on reasonable things and to do what is pleasing to Thee both in words and works. Through Our Lord, etc. *Continue below.*

EPISTLE
1 Thess. 1 ❺

BRETHREN, we give thanks to God always for you all, continually making a remembrance of you in our prayers; being mindful before God our Father of your work of *faith,* and labor, and *charity,* and your enduring *hope* in our Lord Jesus Christ. We know, brethren, beloved of God, how you were chosen. For *our gospel was not delivered to you in word only, but in power also,* and in the Holy Spirit, and in much fullness, as indeed you know what manner of men we have been among you for your sakes. And you became imitators of us and of the Lord, receiving the word in great tribulation, with joy of the Holy Spirit, so that you became a *pattern to all the believers* in Macedonia and in Achaia. For from you the word of the Lord has been spread abroad, not only in *Macedonia* and *Achaia, but in every place* your faith in God has gone forth, so that we need say nothing further. For they themselves report concerning us how we entered among you, and how you turned to God from idols, to serve the living and true God, and to await from heaven Jesus, his Son (Whom He raised from the dead), Who has delivered us from the wrath to come. THANKS BE TO GOD. *Continue below.*

GRADUAL *Ps. 101* ⑥

THE GENTILES shall fear Thy Name, O Lord, and all the kings of the earth Thy glory. For the Lord hath built up Sion, and He shall be seen in His majesty. Alleluia, alleluia. The Lord hath reigned, let the earth rejoice: let many islands be glad. Alleluia. *Turn to* ⑦ *on page 40.*

GOSPEL *Matt. 13* ⑧

AT THAT TIME, another parable Jesus set before them, saying, "The kingdom of heaven is like a *grain of mustard seed,* which a man took and sowed in his field. This indeed is the *smallest of all the seeds;* but when it grows up it is larger than any herb and becomes a tree, so that the *birds of the air come* and *dwell in its branches.*" He told them another parable: "The kingdom of heaven is like leaven, which a woman took and buried in *three measures* of flour, until *all* of it was leavened." All these things Jesus spoke to the crowds in parables, and without parables He did not speak to them; in fulfillment of what was spoken through the prophet, who said, "I will open my mouth in parables, *I will utter things hidden since the foundation of the world.*" *Turn to* ⑨ *on page 41.*

OFFERTORY *Ps. 117* ⑩

THE RIGHT HAND of the Lord hath wrought strength, the right hand of the Lord hath exalted me: I shall not die, but live, and shall declare the works of the Lord. *Turn to* ⑪ *on page 43.*

SECRET ⑫

MAY THIS OFFERING, we pray Thee, O God, cleanse and renew us, govern and protect us. Through Our Lord, etc. *Turn to* ⑬ *on page 47.*

COMMUNION VERSE ⑭

THEY ALL marvelled at the words of grace that came from the mouth of Jesus. *Turn to* ⑮ *on page 62.*

POST-COMMUNION ⑯

HAVING BEEN FED, O Lord, with Thy food of heavenly delight, we beseech Thee that we may ever hunger after those things by which we truly live. Through Our Lord, etc. *Turn to* ⑰ *on page 63.*

⑱ *AFTER MASS, REVIEW YOUR CATECHISM.*

I believe that Jesus will save society in the way of social justice, *only through His Church* which is the Kingdom of God on earth.

I believe that if the majority of individuals *kept His commandments,* if families became again what He wished them to be, if men inspired and *assisted by His Sacrifice,* loved service to one another, there would be prosperity within nations and *peace* amongst nations.

I believe that *personal* reform necessarily leads to *social* reform; that any other type of social reform winds up in failure.

I believe that Christ established *only one Church* to which He wishes all men to belong.

I believe that the one true Church which Christ founded *exists today,* and will *continue to exist* unto the end of time.

PICTURE AND MASS THEME EXPLAINED

"Why do you stand here all day idle? . . . Go you also into the vineyard" (GOSPEL).

As athletes of Christ we are called to a competitive *"race"* (EPISTLE). As workers with Christ we are ordered into the *"vineyard"* (GOSPEL).

It is a *"race"* with death for the *"prize"* of life eternal. Only *"one receives the prize"* by His own right, Christ! But, remember, He still runs in us if we do not lag in this *"race,"* as did Israel under *"Moses"* (EPISTLE).

God comes to us *"early"* in life. Until the last *"hour"* He repeats, *"Why . . . stand . . . idle?"* Each *"hour"* brings us nearer to the *"evening"* of reward, not due to the excellence of our work in itself but mercifully given by God as a recompense (GOSPEL).

NOW BEGIN MASS AT ❶ ON PAGE 35.

INTROIT ❷
Ps. 17

THE GROANS of death surrounded me, the sorrows of hell encompassed me: and *in my affliction I called upon the Lord,* and He heard my voice, from His holy temple.* I will love Thee, O Lord, my strength: the Lord is my firmament, and my refuge and my deliverer. Glory be, etc. *Turn to ❸ on page 38.*

« The "GLORIA," page 39, is not said until Easter »

PRAYER ④

Do Thou, we beg of Thee, O Lord, kindly hear the prayers of Thy people and for the glory of Thy Name *mercifully deliver us from the just afflictions* caused by our sins. Through Our Lord, etc. *Continue below.*

EPISTLE *1 Cor. 9* ⑤

Brethren, do you not know that those who run in a *race,* all indeed run, but one receives the *prize?* So run as to obtain it. And everyone *in a contest* abstains from all things—and they indeed to receive a perishable crown, but we an imperishable. I, therefore, so run as not without a purpose; I so *fight* as not beating the air; but I chastise my body and bring it into subjection, lest perhaps after preaching to others I myself should be rejected. For I would not have you ignorant, brethren, that our fathers were all under the cloud, and all passed through the sea, and all *were baptized* in Moses, in the cloud and in the sea. And all ate the same spiritual food, and all drank the same spiritual drink (for they drank from the spiritual rock which followed them, but the rock was Christ). Yet with most of them God was not well pleased. Thanks be to God. *Continue below.*

GRADUAL *Ps. 9* ⑥

The helper in due time, in tribulation: let them trust in Thee, who know Thee: for Thou dost not forsake them that seek Thee, O Lord. For the poor man shall not be forgotten to the end: the patience of the poor shall not perish for ever: arise, O Lord, let not man be strengthened.

[*Tract.*] From *the depths I have cried to Thee,* O Lord; Lord, hear my voice. Let Thine ears be attentive to the prayer of Thy servant. If Thou shalt observe iniquities, O Lord, Lord, who shall endure it? For with Thee is propitiation, and by reason of Thy law I have waited for Thee, O Lord. *Turn to* 7 *on page 40.*

GOSPEL *Matt. 20* 8

AT THAT TIME, Jesus spoke to His disciples this parable: "The kingdom of heaven is like a householder who went out *early* in the morning to hire laborers for his vineyard. And having agreed with the laborers for a denarius a day, he sent them into his vineyard. And about the third hour, he went out and saw others standing in the market place idle; and he said to them, '*Go you also into the vineyard,* and I will give you whatever is just.' So they went. And again he went out about the sixth, and about the ninth hour, and did as before. But about the eleventh hour he went out and found others standing, and he said to them, '*Why do you stand here all day idle?*' They said to him, 'Because no man has hired us.' He said to them, '*Go you also into the vineyard.*' But when evening had come, the owner of the vineyard said to his steward, 'Call the laborers, and pay them their wages, beginning from the last even to the first.' Now when they of the eleventh hour came, they received each a denarius. And when the first in their turn came, they thought that they would receive more; but they also received each his denarius. And on receiving it, they began to murmur against the householder, saying, 'These last have worked a single hour, and thou hast put them on a level with us, who have borne the burden of the day's heat.' But answering one of them, he said, 'Friend, I do thee no injustice; didst thou not agree with me for a denarius? Take what is thine and go; I choose to give to this last even as to thee. Have I not a right to do what I choose? Or art thou envious because I am generous?' Even so the last shall be first, and the first last; for many are called, but few are chosen." *Turn to* (9) *on page 41.*

OFFERTORY *Ps. 91* (10)

IT IS GOOD to give praise to the Lord, and to sing to Thy Name, O Most High. *Turn to* (11) *on page 43.*

SECRET (12)

ACCEPT OUR OFFERINGS and prayers, we plead with Thee, O Lord, and by these heavenly mysteries cleanse us and graciously hear us. Through Our Lord, etc. *Turn to* (13) *on page 47.*

COMMUNION VERSE (14)

MAKE THY FACE to shine upon Thy servant, and save me in Thy mercy: *Let me not be confounded,* O Lord, for I have called upon Thee. *Turn to* (15) *on page 62.*

POST-COMMUNION (16)

MAY THY FAITHFUL, O God, be strengthened by Thy gift; in receiving may they seek after it more and more and in seeking may they receive it forever. Through Our Lord, etc. *Turn to* (17) *on page 63.*

(18) **Review *"Sacrifice Insufficient",* page 19.**

PICTURE AND MASS THEME EXPLAINED

"The sower went out to sow his seed . . . Now . . . the seed is the word of God" (GOSPEL).

Every springtime God, as it were, rewrites the Book of Genesis and Creation. Appropriate to the coming spring, Jesus is now pictured as the Divine *"Sower."* He sows *"seed"* in the soil of our souls, covered with *"rocks"* of hardening pride, *"thorns"* of softening *"pleasures!"*

The EPISTLE is a vivid picture, moving in quick action over Europe and Asia, but above all moving our souls to action as it describes the sacrifices of Paul, the *"sower,"* sowing the *"word of God,"* despite *passions* from within, *persecutions* from without.

NOW BEGIN MASS AT ❶ ON PAGE 35.

INTROIT *Ps. 43* ❷

ARISE, why sleepest Thou, O Lord? Arise, and cast us not off to the end: why turnest Thou Thy face away, and forgettest our trouble? Our belly hath cleaved to the earth: arise, O Lord, help us and deliver us.* O God, *we have heard with our ears:* our fathers have declared to us. Glory be, etc. *Turn to* ❸ *on page 38.*

PRAYER ④

O God, since Thou dost realize that we put not our trust in anything we do, mercifully grant, by the intercession of St. Paul, that we may be defended *against all adversities*. Through Our Lord, etc. *Continue below.*

EPISTLE *2 Cor. 11-12* ⑤

Brethren, you gladly put up with fools, because you are wise yourselves! For you suffer it if a man enslaves you, if a man devours you, if a man takes from you, if a man is arrogant, if a man slaps your face! I speak to my own shame, as though we had been weak. But wherein any man is bold—I am speaking foolishly—I also am bold. Are they Hebrews? So am I! Are they Israelites? So am I! Are they offspring of Abraham? So am I! Are they ministers of Christ? I—to speak as a fool—am more: in many more labors, in prisons more frequently, in lashes above measure, often exposed to death. From the Jews five times I received forty lashes less one. Thrice I was scourged, once I was stoned, thrice I suffered shipwreck, a night and a day I was adrift on the sea; in journeyings often, in perils from floods, in perils from robbers, in perils from my own nation, in perils from the Gentiles, in perils in the city, in perils in the wilderness, in perils in the sea, in perils from false brethren; in labor and hardships, in many sleepless nights, in hunger and thirst, in fastings often, in cold and nakedness. Besides those outer things, there is my daily pressing anxiety, the care of all the churches! Who is weak, and I am not weak? Who is made to stumble, and I am not inflamed? If I must boast, I will boast of the things that concern my weakness. The God and Father of the Lord Jesus, Who is blessed forevermore, knows that I do not lie. In Damascus the governor under King Aretas was guarding the city of the Damascenes in order to arrest me, but I was lowered in a basket through a window in the wall, and escaped his hands. If I must boast—it is not indeed expedient to do so—but I will come to visions and revelations of the Lord. I know a man in Christ who fourteen years ago—whether in the body I do not know, or out of the body I do not know, God knows—such a one was caught up to the third heaven. And I know such a man—whether in the body or out of the body I do not know, God knows—that he was caught up into paradise and heard secret words that man may not repeat. Of such a man I will boast; but of myself I will glory in nothing save in my infirmities. For if I do wish to boast, I shall not be foolish; for I shall be speaking the truth. But I forbear, lest any man should reckon me beyond what he sees in me or hears from me. And *lest the greatness of the revelations should puff me up,* there was given me a thorn for the flesh, a messenger of Satan, to buffet me. Concerning this I thrice besought the Lord that it might leave me. And He has said to me, *"My grace is sufficient for thee,* for strength is made perfect in weakness." Gladly therefore I will glory in my infirmities, that the strength of Christ may dwell in me. THANKS BE TO GOD. *Continue on next page.*

GRADUAL *Ps. 82* 6

LET THE GENTILES know that God is Thy name: Thou alone art the Most High over all the earth. O my God, make them like a wheel, and as stubble before the face of the wind. [*Tract.*] Thou hast moved the earth, O Lord, and hast troubled it. Heal Thou the breaches thereof, for it hath been moved. That Thy elect may flee from before the bow: that they may be delivered. *Turn to* 7 *on page 40.*

GOSPEL *Luke 8* 8

AT THAT TIME, when a very great crowd was gathering together and men from every town were resorting to him, He said in a parable: "The sower went out to sow his seed. And as he sowed, some seed fell by the wayside and was trodden under foot, and the birds of the air ate it up. And other seed fell upon the rock, and as soon as it had sprung up it withered away, because it had no moisture. And other seed fell among thorns, and the thorns sprang up with it and choked it. And other seed fell upon good ground, and sprang up and yielded fruit a hundredfold." As He said these things He cried out, "He who has ears to hear, let him hear!" But His disciples then began to ask Him what this parable meant. He said to them, "To you it is given to know the mystery of the kingdom of God, but to the rest in parables, that 'Seeing they may not see, and hearing they may not understand.' Now the parable is this: *the seed is the word of God.* And those by the wayside are they who have heard; then the devil comes and takes away the word from their

heart, that they may not believe and be saved. Now those upon the rock are they who, when they have heard, receive the word with joy; and these have no root, but believe for a while, and in time of temptation fall away. And that which fell among the thorns, these are they who have heard, and as they go their way are *choked by the cares and riches and pleasures of life, and their fruit does not ripen.* But that upon good ground, these are they who, with a right and good heart, *having heard the word, hold it fast,* and bear fruit in patience." *Turn to* ⑨ *on page 41.*

OFFERTORY *Ps. 16* ⑩

PERFECT THOU my goings in Thy paths, that my footsteps be not moved; incline Thine ear, and *hear my words:* show forth Thy wonderful mercies, Thou Who savest them that trust in Thee, O Lord. *Turn to* ⑪ *on page 43.*

SECRET ⑫

MAY THIS SACRIFICE, offered to Thee, O Lord, give us life and protect us at all times. Through Our Lord, etc. *Turn to* ⑬ *on page 47.*

COMMUNION VERSE ⑭

I WILL GO IN to the altar of God: to God Who giveth joy to my youth. *Turn to* ⑮ *on page 62.*

POST-COMMUNION ⑯

WE HUMBLY ask Thee, O Almighty God, that we, who have been refreshed by Thy Sacraments, may serve Thee worthily by a life well pleasing to Thee. Through Our Lord, etc. *Turn to* ⑰ *on page 63.*

⑱ **Review "Mass as Sacrifice", page 20.**

PICTURE AND MASS THEME EXPLAINED

Jesus said to him, *"Receive thy sight, thy faith has saved thee"* (GOSPEL).

"We are going up to Jerusalem," city of His Great Sacrifice, during Lent. His intimate followers were spiritually blind to the need of a Good Friday.

In this picture we even see them *"angrily"* trying to hold back one who wanted to *"see."* To strengthen the weak faith of His disciples, He rewards the strong *"faith"* of the *"blind man."* Faith is needed to *"see"* the need of Lenten penance—faith which lives by love: love for God, love for neighbor (EPISTLE). Where there is love, there is no labor; but if there is labor, it is loved. The INTROIT, PRAYER and GRADUAL inspire us with confidence as we too, "go up" with faith (OFFERTORY) and charity (COMMUNION VERSE).

NOW BEGIN MASS AT ❶ ON PAGE 35.

INTROIT ❷
Ps. 30

BE THOU unto me a God, a *protector, and a place of refuge, to save me:* for Thou art my strength, and my refuge; and for Thy Name's sake Thou wilt be my leader, and wilt nourish me.* In Thee, O Lord, have I hoped, let me never be confounded: deliver me in Thy justice, and set me free. Glory be, etc. *Turn to* ❸ *on page 38.*

PRAYER ④

BE Thou gracious to our prayers, O Lord, we implore Thee, and, having released us from the heavy chains of sin, protect us from all adversity. Through Our Lord, etc. *Continue below.*

EPISTLE ⑤
1 Cor. 13

BRETHREN, *if I should speak* with the tongues of men and of angels, but *do not have charity,* I have become as sounding brass or a tinkling cymbal. And if I have prophecy and know all mysteries and all knowledge, and if I have all faith so as to remove mountains, yet *do not have charity, I am nothing.* And if I distribute all my goods to feed the poor, and if I deliver my body to be burned, yet do not have charity, it profits me nothing. Charity is patient, is kind; charity does not envy, is not pretentious, is not puffed up, is not ambitious, is not self-seeking, is not provoked; thinks no evil, does not rejoice over wickedness, but rejoices with the truth; *bears with all things, believes all things, hopes all things, endures all things.* Charity never fails, whereas prophecies will disappear, and tongues will cease, and knowledge will be destroyed. For we know in part and we prophesy in part; but when that which is perfect has come, that which is imperfect will be done away with. When I was a child, I spoke as a child, I felt as a child, I thought as a child. Now that I have become a man, I have put away the things of a child. We see now through a mirror in an obscure manner, but then face to face. Now I know in part, but then I shall know even as I have been known. So there *abide faith, hope and charity,* these three; but the *greatest of these is charity.* THANKS BE TO GOD. *Continue below.*

GRADUAL *Ps. 76* ❻

THOU ART THE GOD that alone dost wonders: Thou hast made Thy power known among the nations. With Thy arm Thou hast redeemed Thy people: the children of Israel and of Joseph. [*Tract.*] Sing joyfully to God, all the earth: serve ye the Lord with gladness. Come in before His presence with exceeding great joy: know ye that the Lord He is God. He made us, and not we ourselves: but we are His people, and the sheep of His pasture. *Turn to* ❼ *on page 40.*

GOSPEL *Luke 18* ❽

AT THAT TIME, Jesus taking to himself the Twelve said to them, *"Behold, we are going up to Jerusalem,* and all things that have been written through the prophets concerning the Son of Man will be accomplished. For He will be delivered to the Gentiles, and will be mocked and scourged and spit upon; and after they have scourged Him, they will put Him to death; and on the third day He will rise again." And *they understood none of these things* and this saying was hidden from them, neither did they get to know the things that were being said. Now it came to pass as He drew near to Jericho, that a certain blind man was sitting by the wayside, begging; but hearing a crowd passing by, he inquired what this might be. And they told him that Jesus of Nazareth was passing by. And he cried out, saying, "Jesus, Son of David, have mercy on me!" And they who went in front angrily tried to silence him. But he cried out all the louder, "Son of David, have mercy on me!" Then Jesus stopped and commanded that he should be brought to Him. And when he drew near, He asked him, saying, "What wouldst thou have Me do for thee?" And he said, *"Lord, that I may see."* And *Jesus said to him, "Receive thy sight, thy faith has saved thee."* And at once he received his sight, and followed Him, glorifying God. And all the people upon seeing it gave praise to God. *Turn to* ⑨ *on page 41.*

OFFERTORY ⑩
Ps. 118

BLESSED ART THOU, O Lord, teach me Thy justifications: with my lips I have pronounced all the judgments of Thy mouth. *Turn to* ⑪ *on page 43.*

SECRET ⑫

MAY THIS VICTIM, we pray Thee, O Lord, take away our sins and sanctify the bodies and minds of Thy servants for the celebration of this sacrifice. Through Our Lord, etc. *Turn to* ⑬ *on page 47.*

COMMUNION VERSE ⑭

THEY DID EAT, and were filled exceedingly, and the Lord gave them their desire: they were not defrauded of that which they craved. *Turn to* ⑮ *on page 62.*

POST-COMMUNION ⑯

WE APPEAL TO THEE, O Almighty God, that we, who have received this heavenly food, may be safeguarded by it against all misfortune. Through Our Lord, etc. *Turn to* ⑰ *on page 63.*

⑱ **Review "Why go to Mass", page 21.**

PICTURE AND MASS THEME EXPLAINED

"Not by bread alone does man live, but by every word that comes forth from the mouth of God" (GOSPEL). 1. In this picture the devil points to the *bread* of *fleshly* desire. *"Now is the acceptable time"* to "ration" our self-indulgence, our worship of physical culture (EPISTLE), and to feed our souls with the Divine Word. This temptation calls for the mortification of self.

2. The *"pinnacle of the temple"* (in the upper left corner), recalls the *pride* of usurping God's *power*, of trying to live beyond His reach. We must topple ourselves from the pinnacle of *pride* and lift ourselves up by prayer to the pinnacle of God Himself.

3. The *"kingdoms of the world,"* seen in the distance (in middle of picture), represent those who covet mere earthly *"glory."* To offset this temptation there must be almsgiving or devoting one's talents to the service of one's neighbor.

The EPISTLE exhorts us not to receive *"in vain"* this plan of personal reformation, first by warning, then by encouraging us in the eternal struggle between Christ and Antichrist.

NOW BEGIN MASS AT ❶ ON PAGE 35.

INTROIT *Ps. 90* ❷

HE SHALL CALL upon Me, and I will hear him; I will deliver him, and glorify him; I will fill him with length of days.* He that dwelleth in the aid of the Most High, shall abide under the *protection* of the God of heaven. Glory be, etc. *Turn to* ❸ *on page 38.*

PRAYER ❹

O GOD, Who dost purify Thy Church by the yearly observance of Lent, grant to us in Thine own family, that whatever we try to gain by abstinence, we may *follow up* with *good works.* Through Our Lord, etc. *Continue below.*

EPISTLE *2 Cor. 6* ❺

BRETHREN, we entreat you *not to receive the grace of God in vain.* For He says, "In an acceptable time I have heard thee, and in the day of salvation I have helped thee." Behold, *now is the acceptable time; behold, now is the day of salvation!* We give no offense to anyone, that our ministry may not be blamed. On the contrary, let us conduct ourselves in all circumstances as God's ministers, in much patience; in tribulations, in hardships, in distresses; in stripes, in imprisonments, in tumults; in labors, in sleepless nights, in fastings; in innocence, in knowledge, in long-sufferings; in kindness, in the Holy Spirit, in unaffected love; in the word of truth, in the power of God; with the armor of justice on the right hand and on the left; in honor and dishonor, in evil report and good report; as deceivers and yet truthful, as unknown and yet well known, as dying and behold, we live, as chastised but not killed, as sorrowful yet always rejoicing, as poor yet enriching many, as having nothing yet possessing all things. THANKS BE TO GOD. *Continue below.*

GRADUAL *Ps. 90* ⑥

GOD hath given His angels charge over thee, to keep thee in all thy ways. In their hands they shall bear thee up, lest thou dash thy foot against a stone. [*Tract.*] He that dwelleth in the aid of the Most High, shall abide under the protection of the God of heaven. He shall say to the Lord, Thou art my protector and my refuge: my God, in Him will I trust. For He hath delivered me from the snare of the hunters, and from the sharp word. He will overshadow thee with His shoulders, and under His wings thou shalt trust. His truth shall compass thee with a shield: thou shalt not be afraid of the terror of the night. Of the arrow that flieth in the day; of the business that walketh about in the dark: of ruin and the noon-day devil. A thousand shall fall at thy side, and ten thousand at thy right hand; but it shall not come nigh thee. For He hath given His angels charge over thee, to keep thee in all thy ways. In their hands they shall bear thee up, lest thou dash thy foot against a stone. Thou shalt walk upon the asp and the basilisk, and thou shalt trample under foot the lion and the dragon. Because he hath hoped in Me, I will deliver him; I will protect him, because he hath known My Name. He shall call upon Me, and I will hear him: I am with him in tribulation. I will deliver him, and I will glorify him; I will fill him with length of days, and I will show him My salvation. *Turn to* ⑦ *on page 40.*

GOSPEL *Matt. 4* ⑧

AT THAT TIME, Jesus was led *into the desert* by the Spirit, to be tempted by the devil. And after fasting forty days and forty nights, He was hungry. And the tempter came and said to Him, "If Thou art the Son of God, command that these stones become loaves of bread." But He answered and said, "It is written, *'Not by bread alone does man live, but by every word* that comes forth from the mouth of God.'" Then the devil took Him into the holy city and set Him on the pinnacle of the temple, and said to Him, "If Thou art the Son of God, throw Thyself down; for it is written, 'He will give His angels charge concerning Thee; and upon their hands they shall bear Thee up, lest Thou dash Thy foot against a stone.'" Jesus said to him, "It is written further, *'Thou shalt not tempt the Lord thy God.'*" Again, the devil took Him to a very high mountain, and showed Him all the *kingdoms of the world* and the glory of them. And he said to Him, "All these things will I give Thee, if Thou wilt fall down and worship me." Then Jesus said to him, "Begone, Satan! for it is written, 'The Lord thy God shalt thou worship and Him only shalt thou serve.'" Then *the devil left* Him; and *behold, angels came* and ministered to Him. *Turn to* ⑨ *on page 41.*

OFFERTORY *Ps. 90* ⑩

THE LORD will overshadow thee with His shoulders, and under His wings thou shalt trust: His truth shall compass thee with a shield. *Turn to* ⑪ *on page 43.*

SECRET ⑫

WE SOLEMNLY OFFER this sacrifice at the beginning of Lent, beseeching Thee, O Lord, that while we abstain from table feasting, we may also *refrain* from harmful pleasures. Through Our Lord, etc. *Turn to* ⑬ *on page 47.*

COMMUNION VERSE ⑭

THE LORD will overshadow thee with His shoulders, and under His wings thou shalt trust: His truth shall compass thee with a shield. *Turn to* ⑮ *on page 62.*

POST-COMMUNION ⑯

MAY THE holy reception of Thy Sacrament give us new strength and, after changing us from our old life, may this saving mystery bring us into a union with Thy Divine Life. Through Our Lord, etc. *Turn to* ⑰ *on page 63.*

⑱ *AFTER MASS, REVIEW YOUR CATECHISM.*

I believe that the Catholic Church is the *one true Church.*

I believe that the Catholic Church is the only *living, infallible guide* which can lead me to eternal life.

I believe that the Catholic Church has the right and duty to *guard the doctrine* of Jesus Christ and to *preach it to every creature,* independent of any human authority.

I believe that the Catholic Church is not a mere organization, but a *living organism;* that it is the very *Mystical* Body of Christ, hence I reverence it as I reverence the *Eucharistic* Body.

I believe that it is *not enough* for me to be a member of the Catholic Church in order to save my soul, but that I *must live in accordance* with the teaching of that Church.

PICTURE AND MASS THEME EXPLAINED

"Behold, there appeared to them Moses and Elias talking together with Him" (GOSPEL).

Last Sunday we beheld Jesus as Man, suffering and conquering the three temptations. Today a faint glimpse of Jesus as God is a further Lenten incentive against discouragement or failure.

We behold Moses, the lawgiver, pointing to the code of the Ten Commandments; Elias, the prophet, pointing to the creed of Divine Truth. *"This is the will of God, ... walking"* in the way of His Commandments (EPISTLE), applying your mind to Divine Truth, so that *"you* (may) *learn how to possess* (your) *vessel in holiness."*

"Your sanctification (EPISTLE) is an *"interior"* obligation in your own private *"life;"* also *"exterior"* (PRAYER), to the extent of helping your neighbor, for *"the Lord is the avenger"* of deception in everyday business (EPISTLE).

NOW BEGIN MASS AT 1 ON PAGE 35.

INTROIT 2
Ps. 24

REMEMBER, O Lord, Thy bowels of compassion, and Thy mercies that are from the beginning of the world, lest at any time our enemies rule over us: deliver us, O God of Israel, from all our tribulations.* To Thee, O Lord, have I lifted up my soul: in Thee, O my God, I put my trust; let me not be ashamed. Glory be, etc. *Turn to* ③ *on page 38.*

PRAYER ④

O God, Who seest how weak we are, guard our *interior* and *exterior* life, that our body may be defended against adversity and our mind cleansed of evil thoughts. Through Our Lord, etc. *Continue below*

EPISTLE *1 Thess. 4* ⑤

Brethren, even as you have learned from us how you ought to walk to please God—as indeed you are walking—we beseech and exhort you in the Lord Jesus to make even greater progress. For you know what precepts I have given to you by the Lord Jesus. For this is the will of God, *your sanctification;* that you abstain from immorality; that every one of you learn how to *possess his vessel in holiness* and honor, not in the passion of lust like the Gentiles who do not know God; that no one transgress *and overreach his brother in the matter,* because *the Lord is the avenger* of all these things, as we have told you before and have testified. For God has not called us unto uncleanness, but unto holiness; in Christ Jesus Our Lord. Thanks be to God. *Continue below.*

GRADUAL *Ps. 24* ⑥

The troubles of my heart are multiplied, deliver me from my necessities, O Lord. See my abjection and my labor, and forgive all my sins. [*Tract.*] Give glory to the Lord, for He is good: for His mercy endureth for ever. Who shall declare the powers of the Lord? Who shall set forth all His praises? Blessed are they that keep judgment, and do justice at all times. Remember us, O Lord, in the favor of Thy people; visit us with Thy salvation. *Turn to* 7 *on page 40.*

GOSPEL *Matt. 17* 8

AT THAT TIME, Jesus took Peter, James and his brother John, and led them up a *high mountain* by themselves, and was transfigured before them. And His face shone as the sun, and His garments became white as snow. And behold, there appeared to them Moses and Elias talking together with Him. Then Peter addressed Jesus, saying, "Lord, *it is good for us to be here.* If Thou wilt, let us set up three tents here, one for Thee, one for Moses, and one for Elias." As he was still speaking, behold, a bright cloud overshadowed them, and behold, a voice out of the cloud said, *"This is My beloved Son,* in Whom I am well pleased; *hear Him."* And on hearing it the disciples fell on their faces and were exceedingly afraid. And Jesus came near and touched them, and said to them, *"Arise, and do not be afraid."* But lifting up their eyes, they *saw no one but Jesus only.* And as they were coming down from the mountain, Jesus cautioned them, saying, "Tell the vision to no one, till the Son of Man has risen from the dead." *Turn to* 9 *on page 41.*

OFFERTORY *Ps. 118* 10

I WILL MEDITATE *on Thy commandments,* which I have loved exceedingly: and I will lift up my hands to Thy commandments, which I have loved. *Turn to* 11 *on page 43.*

SECRET ⑫

We beg Thee, O Lord, to look favorably upon these sacrifices that they may be profitable both to our devotion and salvation. Through Our Lord, etc. *Turn to* ⑬ *on page 47.*

COMMUNION VERSE ⑭

Understand my cry: harken to the voice of my prayer, O my King and my God: for to Thee will I pray, O Lord. *Turn to* ⑮ *on page 62.*

POST-COMMUNION ⑯

Humbly do we pray Thee, O Almighty God, that we whom Thou dost refresh with Thy Sacraments may also *serve Thee by a manner of life* that is pleasing to Thee. Through Our Lord, etc. *Turn to* ⑰ *on page 63.*

⑱ *AFTER MASS, REVIEW YOUR CATECHISM.*

I believe that it *cannot be a matter of indifference* to which church I belong.

I believe that since Christ established one Church, *I am not free* to belong to any other.

I believe that I *cannot conscientiously say* that one religion is as good as another.

I believe that, nevertheless, all those outside the Church through no fault of their own, will be saved if they *follow their conscience* and do not die in mortal sin.

I believe that "those who labor under ignorance of the true religion, if this *ignorance be invincible*, are not before the eyes of God burdened with guilt for this thing."

I believe that those will be lost who are convinced that the Catholic religion is the true religion, and yet *refuse to embrace it.*

I believe that is what I mean when I say: "Outside the Catholic Church there is no salvation."

PICTURE AND MASS THEME EXPLAINED

"When (Jesus) *cast out the devil, the dumb man spoke."* But, as indicated by the little whining group to the right, some complained: *"By Beelzebub, the prince of devils, He casts out devils"* (GOSPEL).

Formerly, on this day, candidates were examined in preparation for Baptism on Holy Saturday. The first effect of Baptism is to free the soul from the power of the devil. The *"house"* of which Jesus speaks, is the human soul before His coming, degraded by idolatry, by sensuality, under the tyranny of the evil spirit.

Mary holding the Infant (pictured in the upper left corner) is a symbol of our Baptism. Mary gives birth to us as members of the Mystical Body of her Christ. Moreover, like her, *"blessed are they who hear the word of God and keep it"* (GOSPEL).

These baptismal duties of "death to sin" and "life in God" (EPISTLE) are meant to gladden, not to oppress the human heart (OFFERTORY), intended by God for Divine possession (COMMUNION VERSE), safe from diabolical obsession.

NOW BEGIN MASS AT 1 ON PAGE 35.

INTROIT *Ps. 24* ❷

MY EYES *are ever towards the Lord:* for He shall pluck my feet out of the snare: look Thou upon me, and have mercy on me, for I am alone and poor.* To Thee, O Lord, have I lifted up my soul: in Thee, O my God, I put my trust; let me not be ashamed. Glory be, etc. *Turn to* ❸ *on page 38.*

PRAYER ❹

BEHOLD THE DESIRES of Thy humble servants, we beg of Thee, O Almighty God, and stretch forth the right hand of Thy Majesty *in our defence.* Through Our Lord, etc. *Continue below.*

EPISTLE *Ephes. 5* ❺

BRETHREN, be you, therefore, imitators of God, as very dear children and *walk in love,* as Christ also loved us and delivered Himself up for us an offering and a sacrifice to God to ascend in fragrant odor. But immorality and every uncleanness or covetousness, let it not even be named among you, as becomes saints; or obscenity or foolish talk or scurrility, which are out of place; but rather thanksgiving. For know this and understand, that no fornicator, or unclean person, or covetous one (for that is idolatry) has any inheritance in the kingdom of Christ and God. Let no one lead you astray with empty words; for because of these things the wrath of God comes upon the children of disobedience. Do not, then, become partakers with them. *For you were once darkness, but now you are light in the Lord.* Walk, then, as hildren of light (for the fruit of the light is in ll goodness and justice and truth). THANKS E TO GOD. *Continue below.*

GRADUAL *Ps. 9* ⑥

ARISE, O LORD, let not man be strengthened; et the Gentiles be judged in Thy sight. When ny enemy shall be turned back, they shall be veakened and perish before Thy face. [*Tract.*] To Thee have I lifted up my eyes, Who dwellest n heaven. Behold as the eyes of servants are n the hands of their masters. And as the eyes f the handmaid are on the hands of her misress: so are our eyes unto the Lord our God, ntil He have mercy on us. Have mercy on us,) Lord, have mercy on us. *Turn to* ⑦ *on page* *'0.*

GOSPEL *Luke 11* ⑧

AT THAT TIME, Jesus was casting out a devil, and he same was dumb; and when He had cast out he devil, the dumb man spoke. And the crowds narvelled. But some of them said, "By Beelzebub, he prince of devils, He casts out devils." But thers, to test Him, demanded from Him a sign rom heaven. But He, seeing their thoughts, said o them: "Every kingdom divided against itself s brought to desolation, and house will fall upon ouse. If, then, Satan also is divided against imself, how shall his kingdom stand? Because ou say that I cast out devils by Beelzebub. Now, f I cast out devils by Beelzebub, by whom do our children cast them out? Therefore they hall be your judges. But if I cast out devils by he finger of God, then the kingdom of God has come upon you. When the strong man, fully armed, guards his courtyard, his property is undisturbed. But if a stronger than he attacks and overcomes him, he will take away his whole armor on which he was depending, and will divide his spoils. *He who is not with Me is against Me;* and he who does not gather with Me scatters. When the unclean spirit has gone out of a man, he roams through waterless places in search of a resting place; and finding none, he says, 'I will return to my house which I left.' And when he has come, he finds the place swept. And then he goes and takes seven other spirits more evil than himself, and they enter in and dwell there; and *the last state of that man becomes worse than the first.*" Now it came to pass as He was saying these things, that a certain woman lifted up her voice from the crowd, and said to Him, "Blessed is the womb that bore Thee, and the breasts that nursed Thee." But He said, *"Rather, blessed are they who hear the word of God and keep it."* *Turn to ⑨ on page 41.*

OFFERTORY *Ps. 18* ⑩

THE JUSTICES of the Lord are right, rejoicing hearts, and His judgments are sweeter than honey and the honeycomb: for Thy servant keepeth them. *Turn to ⑪ on page 43.*

SECRET ⑫

MAY THIS VICTIM, we pray Thee, O Lord, *take away our sins* and sanctify the bodies and minds of Thy servants for the celebration of this sacrifice. Through Our Lord, etc. *Turn to ⑬ on page 47.*

COMMUNION VERSE ⑭

THE SPARROW hath found herself a house, and the turtle a nest, where she may lay her young ones: Thy altars, O Lord of hosts, my King, and my God: *blessed are they that dwell in Thy house,* they shall praise Thee for ever and ever. *Turn to ⑮ on page 62.*

POST-COMMUNION ⑯

IN THY MERCY, we beseech Thee, O Lord, from all guilt absolve us and from all *evil deliver us,* who partake of so great a Sacrament. Through Our Lord, etc. *Turn to ⑰ on page 63.*

⑱ *AFTER MASS, REVIEW YOUR CATECHISM.*

I believe that the present Pope is the successor of St. Peter, the first Pope.

I believe that the Pope is the *representative of Christ* on earth and the visible head appointed by Christ to be the spiritual father of all the faithful.

I believe that the Pope is *infallible in matters of faith and morals* when he speaks "from the chair" as sovereign Pontiff for the whole Church, that is, he cannot make a mistake when he tells me what to believe, or what to do, in order to save my soul.

I believe that I can consistently be a loyal Catholic, and at the same time a loyal citizen of my country.

I believe that I can "render to Cæsar the things that are Cæsar's and to God the *things that are God's.*"

I believe that HABITUAL OR SANCTIFYING grace is a supernatural *quality actually dwelling in the soul,* bestowed by God not by any right on our part, but solely through the merits of Jesus Christ.

I believe that by habitual grace man is *lifted up above* his human nature, becomes a *partaker* in the Divine Nature, an adopted *son of God* and an *heir* to the glory of heaven.

PICTURE AND MASS THEME EXPLAINED

"Jesus then took the loaves and . . . distributed them to those reclining, . . . as much as they wished" (GOSPEL).

We all "wish" to be fed with joy, now and forever. The discipline of Lent may sadden our poor frail nature, so the Church analyzes the causes of true joy on this *"Rejoice"* or Laetare Sunday (INTROIT). The first source of genuine *"joy"* is a sincere Easter Confession; it emancipates us from the slavery of sin. We now enjoy the *"freedom"* of Christ's *Gospel* of love, because we have been freed from the "*bondage*" of that fear which prevailed in the days before Christ (EPISTLE).

The second source of genuine *"joy"* is a fruitful Easter Communion, for which proper preparation and thanksgiving have been made. The soul's instinctive hunger is satisfied by this *personal* com-muning with God. In the picture above, the Host and Chalice are seen descending upon men of all races (symbolized by the awaiting crowd). Humanity thus fed with Divinity, is joyously united in a real *social* and mystical union. Men will then work for one another in *"a city which is compact together"* (COMMUNION VERSE).

NOW BEGIN MASS AT 1 ON PAGE 35.

INTROIT *Is. 66* ❷

REJOICE, O Jerusalem, and come together, all you that love her; *rejoice with joy, you that have been in sorrow:* that you may exult and *be filled* from the breasts of your consolation.* I rejoiced at the things that were said to me: We shall go into the house of the Lord. Glory be, etc. *Turn to* ❸ *on page 38.*

PRAYER ❹

GRANT, we beseech Thee, O Almighty God, that we, who suffer justly for our deeds, may be relieved by the consolation of Thy grace. Through Our Lord, etc. *Continue below.*

EPISTLE *Gal. 4* ❺

BRETHREN, it is written that Abraham had two sons, the one by a *slave-girl* and the other by a *free woman.* And the son of the slave-girl was born according to the flesh, but the son of the free woman in virtue of the promise. This is said by way of allegory. For these are the two covenants: one indeed from Mount Sinai, bringing forth children unto *bondage,* which is Agar. For Sinai is a mountain in Arabia, which corresponds to the present Jerusalem, and is in slavery with her children. But that Jerusalem which is above is free, which is our mother. For it is written, "*Rejoice* thou barren, that dost not bear; break forth and cry, thou that dost not travail; for many are the children of the desolate, more than of her that has a husband." Now we, brethren, are the children of promise, as Isaac was. But as then he who was born according to the flesh persecuted him who was born according to the spirit, so also it is now. But what does the

Scripture say? "Cast out the slave-girl and her son, for the son of the slave-girl shall not be heir with the son of the free woman." Therefore, brethren, we are not children of a slave-girl, *but of the free woman*—in virtue of the freedom wherewith *Christ has made us free.* THANKS BE TO GOD. *Continue below.*

GRADUAL *Ps. 121* ❻

I REJOICED at the things that were said to me: We shall go into the house of the Lord. Let peace be in thy strength, and abundance in thy towers. [*Tract.*] They that trust in the Lord shall be as Mount Sion: he shall not be moved for ever that dwelleth in Jerusalem. Mountains are round about it: so the Lord is round about His people, from henceforth, now and for ever. *Turn to* ❼ *on page 40.*

GOSPEL *John 6* ❽

AT THAT TIME, Jesus went away to the other side of the sea of Galilee, which is that of Tiberias. And there followed Him a great crowd, because they were witnessing the signs He worked on those who were sick. Jesus therefore went up the mountain, and was sitting there with His disciples. Now the Passover, the feast of the Jews, was near. When, therefore, Jesus had lifted up His eyes and seen that a very great crowd had come to Him, He said to Philip, *"Whence shall we buy bread that these may eat?"* But He said this to try him, for He Himself knew what He would do. Philip answered Him, "Two hundred denarii worth of bread is not enough for them, that each one may receive a little." One of His disciples, Andrew, the brother of Simon Peter, said to Him, "There is a young boy here who has five barley loaves and two fishes; but what are these among so many?" Jesus then said, "Make the people recline." Now there was much grass in the place. The men therefore reclined, in number about five thousand. Jesus then took the loaves, and when *He had given thanks,* distributed them to those reclining; and likewise the fishes, as much as they wished. But when they were filled, He said to His disciples, "Gather the fragments that are left over, *lest they be wasted.*" They therefore gathered them up; and they filled twelve baskets with the fragments of the five barley loaves left over by those who had eaten. When the people, therefore, had seen the sign which Jesus had worked, they said, "This is indeed the Prophet who is to come into the world." So when Jesus perceived that they would come to take Him by force and make Him king, He fled again to the mountain, Himself alone. *Turn to* 9 *on page 41.*

OFFERTORY 10
Ps. 134

PRAISE YE THE LORD, for He is good: sing ye to His Name, for He is sweet: whatsoever He pleased He hath done in heaven and in earth. *Turn to* 11 *on page 43.*

SECRET 12

DO THOU, we beseech Thee, O Lord, give heed and be appeased by the sacrifices here before Thee, that they may be of profit both to our devotion and salvation. Through Our Lord, etc. *Turn to* 13 *on page 47.*

COMMUNION VERSE ⑭

JERUSALEM, which is built as *a city, which is compact together;* for thither did the tribes go up, the tribes of the Lord, to praise Thy Name, O Lord. *Turn to* ⑮ *on page 62.*

POST-COMMUNION ⑯

O LORD, we beseech Thee, dispose us to handle with sincere worship and to receive with ever faithful minds Thy holy Sacrament with which we are continually fed. Through Our Lord, etc. *Turn to* ⑰ *on page 63.*

⑱ *AFTER MASS, REVIEW YOUR CATECHISM.*

I believe that by habitual grace man becomes *capable of performing acts* on earth which will one day in heaven perfect his union with God.

I believe that habitual grace can be *lost by mortal sin* but can be *restored* by an act of *perfect contrition* (page 316) or by the *Sacrament of Penance.*

I believe that Angels are *spirits without physical body* but endowed with intellect and will.

I believe that all the *angels who co-operated* with the grace of God now enjoy the beatific *vision* of and *union* with God; that those who did not, were thrust into hell; no longer angels ***but devils,*** whose chief is Lucifer or Satan.

I believe that it is very helpful to my Christian life to have *special devotion to my Guardian Angel,* reverencing him and calling on him, especially in time of temptation; following his suggestions, thanking him for his help and never vexing his presence by sin.

✝ This cross in margin of Ordinary (pages 35, 36, 39, 45), indicates paragraph is omitted in today's Mass.

PICTURE AND MASS THEME EXPLAINED

"They therefore took up stones to cast at Him; but Jesus hid Himself and went out from the temple" (GOSPEL).

The poor forlorn beggar (to the right in the picture), looking at the departing Christ, Whose shadow may still be seen, is a symbol of us beholding the veiled crucifix on the altar today. Christ voices His terrifying analysis of those who ignore His miracles, His sinlessness: *"The reason why you do not hear is that you are not of God."*

Aware how much He will endure from an *unholy* nation on the *"hill"* of Calvary (INTROIT), Jesus appeals to His Eternal Father, recalling how *"they have fought against me from my youth"* (GRADUAL). Yet for them, for us, He will shed His Precious Blood to *"cleanse* (our) *conscience from dead works to serve the living God"* (EPISTLE).

NOW BEGIN MASS AT ❶ ON PAGE 35.

INTROIT ❷
Ps. 42

JUDGE ME, O God, and distinguish my cause from the *nation that is not holy;* deliver me from the unjust and deceitful man. For Thou art God and my strength.* Send forth Thy light and Thy truth: they have conducted me, and brought me unto Thy *holy hill,* and into Thy tabernacles. Judge me. *Turn to* ❸ *on page 38.*

PRAYER ❹

WE IMPLORE THEE, O Almighty God, look down mercifully upon this Thy family; may its body be governed by Thy generosity and may its spirit be guarded by Thy safekeeping. Through Our Lord, etc. *Continue below.*

EPISTLE *Heb. 9* ❺

BRETHREN, when Christ appeared as high priest of the good things to come, He entered once for all through the greater and more perfect tabernacle, not made by hands (that is, not of this creation), nor again by virtue of blood of goats and calves, but by virtue of His own Blood: into the Holies, having obtained eternal redemption. For if the blood of goats and bulls and the sprinkled ashes of a heifer sanctify the unclean unto the cleansing of the flesh, *how much more will the Blood of Christ,* Who through the Holy Spirit offered Himself unblemished unto God, *cleanse your conscience from dead works* to serve the living God? And this is why He is Mediator of a new covenant, that whereas a death has taken place for redemption from the transgressions committed under the former covenant, they who have been called may receive eternal inheritance according to the promise; in Christ Jesus Our Lord. THANKS BE TO GOD. *Continue on next page.*

GRADUAL
Ps. 142
6

DELIVER ME from my enemies, O Lord, teach me to do Thy will. My deliverer, O Lord, *from the angry nations:* Thou wilt lift me up above them that rise up against me: from the unjust man Thou wilt deliver me. [*Tract.*] *Often have they fought against me from my youth.* Let Israel now say: often have they fought against me from my youth. But they could not prevail over me: the wicked have wrought upon my back. They have lengthened their iniquities: the Lord Who is just will cut the necks of sinners.

Turn to 7 *on page 40.*

GOSPEL
John 8
8

AT THAT TIME, Jesus said to the crowd of the Jews: "Which of you can convict Me of sin? If I speak the truth, why do you not believe Me? He who is of God hears the words of God. *The reason why you do not hear is that you are not of God.*" The Jews therefore in answer said to Him, "Are we not right in saying that Thou art a Samaritan, and hast a devil?" Jesus answered, "I have not a devil, but I honor My Father, and you dishonor Me. Yet I do not seek My own glory; there is one who seeks and who judges. Amen, amen, I say to you, if anyone keep My word, he will never see death." The Jews therefore said, "Now we know that Thou hast a devil. Abraham is dead, and the prophets, and Thou sayest, 'If anyone keep My word he will never taste death.' Art Thou greater than our father Abraham, who is dead? And the prophets are dead. Whom dost Thou make thyself?" Jesus answered, "If I glorify Myself, My glory is nothing. It is My Father Who glorifies Me, of

Whom you say that He is your God. And you do not know Him, but I know Him. And if I say that I do not know Him, I shall be like you, a liar. *But I know Him, and I keep His word.* Abraham your father rejoiced that he was to see My day. He saw it and was glad." The Jews therefore said to Him, "Thou art not yet fifty years old, and hast Thou seen Abraham?" Jesus said to them, "Amen, amen, I say to you, before Abraham came to be, I am." *They therefore took up stones to cast at Him;* but Jesus hid himself, and went out from the temple. *Turn to* ⑨ *on page 41.*

OFFERTORY *Ps. 118* ⑩

I WILL CONFESS to Thee, O Lord, with my whole heart: render to Thy servant; I shall live and keep Thy words: enliven me according to Thy word, O Lord. *Turn to* ⑪ *on page 43.*

SECRET ⑫

MAY THESE OFFERINGS, we beg of Thee, O Lord, loose the bonds of our wickedness and procure for us the gifts of Thy mercy. Through Our Lord, etc. *Turn to* ⑬ *on page 47.*

COMMUNION VERSE ⑭

"THIS IS MY BODY which shall be given up for you; this cup is the new covenant in My Blood", said the Lord: "Do this as often as you drink it, in remembrance of Me." *Turn to* ⑮ *on page 62.*

POST-COMMUNION ⑯

DRAW NEAR to us, O Lord our God, and by Thy ever-ready assistance defend those whom Thou hast refreshed with Thy Sacraments. Through Our Lord, etc. *Turn to* ⑰ *on page 63.*

⑱ **Review "Acceptable to God", page 21.**

✝ This cross in margin of Ordinary (pages 35, 36, 39, 45), indicates paragraph is omitted in today's Mass.

« *Palms are blessed in a special ceremony before Holy Mass. Make a cross from these branches for a place of honor at the family table today* »

PICTURE AND MASS THEME EXPLAINED

We carry palm branches as a tribute of *waving* joy, before Christ, victorious over death; also as a symbol of our *wavering* fickleness, betraying Christ unto His Death.

Jesus is our *"example;"* let us never lose sight of the eternal joy of *"sharing in His Resurrection,"* when with Him we now *"suffer on a cross"* (PRAYER).

In glorious language we read how the Son of God became the *"slave"* of man; how *"He humbled Himself"* and is now our pledge *"in the glory of God the Father"* (EPISTLE).

Even as Christ adhered to the Father, so must we, despite the seeming *"prosperity of the sinner"* (GRADUAL).

The "long Gospel" enables us, as it were, to be eyewitnesses of Christ's Passion and Death, revealing His love "unto the end" (indicated by Calvary in background).

NOW BEGIN MASS AT 1 ON PAGE 35.

INTROIT
Ps. 21 ❷

O Lord, remove not Thy help to a distance from me, look toward my defence; deliver me from the lion's mouth, and my lowness from the horns of the unicorns.* *O God, my God, look upon me:* why hast Thou forsaken me? Far from my salvation are the words of my sins. O Lord.
Turn to ❸ on page 38.

PRAYER ❹

Almighty and Eternal God, Who hast caused Our Savior to become Man and then *to suffer death on the cross,* so that all mankind might *follow in His example* of humility: mercifully grant that we may deserve to keep in mind both the *record* of His suffering and also our *share in His Resurrection.* Through Our Lord, etc.
Continue below.

EPISTLE
Philip. 2 ❺

Brethren, have this mind in you which was also in Christ Jesus, Who though He was by nature God, did not consider being equal to God a thing to be clung to, but emptied Himself, *taking the nature of a slave* and being made like unto men. And appearing in the form of man, *He humbled Himself,* becoming obedient to death, even to death on a cross. Therefore God also has

---

Receive Holy Communion on Easter Sunday to Unite with the Risen Christ as a Pledge of Your Final Victory over Death.

exalted Him and has bestowed upon Him the Name that is above every name (*here all kneel*), so that at the Name of Jesus every knee should bend of those in heaven, on earth and under the earth, and every tongue should confess that the Lord Jesus Christ is *in the glory of God the Father*. THANKS BE TO GOD. *Continue below.*

GRADUAL *Ps. 72* ⑥

THOU HAST HELD me in Thy right hand, and by Thy will Thou hast conducted me; and with glory Thou hast assumed me. How good is God to Israel, *to them that are of a right heart!* But *my feet were almost moved*, my steps had well nigh slipped; because I was jealous of sinners, seeing the prosperity of sinners. [*Tract.*] O God, my God, look upon me: why hast Thou forsaken me? Far from my salvation are the words of my sins. O my God, I shall cry by day, and Thou wilt not hear: and by night, and it shall not be reputed as folly in me. But Thou dwellest in the holy place, the praise of Israel. In Thee have our fathers hoped, they have hoped, and Thou hast delivered them. They cried to Thee, and they were saved, they trusted in Thee, and were not confounded. But I am a worm and no man: the reproach of men, and the outcast of the people. All they that saw Me have laughed Me to scorn; they have spoken with the lips, and wagged the head. He hoped in the Lord, let Him deliver Him: let Him save Him, seeing He delighteth in Him. But they have looked and stared upon Me: they parted My garments amongst them, and upon my vesture they cast lots. Deliver me from the lion's mouth: and my lowness from the horns of the unicorns. Ye that fear the Lord, praise Him: all ye the seed of Jacob, glorify Him. There shall be declared to the Lord a generation to come: and the heavens shall show forth His justice. To a people that shall be born, which the Lord had made. *Continue below.*

The Passion of Our Lord Jesus Christ according to St. Matthew

PROPHECY and CONSPIRACY

GOSPEL *Matt. 26-27* 8

AT THAT TIME, Jesus said to His disciples: "You know that after two days the Passover will be here; and the *Son of Man will be delivered up to be crucified.*" Then the chief priests and the elders of the people gathered together in the court of the high priest, who was called Caiphas, and they *took counsel together* how they might seize Jesus by stealth and put Him to death. But they said, "Not on the feast, or there might be a riot among the people."

JUDAS SEEKS to BETRAY CHRIST

NOW WHEN JESUS was in Bethany, in the house of Simon the leper, a woman came up to Him with an alabaster jar of precious ointment, and she poured it on His head, as He reclined at table. But when the disciples saw this, they were indignant, and said, "To what purpose is this waste? for this might have been sold for much and given to the poor." *But Jesus, perceiving it, said to them, "Why do you trouble the woman?* She has done Me a good turn. For the poor you have always with you, but you do not always have Me. For in pouring this ointment on My Body, she has done it for My burial. Amen I say to you, wherever in the whole world this gospel is preached, *this also that she has done shall be told in memory of her."* Then one of the Twelve, called Judas Iscariot, went to the chief priests, and said to them, "What are you willing to give me, and I will deliver Him to you?" But they counted him out thirty pieces of silver. And from then on he was watching for an opportunity to betray Him.

THE LAST SUPPER

Now on the first day of the Unleavened Bread, the disciples came to Jesus and said, "Where dost Thou want us to prepare for Thee to eat the passover?" But Jesus said, "Go into the city to a certain man, and say to him, 'The Master says, My time is near at hand; at thy house I am keeping the Passover with My disciples.'" And the disciples did as Jesus bade them, and prepared the passover. *Now when evening arrived, He reclined at table with the twelve disciples.* And while they were eating, He said, "Amen I say to you, one of you will betray Me." And being very much saddened they began each to say, "Is it I, Lord?" But He answered and said, "He who dips his hand with Me in the dish, he will betray Me. The Son of Man indeed goes His way, as it is written of Him; but woe to that man by whom the Son of Man is betrayed! It were better for that man if he had not been born." And Judas who betrayed Him answered and said, "Is it I, Rabbi?" He said to him, "Thou hast said it."

JESUS INSTITUTES BLESSED SACRAMENT

AND WHILE they were at supper, Jesus took bread, and blessed and broke, and gave it to His disciples, and said, "Take and eat; *this is My Body.*" And taking a cup, He gave thanks and gave it to them, saying, "All of you drink of this; *for this is My Blood of the new covenant,* which is being shed for many unto the forgiveness of sins. But I say to you, I will not drink henceforth of this fruit of the vine, until that day when I shall drink it new with you in the kingdom of My Father." *And after reciting a hymn,* they went out to Mount Olivet.

JESUS PREDICTS THEIR DISLOYALTY

THEN JESUS said to them, *"You will all be scandalized this night because of Me;* for it is written, 'I will smite the shepherd, and the sheep of the flock will be scattered.' But after I have risen, I will go before you into Galilee." But Peter answered and said to Him, "Even though all shall be scandalized because of Thee, I will never be scandalized." Jesus said to him, "Amen I say to thee, this very night, before a cock crows, *thou wilt deny Me thrice.*" Peter said to Him, "Even if I should have to die with Thee, I will not deny Thee!" And all the disciples said th same thing.

THE AGONY in the GARDEN

THEN JESUS came with them to a country place called Gethsemani, and He said to His disciples, "Sit down here, while I go over yonder and pray." And He took with Him Peter and the two sons of Zebedee, and *He began to be saddened and exceedingly troubled.* Then He said to them, "My soul is sad, even unto death. Wait here and watch with Me." And going forward a little, He fell on His face, and prayed, saying, "Father, if it is possible, let this cup pass away from Me; yet not as I will, but as Thou willest." Then He came to the disciples and found them sleeping. And He said to Peter, *"Could you not then watch one hour with Me?* Watch and pray, that you may not enter into temptation. The spirit indeed is willing, but the flesh is weak." Again a second time He went away and prayed, saying, "My Father, if this cup cannot pass away unless I drink it, Thy will be done." And He came again and found them sleeping, for their eyes were heavy. And leaving them He went back again, and prayed a third time, saying the same words over. Then He came to His disciples, and said to them, "Sleep on now, and take your rest! Behold, *the hour is at hand,* and the *Son of Man will be betrayed into the hands of sinners.* Rise, let us go. Behold, he who betrays Me is at hand."

TREACHERY and FLIGHT

AND WHILE He was yet speaking, behold Judas, one of the Twelve, came and with him a great crowd with swords and clubs, from the chief priests and elders of the people. Now His betrayer had given them a sign, saying, *"Whomever I kiss, that is He;* lay hold of Him." And he went straight up to Jesus and said, "Hail, Rabbi!" and kissed Him. And Jesus said to him, *"Friend, for what purpose hast thou come?"* Then they came forward and set hands on Jesus and took Him. And behold, one of those who were with Jesus, stretching forth his hand, drew his sword, and striking the servant of the high priest, cut off his ear. Then Jesus said to him, "Put back thy sword into its place; for all those who take the sword will perish by the sword. Or dost thou suppose that I cannot entreat My Father, and He will even now furnish Me with more than twelve legions of angels? How then are the Scriptures to be fulfilled, that thus it must happen?" In that hour Jesus said to the crowds, "As against a robber you have come out, with swords and clubs to seize Me. *I sat daily with you in the temple teaching, and you did not lay hands on Me.*" Now all this was done that the Scriptures of the prophets might be fulfilled. Then all the disciples left Him and fled.

JESUS AFFIRMS HE IS GOD

Now those who had taken Jesus led Him away to Caiphas the high priest, where the Scribes and the elders had gathered together. But Peter was following Him at a distance, even to the courtyard of the high priest, and he went in and sat with the attendants to see the end. Now the chief priests and all the Sanhedrin were seeking *false witness* against Jesus, that they might put Him to death, but they found none, though many false witnesses came forward. But last of all there came forward two false witnesses, and said, "This man said, 'I am able to destroy the temple of God, and to rebuild it after three days.' " Then the high priest, standing up, said to Him, "Dost Thou make no answer to the things that these men prefer against Thee?" But Jesus kept silence. And the high priest said to Him, "I adjure Thee by the living God that Thou *tell us whether Thou art the Christ, the Son of God."* Jesus said to him, *"Thou hast said it.* Nevertheless, I say to you, hereafter you shall see the Son of Man sitting at the right hand of the Power and coming upon the clouds of heaven." Then the high priest tore his garments, saying, "He has blasphemed; what further need have we of witnesses? Behold, now you have heard the blasphemy. What do you think?" And they answered and said, "He is liable to death." Then *they spat in His face and buffeted Him;* while others struck His face with the palms of their hands, saying, "Prophesy to us, O Christ! who is it that struck Thee?"

DENIAL by PETER

Now Peter was sitting outside in the courtyard; and a maidservant came up to him and said, *"Thou also wast with Jesus* the Galilean." But he denied before them all, saying, "I do not know what thou art saying." And when he had gone out to the gateway, another maid saw him, and said to those who were there, "This man also was with Jesus of Nazareth." And again he denied with an oath, *"I do not know the Man!"* And after a little while the bystanders came up and said to Peter, "Surely thou also art one of them, for even thy speech betrays thee." Then he began to curse and to swear that he did not know the Man. And at that moment a cock crowed. And Peter remembered the word that Jesus had said, "Before a cock crows, thou wilt deny Me thrice." *And he went out and wept bitterly.*

THE DESPAIR of JUDAS

NOW WHEN MORNING came all the chief priests and the elders of the people took counsel together against Jesus in order to put Him to death. And they bound Him and led Him away, and delivered him to Pontius Pilate the procurator. Then Judas, who betrayed Him, when he saw that He was condemned, repented and brought back the thirty pieces of silver to the chief priests and the elders, saying, *"I have sinned in betraying innocent blood."* But they said, "What is that to us? See to it thyself." And he flung the pieces of silver into the temple, and withdrew; and went away and *hanged himself with a halter.* And the chief priests took the pieces of silver, and said, "It is not lawful to put them into the treasury, seeing that it is the price of blood." And after they had consulted together, they bought with them the potter's field, as a burial place for strangers. For this reason that field has been called even to this day, Haceldama, that is, *the Field of Blood.* Then was fulfilled what was spoken through Jeremias the prophet, saying, "And they took the thirty pieces of silver, the price of him who was priced, upon whom the children of Israel set a price; and they gave them for the potter's field, as the Lord directed me."

BARABBAS CHOSEN—CHRIST REJECTED

NOW JESUS stood before the procurator; and the procurator asked Him, saying, *"Art Thou the King of the Jews?"* Jesus said to him, "Thou sayest it." And when He was accused by the chief priests and the elders, He made no answer. Then Pilate said to Him, "Dost Thou not hear how many things they prefer against Thee?" But He did not answer him a single word, so that the procurator wondered exceedingly. Now at festival time the procurator used to release to the crowd a prisoner, whomever they would. Now he had at that time a notorious prisoner called Barabbas. Therefore, when they had gathered together, Pilate said, *"Whom do you wish that I release to you? Barabbas, or Jesus Who is called Christ?"* For he knew that they had delivered Him up out of envy. Now, as he was sitting on the judgment-seat, his wife sent to him, saying, *"Have nothing to do with that Just Man,* for I have suffered many things in a dream today because of Him." But the chief priests and the elders persuaded the crowds to ask for Barabbas and to destroy Jesus. But the procurator addressed them, and said to them, "Which of the two do you wish that I release to you?" And they said, "Barabbas." Pilate said to them, *"What then am I to do with Jesus Who is called Christ?"* They all said, "Let him be crucified!" The procurator said to them, "Why, what evil has He done?" But they kept crying out the more, saying, *"Let Him be crucified!"* Now Pilate, seeing that he was doing no good, but rather that a riot was breaking out, took water and washed his hands in sight of the crowd, saying, "I am innocent of the blood of this Just Man; see to it yourselves." And all the people answered and said, *"His blood be on us and on our children."* Then he released to them Barabbas; but Jesus he scourged and delivered to them to be crucified.

JESUS MOCKED and SPAT UPON

THEN THE SOLDIERS of the procurator took Jesus into the prætorium, and gathered together about Him the whole cohort. And they stripped Him and put on Him a scarlet cloak; and plaiting *a crown of thorns,* they put it upon His head, and a reed into His right hand; and bending the knee before Him *they mocked Him,* saying, "Hail, King of the Jews!" And *they spat on Him,* and took the reed and kept striking Him on the head. And when they had mocked Him, they took the cloak off Him and put on Him His own garments, and led Him away to crucify Him.

JESUS CRUCIFIED

NOW as they went out, they found a man of Cyrene named Simon; him they forced to *take up His cross.* And they came to the place called Golgotha, that is, the Place of the Skull. And they gave Him wine to drink mixed with gall; but when He had tasted it, He would not drink. And after they had crucified Him, *they divided His garments,* casting lots, [to fulfill that which was spoken through the prophets, saying, "They divided My garments among them, and upon My vesture they cast lots."] And *sitting down they kept watch over Him.* And they put above His head the charge against Him, written "THIS IS JESUS, THE KING OF THE JEWS." Then two robbers were crucified with Him, one on His right hand and one on His left.

SUFFERING of JESUS on the CROSS

Now the passers-by were jeering at Him, *shaking their heads,* and saying, "Thou Who destroyest the temple, and in three days buildest it up again, *save Thyself! If Thou art the Son of God, come down from the cross!"* In like manner, the chief priests with the Scribes and the elders, mocking, said, "He saved others, Himself He cannot save! If He is the King of Israel, *let Him come down now from the cross,* and *we will believe Him.* He trusted in God; let Him deliver Him now, if He wants Him; for He said, 'I am the Son of God.'" And the robbers also, who were crucified with Him, reproached Him in the same way.

JESUS DIES

Now from the sixth hour there was darkness over the whole land until the ninth hour. But about the ninth hour Jesus cried out with a loud voice, saying, "Eli, Eli, lama sabacthani," that is, *"My God, My God, why hast Thou forsaken Me?"* And some of the bystanders on hearing this said, "This man is calling Elias." And immediately one of them ran and, taking a sponge, soaked it in common wine, put it on a reed and offered it to Him to drink. But the rest said, "Wait, let us see whether Elias is coming to save Him." But Jesus again *cried out with a loud voice, and gave up His spirit.*

Here all kneel, and pause a little while.

RECOGNIZES JESUS IS GOD

And behold, the curtain of the temple was torn in two from top to bottom; and the *earth quaked,* and the *rocks were rent,* and the tombs were opened, and many bodies of the saints who had fallen asleep arose; and coming forth out of the tombs after His resurrection, they came into the holy city, and appeared to many. Now when the centurion, and those who were with him *keeping guard over Jesus,* saw the earthquake and the things that were happening, they were very much afraid, and they said, *"Truly He was the Son of God."*

BURIAL of JESUS

AND MANY WOMEN were there, looking on from a distance, *who had followed Jesus* from Galilee, *ministering to Him.* Among them were Mary Magdalene, and Mary the mother of James and Joseph, and the mother of the sons of Zebedee. Now when it was evening, there came a certain rich man of Arimathea, Joseph by name, who also himself was a disciple of Jesus. He went to Pilate and *asked for the body of Jesus.* Then Pilate ordered the body to be given up. And Joseph taking the body, wrapped it in a clean linen cloth, and *laid it in his new tomb,* which he had hewn out in the rock. Then he rolled a great stone to the entrance of the tomb, and departed. But Mary Magdalene and the other Mary were there, sitting opposite the sepulchre.

The celebrant now goes to the middle of the altar, recites the **"Cleanse My Heart"** (7) *on page 40, returns to the Gospel side, and reads the following passage:*

The TOMB is GUARDED

AND THE NEXT DAY, which is the day after the Preparation, the chief priests and the Pharisees went in a body to Pilate, saying, "Sir, we have remembered how that deceiver said, while He was yet alive, 'After three days I will rise again.' *Give orders, therefore, that the sepulchre be guarded until the third day,* or else His disciples may come and steal Him away, and say to the people, *'He has risen from the dead'*; and the last imposture will be worse than the first." Pilate said to them, "You have a guard; go, guard it as well as you know how." So they went and made the stone secure, sealing the stone, and setting the guard. *Turn to* ⑨ *on page 41.*

OFFERTORY *Ps. 68* ⑩

MY HEART hath expected reproach and misery; and I looked for one that would grieve together with Me, and there was none: I sought for one to comfort Me, and I found none; and they gave Me gall for My food, and in My thirst they gave Me vinegar to drink. *Turn to* ⑪ *on page 43.*

SECRET ⑫

GRANT, we beseech Thee, O Lord, that this gift, offered before the eyes of Thy Majesty, may obtain for us the grace of devotion and the reward of everlasting happiness. Through Our Lord, etc. *Turn to* ⑬ *on page 47.*

COMMUNION VERSE ⑭

"FATHER, if this cup cannot pass away, unless I drink it, Thy will be done." *Turn to* ⑮ *on page 62.*

POST-COMMUNION ⑯

THROUGH the action of this Sacrament within us, O Lord, may our vices be purged away and our just desires be fulfilled. Through Our Lord, etc. *Turn to* ⑰ *on page 63.*

⑱ *Meditate on Christ's Passion.*

PICTURE AND MASS THEME EXPLAINED

"You are looking for Jesus of Nazareth, Who was crucified. He has risen, He is not here . . . Go, tell His disciples . . . that He goes before you" (GOSPEL).

Yes; we, too, searchers after Christ, now confess we have found Him. The task before us is to *"tell"* others of His victory, that all may be *"of one mind and heart"* (POSTCOMMUNION).

Why? Because if Christmas is the loveliest Feast as we behold God *born of Mary* unto man's life, certainly Easter is the greatest as we behold Jesus *born of a tomb* so that man may rise unto God's Life.

Our faith in His Divinity is confirmed because He *"overcame death;"* our hope is enlivened because He has *"opened unto us the Gate of Eternity"* (PRAYER). Is it any wonder that the *"earth trembled . . . when God arose"* (OFFERTORY)?

How are we to prepare for our Easter Communion? A Resurrection Day effort to *"purge out the old"* life for the *"new!"* How could we be nourished by the *"sincerity and truth"* of Divine Bread if it were spoiled by the *"leaven"* of an insincere will, of an untrue mind (EPISTLE)?

NOW BEGIN MASS AT 1 ON PAGE 35.

INTROIT *Ps. 138* ❷

I AROSE and *am still with Thee,* alleluia: Thou hast laid Thy hand upon Me, alleluia: Thy knowledge is become wonderful, alleluia, alleluia.* Lord, Thou hast proved Me, and known Me: Thou hast known My sitting down, and My rising up. Glory be, etc. *Turn to* ❸ *on page 38.*

PRAYER ❹

O GOD, Who, on this day, through Thine only-begotten Son, hast overcome death and opened unto us the Gate of Eternity; even as by Thy grace Thou dost inspire our desires, so also follow them up with Thy continual help. Through the same Lord, etc. *Continue below.*

EPISTLE *1 Cor. 5* ❺

BRETHREN, purge out the old leaven, that you may be a new dough, as you really are without leaven. For Christ, our Passover, has been sacrificed. Therefore let us keep festival, not with the old leaven, nor with the leaven of malice and wickedness, but with the unleavened bread of sincerity and truth. THANKS BE TO GOD. *Continue below.*

GRADUAL *Ps. 117* ❻

THIS IS THE DAY which the Lord hath made: *let us be glad and rejoice* therein. Give praise to the Lord, for He is good: for His mercy endureth for ever. Alleluia, alleluia. Christ, our Passover, has been sacrificed. *Continue with SEQUENCE below.*

SEQUENCE FOR EASTER

BRING, oh, bring, all you Christians, bring
Praise and sacrifice to your King.

That spotless Lamb, Who more than due
Paid for His sheep, and those sheep you;

That guiltless Son, Who wrought your peace,
And made His Father's anger cease.

Life and death together fought,
Each to a *strange duel* was brought,

Life died, but soon revived again,
And even death by Life was slain.

Say, happy Magdalen! oh, say,
What didst thou see there by the way?

I saw the tomb of my dear Lord;
I saw Himself, and Him adored.

I saw the Holy Winding Sheet,
That bound His head and wrapt His feet.

I heard the Angels witness bear,
"Jesus is risen; He is not here:

Go, tell His followers, they shall see
Thine and their Hope in Galilee."

We, Lord! with faithful heart and cheerful voice,
On this Thy Resurrection day rejoice.

O Thou, Whose conquering Life overcame the grave,
By Thy victorious grace, us sinners save.

Turn to ❼ *on page 40.*

GOSPEL *Mark 16* ❽

AT THAT TIME, Mary Magdalene, Mary the mother of James, and Salome, bought spices, that they might go and anoint Jesus. And very early on the first day of the week, they came to the tomb, when the sun had just risen. And they were saying to one another, "Who will roll the stone back from the doorway of the tomb for us?" And looking up they saw that the stone had been rolled back, for it was very large. But on entering the tomb, they saw a young man sitting at the right side, clothed in a white robe, and they were amazed. He said to them, "Do not be terrified. You are looking for Jesus of Nazareth, Who was crucified. He has risen, He is not here. Behold the place where they laid Him. But go, tell His disciples and Peter that He goes before you into Galilee; there you shall see Him, as He told you." *Turn to* 9 *on page 41.*

OFFERTORY 10
Ps. 75

THE EARTH *trembled* and was still, *when God arose* in judgment. Alleluia. *Turn to* 11 *on page 43.*

SECRET 12

RECEIVE, we implore Thee, O Lord, the prayers of Thy people, together with our offering of sacrifice; so that what we have begun on this feast of Easter may by Thy grace become a healing remedy unto life everlasting. Through Our Lord, etc. *Turn to* 13 *on page 47.*

COMMUNION VERSE 14

CHRIST, our Passover, has been sacrificed, alleluia: therefore let us keep festival with the unleavened bread of sincerity and truth. Alleluia, alleluia, alleluia. *Turn to* 15 *on page 62.*

POST-COMMUNION 16

POUR FORTH upon us, O Lord, the spirit of Thy love, and in Thy goodness make us to be *of one mind and heart,* whom Thou hast fed with Thy Easter Sacrament. Through Our Lord, etc. *Turn to* 17 *on page 63.*

18 ***Review "Mass Vestments", page 25.***

PICTURE AND MASS THEME EXPLAINED

"Bring here thy finger, and see My hands; and bring here thy hand, and put it into My side; and be not unbelieving, but believing" (GOSPEL).

Be a witness to the Divinity of Jesus Christ! Thus did the ancient Church speak to the newly baptized on this Sunday. Since their Baptism on Holy Saturday these converts wore white robes. Now in their everyday dress they must go out as witnesses that *"Christ is the Truth"* (EPISTLE).

God the *"Father"* bore *"witness"* to this at Christ's Baptism by *"water;"* God the *"Word"* became our *"Blood"* witness on the Cross; God the *"Spirit"* gave witness when by Him Jesus was conceived in the womb of Mary. Yes, this is the triple *"testimony of God"* which we, too, must witness unto others— that *"Jesus is God"* (EPISTLE).

To the "doubting Thomases" of all future ages, Jesus gave a new proof of His Divinity in today's GOSPEL, *"written that you may believe . . . and that believing you may have life."*

NOW BEGIN MASS AT 1 ON PAGE 35.

INTROIT *1 Pet. 2* ❷

CRAVE, as newborn babes, alleluia, pure spiritual milk, alleluia, alleluia, alleluia.* Rejoice to God our helper: sing aloud to the God of Jacob. Glory be, etc. *Turn to* ❸ *on page 38.*

PRAYER ❹

GRANT, we pray Thee, O Almighty God, that we who have now come to the end of Easter festivities, may through Thy goodness, always keep its spirit in our life and conduct. Through Our Lord, etc. *Continue below.*

EPISTLE *1 John 5* ❺

DEARLY BELOVED, all that is born of God overcomes the world; and this is the victory *that overcomes the world, our faith.* Who is there that overcomes the world if not he who believes that Jesus is the Son of God? This is He Who came in water and in blood, Jesus Christ; not in the water only, but in the water and in the blood. And it is the Spirit that bears witness that *Christ is the Truth.* For *there are three that bear witness in heaven:* the Father, the Word, and the Holy Spirit; and these three are one. *And there are three that bear witness on earth:* the *Spirit,* and the *water,* and the *blood*; and these three are one. If we receive the testimony of men, the testimony of God is greater; for this is the testimony of God which is greater, that He has borne witness concerning His Son. He who believes in the Son of God has the testimony of God in himself. THANKS BE TO GOD. *Continue on next page.*

ALLELUIA VERSE ⑥

ALLELUIA, alleluia. "In the day of My resurrection," said the Lord, "I will go before you into Galilee." Alleluia. After eight days, Jesus came, the doors being closed, and stood in the midst of His disciples and said: "Peace be to you." Alleluia. *Turn to* ❼ *on page 40.*

GOSPEL ⑧
John 20

AT THAT TIME, when it was late that same day, the first of the week, though the doors where the disciples gathered had been closed for fear of the Jews, Jesus came and stood in the midst and said to them, "Peace be to you!" And when He had said this, He showed them His hands and His side. The disciples therefore rejoiced at the sight of the Lord. He therefore said to them again, *"Peace be to you!* As the Father has sent Me, I also send you." When He had said this, He breathed upon them, and said to them, "Receive the Holy Spirit; whose sins you shall forgive, they are forgiven them; and whose sins you shall retain, they are retained." Now Thomas, one of the Twelve, called the Twin, was not with them when Jesus came. The other disciples therefore said to him, "We have seen the Lord." But he said to them, "Unless I see in His hands the print of the nails, and put my finger into the place of the nails, and put my hand into His side, *I will not believe."* And after eight days, His disciples were again inside, and Thomas with them. Jesus came, the doors being closed, and stood in their midst, and said, "Peace be to you!" Then He said to Thomas, *"Bring here thy finger,* and see My hands; and *bring here thy hand, and put it into My side; and be not unbelieving, but believing."* Thomas answered and said to him, "My Lord and my God!" Jesus said to him, "Because thou hast seen Me, thou hast believed. *Blessed are they who have not seen, and yet have believed."* Many other signs also Jesus worked in the sight of His disciples, which are not written in this book. But *these are written that you may believe that Jesus is the Christ, the Son of God,* and that *believing you may have life* in His Name. *Turn to* 9 *on page 41.*

OFFERTORY *Matt. 28* 10

AN ANGEL *of the Lord came down* from heaven, and said to the women: "He Whom you seek has risen even as He said", alleluia. *Turn to* 11 *on page 43.*

SECRET 12

WE ASK THEE, O Lord, to receive the gifts of Thy rejoicing Church and, even as Thou hast given her cause for such great joy, so also grant her the fruit of perpetual gladness. Through Our Lord, etc. *Turn to* 13 *on page 47.*

COMMUNION VERSE 14

"BRING here thy hand, and put it into My side"; alleluia; *"and be not unbelieving, but believing,"* alleluia, alleluia. *Turn to* 15 *on page 62.*

POST-COMMUNION 16

O LORD, OUR GOD, we beseech Thee to make this most holy Sacrament a remedy for us both *in the present and the future,* since Thou hast given it as the sure defence of our salvation. Through Our Lord, etc. *Turn to* 17 *on page 63.*

18 **Review** "Symbols of Service", page 26.

PICTURE AND MASS THEME EXPLAINED

"I am the Good Shepherd . . . I lay down My life for My sheep . . . but the hireling flees because he is a hireling, and has no concern for the sheep" (GOSPEL).

Jesus organized the visible Church along the lines of a *sheepfold.* St. Peter, first shepherd of the visible Church, depicts Jesus as the invisible *"shepherd . . . of your souls"* (EPISTLE). He tenderly remembers all that Jesus suffered for us *"sheep going astray."*

On Catacomb walls, early Christians delighted to draw pictures and to write explanations of the perfect understanding and love between the Good Shepherd and His sheep, such as that which exists between the *"Father"* and *"Me."*

We are not only fed through the *visible guidance of His Church,* but also through the *invisible grace of the Sacraments,* especially *"in the breaking of bread"* (ALLELUIA VERSE).

NOW BEGIN MASS AT 1 ON PAGE 35.

INTROIT *Ps. 32* 2

THE EARTH *is full of the mercy of the Lord,* alleluia: by the word of the Lord the heavens were established, alleluia, alleluia.* Rejoice in the Lord, ye just: praise becometh the upright. Glory be, etc. *Turn to* ❸ *on page 38.*

PRAYER ❹

O God, Who, by the humility of Thy Son, hast lifted up a fallen world, grant perpetual happiness to Thy faithful ones, and since Thou hast rescued them from the perils of eternal death, bring them likewise to the realization of eternal joy. Through the same Lord, etc. *Continue below.*

EPISTLE *1 Peter 2* ❺

DEARLY BELOVED, Christ also has suffered for you, leaving you an example that you may *follow in His steps*: "Who did no sin, neither was deceit found in His mouth." Who, when He was reviled, did not revile, when He suffered, did not threaten, but yielded Himself to him who judged Him unjustly; Who Himself bore our sins in His body upon the tree, that we, *having died to sin, might live to justice;* and by His stripes you were healed. For you were as *sheep going astray,* but now you have returned to the *shepherd and guardian of your souls.* THANKS BE TO GOD. *Continue below.*

ALLELUIA VERSE ❻

ALLELUIA, alleluia. The disciples recognized the Lord Jesus *in the breaking of bread.* Alleluia. "I am the Good Shepherd: and I know Mine, and Mine know Me." Alleluia. *Turn to* ❼ *on page 40.*

GOSPEL *John 10* ❽

AT THAT TIME, Jesus said to the Pharisees: "I am the *Good Shepherd.* The Good Shepherd lays down His life for His sheep. But the hireling, who is not a shepherd, whose own the sheep are not, sees the wolf coming and leaves the sheep and flees. And the wolf snatches and scatters the sheep; but the *hireling flees* because he is a hireling, and *has no concern* for the sheep. I am the Good Shepherd, and *I know mine* and Mine know Me, even as the Father knows Me and I know the Father; and *I lay down My life for My sheep*. And *other sheep I have* that are not of this fold. Them also I must bring, and they shall hear My voice, and there shall be one fold and one shepherd." *Turn to* (9) *on page 41.*

OFFERTORY *Ps. 62* (10)

O God, my God, to Thee do I watch at break of day: and in Thy Name I will lift up my hands, alleluia. *Turn to* (11) *on page 43.*

SECRET (12)

Let this sacred offering ever bestow upon us Thy healthful blessing, and what it performs in mystery, may it produce in virtue. Through Our Lord, etc. *Turn to* (13) *on page 47.*

COMMUNION VERSE (14)

"I am the good shepherd," alleluia: "and I know Mine, and Mine know Me," alleluia, alleluia. *Turn to* (15) *on page 62.*

POST-COMMUNION (16)

Grant us, we beseech Thee, O Almighty God, that we, who have obtained from Thee the grace of a new life, may ever glory in Thy gift. Through Our Lord, etc. *Turn to* (17) *on page 63.*

(18) **Review** *"The Mass Year"*, **page 31.**

PICTURE AND MASS THEME EXPLAINED

"A little while and you shall see Me no longer, ... because I go to the Father ... And you therefore have sorrow now; but I will see you again, and your heart shall rejoice, and your joy no one shall take from you" (GOSPEL).

Christianity is a religion of joy! (INTROIT). May *"those ... in error"* receive this *"light"* (PRAYER). Jesus predicts, however, that our joy can never be perfect here. The "cross before the crown" (ALLELUIA VERSE) would indeed be a mystery had not Jesus lived it out for us.

An unbelieving *"world shall rejoice"* because it regards Him as dead and gone. But Christ departs only for a *"little while"* (GOSPEL) to test our love and loyalty. He shall return (as indicated by little figure of Christ in the clouds).

Prepare for His coming *"in the day of visitation"* by good example. *"Behave yourselves honorably among ... pagans; that ... they ... observing ...*

your good works" for God and country (described in the EPISTLE) may recognize that Christianity is a religion of joy, now and forever!

NOW BEGIN MASS AT 1 ON PAGE 35.

INTROIT *Ps. 65* 2

SHOUT WITH JOY to God, all the earth, alleluia; sing ye a psalm to His Name, alleluia: give glory to his praise. Alleluia, alleluia, alleluia.* Say unto God: How terrible are Thy *works,* O Lord! In the multitude of Thy strength Thy *enemies* shall lie to Thee. Glory be, etc. *Turn to 3 on page 38.*

PRAYER 4

O GOD, since Thou dost show the light of Thy truth to those who are in error, so that they might return to the path of right living; grant unto all *who go by the name of Christian,* both to reject what is opposed and to uphold what is becoming to this name. Through Our Lord, etc. *Continue below.*

EPISTLE *1 Peter 2* 5

DEARLY BELOVED, I exhort you as strangers and pilgrims to abstain from carnal desires which war against the soul. Behave yourselves honorably among the pagans; that, whereas they slander you *as evildoers,* they may through observing you by reason of your good works glorify God in the day of visitation. Be subject to every human creature for God's sake, whether to the king as supreme, or to governors as sent through him for vengeance on evildoers and for the praise of the good. For such is the will of God, that by *doing good you should put to silence the ignorance of foolish men.* Live as freemen, yet not using your freedom as a cloak for malice but as servants of God. Honor all men; love the brotherhood; fear God; honor the king. Servants, be subject to your masters in all fear, not only to the good and moderate, but also to the severe. This is indeed a grace, in Christ Jesus Our Lord. THANKS BE TO GOD. *Continue below.*

ALLELUIA VERSE 6

ALLELUIA, alleluia. The Lord hath sent redemption to His people. Alleluia. It behooved Christ *to suffer these things, and so to enter into His glory.* Alleluia. *Turn to* 7 *on page 40.*

GOSPEL
John 16 8

AT THAT TIME, Jesus said to His disciples: "A little while and you shall see Me no longer; and again a little while and you shall see Me, *because I go to the Father.*" Some of His disciples therefore said to one another, "What is this He says to us, 'A little while and you shall not see Me, and again a little while and you shall see Me'; and, 'I go to the Father'?" They kept saying therefore, "What is this 'little while' of which He speaks? We do not know what He is saying." But Jesus knew that they wanted to ask Him, and He said to them, "You inquire about this among yourselves because I said, 'A little while and *you shall not see Me,* and again a little while and *you shall see Me.'* Amen, amen, I say to you, that *you shall weep* and lament, but the world shall rejoice; and you shall be sorrowful, but *your sorrow* shall *be turned into joy.* A woman about to give birth has sorrow, because her hour has come. But when she has brought forth the child, she no longer remembers the anguish for her joy that a man is born into the world. And *you therefore have sorrow now;* but I will see you again, and your heart shall rejoice, and *your joy no one shall take from you."* *Turn to* ⑨ *on page 41.*

OFFERTORY *Ps. 145* ⑩

PRAISE THE LORD, O my soul, in my life I will praise the Lord: I will sing to my God as long as I shall be. Alleluia. *Turn to* ⑪ *on page 43.*

SECRET ⑫

BY THESE MYSTERIES, O Lord, confer upon us the grace to *restrain our earthly desires,* so that we might learn how to *love the things of heaven.* Through Our Lord, etc. *Turn to* ⑬ *on page 47.*

COMMUNION VERSE ⑭

"A LITTLE WHILE and you shall see Me no longer," alleluia; "and again a little while and you shall see Me, *because I go to the Father."* Alleluia, alleluia. *Turn to* ⑮ *on page 62.*

POST-COMMUNION ⑯

MAY THE SACRAMENT we have received, O Lord we pray Thee, be a life-giving food to our souls and a life-saving help to our bodies. Through Our Lord, etc. *Turn to* ⑰ *on page 63.*

⑱ **Review "Spring", page 32.**

The Easter Season is drawing to a close. If anyone in your family has failed to make his "EASTER DUTY," it is your duty to pray for him and to urge him to receive the Sacraments.

PICTURE AND MASS THEME EXPLAINED

"If I do not go, the Advocate will not come; . . . but if I go, I will send Him to you . . . He will (convince) *the world . . . of justice"* (GOSPEL).

The Sunday of Justice, interior and social! The Holy Spirit descends upon us with His seven Gifts at our Confirmation (symbolized by the Dove). He puts before us the imitation of Christ's sinless example, since *"the prince of this world"* had tried to confuse and even destroy the correct ideas of right and wrong. Hence we may now sing *"a new canticle,"* because God *"hath revealed His justice"* (INTROIT).

The EPISTLE and OFFERTORY extol the gifts of interior *"justice;"* the PRAYER, evidently referring to social *"justice,"* makes us realize that only God can *"make* (all) *of one will."*

How do we react in thought and action to this twofold standard of *"justice"* revealed in the Life of Christ and taught us by the *"Spirit of truth?"*

NOW BEGIN MASS AT 1 ON PAGE 35.

INTROIT *Ps. 97* 2

SING YE to the Lord a *new* canticle, alleluia; for the Lord hath done wonderful things, alleluia; *He hath revealed His justice* in the sight of the

Gentiles, alleluia, alleluia.* His right hand hath wrought for Him salvation; and His arm is holy. Glory be, etc. *Turn to* ❸ *on page 38.*

PRAYER ❹

O God, Who dost make the faithful *to be of one mind and will,* grant that we, Thy people, may love what Thou dost command and desire what Thou dost promise; so that, amid the changing things of this world, our hearts may be fixed where true joys are to be found. Through Our Lord, etc. *Continue below.*

EPISTLE ❺
James 1

Dearly beloved, *every good gift* and *every perfect gift is from above,* coming down from the Father of Lights, with Whom there is no change, nor shadow of alteration. Of His own will *He has begotten* us by the word of truth, that we might be, as it were, the first-fruits of His creatures. You know this, my beloved brethren. But let every man be swift to hear, slow to speak, and slow to wrath. For the wrath of man does not work the justice of God. Therefore, *casting aside all uncleanness* and abundance of malice, with meekness *receive the ingrafted word,* which is able to save your souls. Thanks be to God. *Continue below.*

ALLELUIA VERSE ❻

Alleluia, alleluia. The right hand of the Lord hath wrought power; the right hand of the Lord hath exalted me. Alleluia. Christ, having risen from the dead, dies now no more, death shall no longer have dominion over Him. Alleluia. *Turn to* ❼ *on page 40.*

GOSPEL
John 16 ⑧

AT THAT TIME, Jesus said to His disciples, "Now I am going to Him Who sent Me, and *no one of you asks me, 'Where art Thou going?'* But because I have spoken to you these things, sadness has filled your heart. But I speak the truth to you; it is expedient for you that I depart. For *if I do not go, the Advocate will not come to you; but if I go, I will send Him to you.* And *when He has come He will convict the world of sin, and of justice,* and of judgment: of sin, because they do not believe in Me; of justice, because I go to the Father, and you will see Me no more; and of judgment, because *the prince of this world* has already been judged. Many things yet I have to say to you, but you cannot bear them now. But when He, the Spirit of truth, has come, He will teach you all the truth. For He will not speak on His own authority, but whatever He will hear He will speak, and the things that are to come He will declare to you. He will glorify Me, because He will receive of what is Mine and declare it to you." *Turn to* ⑨ *on page 41.*

OFFERTORY
Ps. 65 ⑩

SHOUT WITH JOY to God, all the earth, sing ye a psalm to His Name: come, and hear, and I will tell you, all you that fear God, *what things the Lord hath done for my soul,* alleluia. *Turn to* ⑪ *on page 43.*

SECRET ⑫

O GOD, Who, by the Holy Communion of this Sacrifice, hast made us partakers of Thy one and supreme Divine Nature, grant that we who know Thy truth, may also follow it by a worthy life. Through Our Lord, etc. *Turn to* ⑬ *on page 47.*

COMMUNION *John 16* ⑭

"When the Advocate has come, the Spirit of truth, *He will convict the world* of sin, and *of justice,* and of judgment," alleluia, alleluia. *Turn to* ⑮ *on page 62.*

POST-COMMUNION ⑯

Help us, O Lord, our God, so that by this Sacrament which we have received in all faith, we may be cleansed from sin and rescued from all dangers. Through Our Lord, etc. *Turn to* ⑰ *on page 63.*

⑱ *AFTER MASS, REVIEW YOUR CATECHISM.*

I believe that Mary is the Virgin Mother of God, because she is the Mother of Jesus Christ, Who is truly our God as well as true Man.

I believe that Mary was conceived Immaculate, preserved free from the stain of original sin; that she was always "full of grace".

I believe that shortly after death, her Immaculate soul was reunited to her incorrupt body, and that she was then assumed into heaven as Queen above all the angels and saints.

I believe that Mary became our true heavenly Mother, because of our adoption as Sons of God and brethren of her Christ at the time of our Baptism.

I believe that Jesus, from the cross, bequeathed His Mother to be our Mother, when, in the person of St. John He confided all men to be her children.

I believe that I owe the greatest love, reverence and respect to Mary, my Mother.

PICTURE AND MASS THEME EXPLAINED

"If you ask the Father anything in My Name, He will give it to you . . . Ask, and you shall receive, that your joy may be full" (GOSPEL).

Petition Sunday, followed by Rogation Days! We petition the Father's blessing upon springtime planting in the fields; yes, and in our souls. We ask in the *"Name"* of Jesus. He intercedes for us with the Father.

We must ask only for what keeps us on the Christian road. *"I go to the Father,"* is the signpost on this road to which Jesus points. The EPISTLE warns us of a dangerous detour, if we ignore this roadguide. Religion is vain unless one be a *"doer"* and not a *"hearer"* only. *"Religion pure and undefiled"* in our interior life, means keeping *"oneself unspotted;"* in our social life, it means the spiritual and corporal works of mercy to all *"in their tribulation."*

NOW BEGIN MASS AT ❶ ON PAGE 35.

INTROIT
Is. 48 ❷

DECLARE the voice of joy, and let it be heard, alleluia: declare it even unto the ends of the earth: The Lord hath delivered His people, alleluia, alleluia.* Shout with joy to God, all the earth: sing ye a psalm to His Name, give glory to His praise. Glory be, etc. *Turn to* ❸ *on page 38.*

PRAYER ❹

O GOD, from Whom all good things proceed, grant a favorable reply to our lowly petitions, that by Thy holy inspiration we may ever think on such things as are right and by Thy guidance ever do what is correct. Through Our Lord, etc. *Continue below.*

EPISTLE
James 1 ❺

DEARLY BELOVED, be *doers* of the word, and *not hearers* only, deceiving yourselves. For if anyone is a *hearer* of the word, and not a *doer,* he is like a man looking at his natural face in a mirror: for he looks at himself and goes away, and presently he forgets what kind of man he is. But he who has looked carefully into the perfect law of liberty and has remained in it, not becoming a forgetful hearer but a doer of the work, shall be blessed in his deed. And if anyone thinks himself to be religious, not restraining his tongue but deceiving his own heart, that man's religion is vain. *Religion pure* and *undefiled* before God the Father is this: to give aid to orphans and widows *in their tribulation,* and to *keep oneself unspotted* from this world. THANKS BE TO GOD. *Continue on next page.*

ALLELUIA VERSE ⑥

ALLELUIA, alleluia. Christ is risen, and hath shone His light upon us whom He hath redeemed with His Blood. Alleluia. "I came forth from the Father and have come into the world. Again I leave the world and *go to the Father.*" Alleluia. *Turn to* ⑦ *on page 40.*

GOSPEL ⑧
John 16

AT THAT TIME, Jesus said to His disciples: "Amen, amen, I say to you, if you ask the Father anything *in My Name,* He will give it to you. Hitherto you have not asked anything *in My Name.* Ask, and you shall receive, that your joy may be full. These things I have spoken to you in parables. The hour is coming when I will no longer speak to you in parables, but will speak to you plainly of the Father. In that day you shall ask *in My Name;* and I do not say to you that I will ask the Father for you, for the Father Himself loves you because you have loved Me, and have believed that I came forth from God. I came forth from the Father and have come into the world. Again *I leave the world and go to the Father.*" His disciples said to Him, "Behold, now Thou speakest plainly, and utterest no parable. Now we know that Thou knowest all things, and dost not need that anyone should question Thee. For this reason we believe that Thou camest forth from God." *Turn to* ⑨ *on page 41.*

OFFERTORY ⑩
Ps. 65

O BLESS THE LORD our God, ye Gentiles, and make the voice of His praise to be heard: Who hath set my soul to live, and hath not suffered my feet to be moved: blessed be the Lord, Who hath not turned away my prayer, nor His mercy from me, alleluia. *Turn to* ⑪ *on page 43.*

SECRET ⑫

RECEIVE, O LORD, the prayers of those who believe in Thee, together with our offering of sacrifice, so that, through this service of loving devotion, we may enter into the glory of heaven. Through Our Lord, etc. *Turn to* ⑬ *on page 47.*

COMMUNION VERSE ⑭

SING YE to the Lord, alleluia; sing ye to the Lord, and bless His Name; show forth His salvation from day to day, alleluia, alleluia. *Turn to* ⑮ *on page 62.*

POST-COMMUNION ⑯

DO THOU, O Lord, grant unto us who have been nourished and strengthened at Thy heavenly table, both to desire what is right and to obtain what we desire. Through Our Lord, etc. *Turn to* ⑰ *on page 63.*

⑱ *AFTER MASS, REVIEW YOUR CATECHISM.*

I believe that the recitation of the Rosary, together with meditation on its various mysteries, is the type of devotion to Mary most recommended by the Church; because in the first part of the "Hail Mary" we salute her extraordinary privileges and gifts; and in the second part we implore her protection for our present needs, but above all, at the great crisis of life, "at the hour of our death".

I believe that my salvation depends upon Mary's Mediation in union with Christ, because of her exalted position as Mediatrix of all Grace and nearness to her Divine Son.

PICTURE AND MASS THEME EXPLAINED

"*'You shall be witnesses for Me . . . to the very ends of the earth.'* (Then) *He was lifted up, . . . and a cloud took Him out of their sight*" (EPISTLE).

"I go to prepare a place for you." The Valedictory Address of the Divine Teacher as He enters into His Commencement Day in heaven! Hence we pray *"that our minds also may dwell in heavenly places"* (PRAYER); that we may not be guilty of any *"lack of faith"* or *"hardness of heart"* (GOSPEL).

We must *"be witnesses"* of all that *"Jesus did and taught"* (EPISTLE), making clear that Jesus did not come to *"restore the kingdom"* as a material or political affair.

Let us renew our enthusiasm, *"O clap your hands, . . . shout with the voice of joy unto God"* (INTROIT); unto neighbor, even as the first Christians *"went forth and preached everywhere"* (GOSPEL).

NOW BEGIN MASS AT ❶ ON PAGE 35.

INTROIT *Acts 1* ❷

"MEN OF GALILEE, why do you stand looking up to heaven?" alleluia: "He will come in the same way as you have seen Him going up into heaven," alleluia, alleluia, alleluia.* O clap your hands, all ye nations; shout unto God with the voice of joy. Glory be, etc. *Turn to* ❸ *on page 38.*

PRAYER ④

GRANT, we implore Thee, O Almighty God, according to our belief in the Ascension into heaven of Thine only-begotten Son, Our Redeemer, that *our minds also may dwell in heavenly places.* Through the same Lord, etc. *Continue below.*

EPISTLE ⑤
Acts 1

IN THE FORMER BOOK, O Theophilus, I spoke of all that Jesus did and taught from the beginning until the day on which He was taken up, after He had given commandments through the Holy Spirit to the apostles whom He had chosen. To them also *He showed Himself alive* after His passion by many proofs, *during forty days appearing to them* and speaking of the kingdom of God. And while eating with them, He charged them not to depart from Jerusalem, but to wait for the promise of the Father, "of which you have heard," said He, "by My mouth; for John indeed baptized with water, but you shall be baptized with the Holy Spirit not many days hence." They therefore who had come together began to ask Him, saying, "Lord, wilt Thou at this time *restore the kingdom to Israel?"* But He said to them, "It is not for you to know the times or dates which the Father has fixed by His own authority; but you shall receive *power when the Holy Spirit comes upon you,* and *you shall be witnesses for Me* in Jerusalem and in all Judea and Samaria and *even to the very ends of the earth."* And when He had said this, *He was lifted up before their eyes,* and a cloud took Him out of their sight. And while they were gazing up to heaven as He went, behold, two men stood by them in white garments, and said to them, "Men of Galilee, why do you stand looking up to heaven? This Jesus Who has been taken up from you into heaven, will come in the same way as you have seen Him going up to heaven." THANKS BE TO GOD. *Continue below.*

ALLELUIA VERSE ⑥

ALLELUIA, alleluia. God hath ascended in jubilation, and the Lord with the sound of the trumpet. Alleluia. The Lord is in Sina, in His holy place; ascending on high, He hath led captivity captive. Alleluia. *Turn to* ⑦ *on page 40.*

GOSPEL *Mark 16* ⑧

AT THAT TIME, Jesus appeared to the Eleven as they were at table; and He upbraided them for *their lack of faith* and *hardness of heart,* in that they had not believed those who had seen Him after He had risen. And He said to them, "*Go into the whole world* and preach the gospel to every creature. He who believes and is baptized shall be saved, but he who does not believe shall be condemned. And these signs shall attend those who believe: in My Name they shall cast out devils; they shall speak in new tongues; they shall take up serpents; and if they drink any deadly thing, it shall not hurt them; they shall lay hands upon the sick and they shall get well." So then the Lord, after He had spoken to them, was taken up into heaven, and sits at the right hand of God. But *they went forth and preached everywhere,* while the Lord worked with them and confirmed the preaching by the signs that followed. *Turn to* ⑨ *on page 41.*

OFFERTORY *Ps. 46* ⑩

GOD is ascended in jubilee, and the Lord with the sound of trumpet. Alleluia. *Turn to* ⑪ *on page 43.*

SECRET ⑫

ACCEPT, O Lord, the gifts that we bring to Thee for the glorious Ascension of Thy Son, and mercifully grant that we may be freed from present dangers and finally arrive at everlasting life. Through the same Lord, etc. *Turn to* ⑬ *on page 47.*

COMMUNION VERSE ⑭

SING YE to the Lord, Who mounteth above the heaven of heavens to the east. Alleluia. *Turn to* ⑮ *on page 62.*

POST-COMMUNION ⑯

GRANT, we beseech Thee, O Almighty and Merciful God, that what we have received in this visible Sacrament may profit us by its invisible grace. Through Our Lord, etc. *Turn to* ⑰ *on page 63.*

⑱ *AFTER MASS, REVIEW YOUR CATECHISM.*

I believe that ACTUAL grace is a supernatural help from God to *enlighten our minds* or *move our wills* to do good or shun evil for His sake and our eternal life.

Sunday within Octave of Ascension

PICTURE AND MASS THEME EXPLAINED

"When . . . the Spirit of truth . . . has come, He will bear witness concerning Me. And you also bear witness . . . The hour is coming for everyone who kills you to think that he is offering worship to God" (GOSPEL).

The Apostles make *the first Novena,* recommended by Christ Himself, in preparation for the coming of the Holy Spirit. The INTROIT presents their Novena prayer, and ours, too.

In the background St. Stephen is shown being stoned to death. The cross upside down, indicates how St. Peter was crucified. We are to *"bear witness"* to Christ and His Church against a world that will condemn us to death, *thinking that* they are *"offering worship to God"* (GOSPEL).

A witness! Yes, interiorly, to *"be watchful in prayers;"* exteriorly, by *"mutual charity among yourselves"* (EPISTLE). For this we now offer *"this . . . sacrifice"* (SECRET), to *"purify us"* from past disloyalties and to *"strengthen"* us for future testimony.

NOW BEGIN MASS AT (1) ON PAGE 35.

INTROIT *Ps. 26* ❷

HEAR, O LORD, my voice with which I have cried to Thee, alleluia: my heart hath said to Thee, *I have sought Thy face,* Thy face, O Lord, I will seek: turn not away Thy face from me, alleluia, alleluia.* *The Lord is my light* and my salvation; whom shall I fear? Glory be, etc. *Turn to* ❸ *on page 38.*

PRAYER ❹

O ALMIGHTY and Everlasting God, grant that we may always have a will devoted to Thee and a *sincere* heart to serve Thy Majesty. Through Our Lord, etc. *Continue below.*

« The prayer from the "Feast of the Ascension" is also said: »

GRANT, we implore Thee, O Almighty God, according to our belief in the Ascension into heaven of Thine only-begotten Son, Our Redeemer, that our minds also may dwell in heavenly places. Through the same Lord, etc. *Continue below.*

EPISTLE *1 Peter 4* ❺

DEARLY BELOVED, be prudent therefore and *watchful in prayers.* But above all things have a constant *mutual charity among yourselves;* for charity covers a multitude of sins. Be hospitable to one another without murmuring. According to the *gift* that each has received, administer it to one another as good stewards of the manifold grace of God. If anyone speaks, let it be as with words of God. If anyone ministers, let it be as from the strength that God furnishes; that in all things God may be honored through Jesus Christ, Our Lord. THANKS BE TO GOD. *Continue on next page.*

ALLELUIA VERSE ⑥

ALLELUIA, alleluia. The Lord hath reigned over all the nations; God sitteth on His holy throne. Alleluia. "I will not leave you orphans; I go away and I am coming to you, and your heart shall rejoice." Alleluia. *Turn to* ⑦ *on page 40.*

GOSPEL ⑧
John 15-16

AT THAT TIME, Jesus said to His disciples, "When *the Advocate* has come, *Whom I will send you from the Father, the Spirit of truth Who proceeds from the Father,* He will bear witness concerning Me. And *you also bear witness,* because from the beginning you are with Me. These things I have spoken to you that you may not be scandalized. They will expel you from the synagogues. Yes, the hour is coming for everyone who kills you to *think that he is offering worship to God.* And these things they will do because they have not known the Father nor Me. But these things I have spoken to you, that when the time for them has come you may remember that I told you." *Turn to* ⑨ *on page 41.*

OFFERTORY ⑩
Ps. 46

GOD IS ascended with jubilee; and the Lord with the sound of trumpet. Alleluia. *Turn to* ⑪ *on page 43.*

SECRET ⑫

MAY THIS IMMACULATE sacrifice purify us, O Lord, and *strengthen our souls* with grace from heaven. Through Our Lord, etc. *Continue on next page.*

« The Secret from the "Feast of the Ascension" is also said: »

ACCEPT, O Lord, the gifts that we bring to Thee for the glorious Ascension of Thy Son, and mercifully grant that we may be freed from present dangers and finally arrive at everlasting life. Through the same Lord, etc. *Turn to* ⑬ *on page 47.*

COMMUNION VERSE ⑭

"FATHER, while I was with them, I kept them whom Thou hast given Me," alleluia; "but now I am coming to Thee; I do not pray that Thou take them out of the world, but that Thou keep them from evil," alleluia, alleluia. *Turn to* ⑮ *on page 62.*

POST-COMMUNION ⑯

HAVING BEEN FILLED, O Lord, with Thy heavenly gifts, grant, we beseech Thee, that we may ever continue in the spirit of thanksgiving. Through Our Lord, etc. *Continue below.*

« The Postcommunion from the "Feast of the Ascension" is also said »

GRANT, we beseech Thee, O Almighty God, that what we have received in this visible Sacrament may profit us by its invisible grace. Through Our Lord, etc. *Turn to* ⑰ *on page 63.*

⑱ AFTER MASS, REVIEW YOUR CATECHISM.

I believe that actual grace is different from habitual grace which is a quality dwelling *within* the soul; whereas actual grace is a divine movement *from without,* helping the soul beyond its natural powers, either to think or to act along certain lines, such as making an act of contrition.

PICTURE AND MASS THEME EXPLAINED

"Suddenly there came a sound from heaven, as of a violent wind . . . it filled the whole house . . . And there appeared to them parted tongues as of fire, which settled upon each of them. And they were all filled with the Holy Spirit" (EPISTLE).

On Christmas we celebrate the birthday of Christ in His Physical Body. Today is the birthday of the Church, of all those who have been reborn into His Mystical Body.

How did the first Christians prepare? They were all "in prayer" with Mary; and they were "all of one mind," under the leadership of Peter, making ready to tell *"men from every nation under heaven . . . of the wonderful works of God"* (EPISTLE). Yes, prayer and action are the marks of the true Christian.

In the OFFERTORY we ask the Holy Spirit to *"confirm"* the graces *"wrought in us"* when we were baptized and confirmed. We pray also *"to relish"* things of the Spirit and to benefit by *"His consolation"* (PRAYER) in the struggle of Church and soul against *"the prince of the world"* (GOSPEL).

NOW BEGIN MASS AT 1 ON PAGE 35.

INTROIT *Wis. 1* **2**

THE SPIRIT *of the Lord hath filled the whole*

earth, alleluia; and that which containeth all things hath knowledge of the voice, alleluia, alleluia, alleluia.* *Let God arise, and His enemies be scattered;* and let them that hate Him fly before His face. Glory be, etc. *Turn to* ❸ *on page 38.*

PRAYER ❹

O God, Who on this day didst instruct the hearts of Thy faithful by the light of the Holy Spirit, grant us, by the same Spirit, to *relish* what is right and evermore to rejoice in His *consolation.* Through Our Lord . . . in the unity of the same Holy Spirit, etc. *Continue below.*

EPISTLE ❺
Acts. 2

When the days of Pentecost were drawing to a close, they were all together in one place. And suddenly there came a sound from heaven, as of a violent wind coming, and it filled the whole house where they were sitting. And there appeared to them *parted tongues as of fire,* which settled upon each of them. And *they were* all *filled with the Holy Spirit* and began to speak in foreign tongues, even as the Holy Spirit prompted them to speak. Now there were staying at Jerusalem Jews, devout men from every nation under heaven. And when this sound was heard, the multitude gathered and were bewildered in mind, because each heard them speaking in his own language. But they were all amazed and marvelled, saying, "Behold, are not all these that are speaking Galileans? And how have we heard each his own language in which he was born? Parthians and Medes and Elamites, and inhabitants of Mesopotamia, Judea, and

Cappadocia, Pontus and Asia, Phrygia and Pamphylia, Egypt and the parts of Libya about Cyrene, and visitors from Rome, Jews also and proselytes, Cretans and Arabians, we have heard them speaking in our own languages of *the wonderful works of God."* THANKS BE TO GOD. *Continue below.*

ALLELUIA VERSE 6

ALLELUIA, alleluia. Send forth Thy Spirit and they shall be created: and Thou shalt renew the face of the earth. Alleluia. (*Here all kneel*) Come, O Holy Spirit, fill the hearts of Thy faithful: and kindle in them the fire of Thy love.

SEQUENCE FOR PENTECOST

COME, O Holy Spirit, come;
And from Thy heavenly Home
Shed a ray of Light divine.
Come, Thou, Father of the poor;
Come, with treasures that endure;
Come, to light this heart of mine.

Thou of all consolers best,
Thou the soul's most welcome guest,
Grace, refreshment now bestow.
Thou in toil our comfort sweet,
Thou our Peace in passion's heat,
Solace in the midst of woe.

Light immortal! Light Divine!
Visit Thou these hearts of Thine
And our inmost being fill.
If Thou take Thy grace away,
Nothing pure in man will stay;
All his good is turned to ill.

Heal our wounds; our strength renew;
On our dryness pour Thy dew;
Wash the stains of guilt away.
Do Thou bend the rigid will;
The frozen heart with fervor fill;
Guide the steps that go astray.

Upon those who trust Thee evermore,
Thee believe and Thee adore,
In Thy sevenfold gifts descend.
Give them virtue's sure reward;
Give them Thy salvation, Lord;
Give them joys that never end.

Amen. Alleluia.

Turn to 7 *on page 40.*

GOSPEL *John 14* 8

AT THAT TIME, Jesus said to His disciples, "If anyone love Me, he will keep My word, and My Father will love him, and *We will come to him* and make Our abode with him. He who does not love Me does not keep My words. And the word that you have heard is not Mine, but the Father's Who sent Me. These things I have spoken to you while yet dwelling with you. But the Advocate, the Holy Spirit, Whom the Father will send in My Name, He will teach you all things, and bring to your mind whatever I have said to you. Peace I leave with you, *My peace I give to you;* not as the world gives do I give to you. *Do not let your heart be troubled, or be afraid.* You have heard Me say to you, 'I go away and I am coming to you.' If you loved Me, you would indeed rejoice that I am going to the Father, for the Father is greater than I. And now I have told you before it comes to pass, that when it has come to pass you may believe. I will no longer speak much with you, for the *prince of the world is coming,* and in Me he has nothing. But he comes that the world may know that I love the Father, and that I do as the Father has commanded Me." *Turn to* ⑨ *on page 41.*

OFFERTORY *Ps. 67* ⑩

CONFIRM THIS, O God, which Thou hast wrought in us: from Thy temple, which is in Jerusalem, kings shall offer presents to Thee, alleluia. *Turn to* ⑪ *on page 43.*

SECRET ⑫

SANCTIFY these gifts offered unto Thee, we plead, O Lord, and cleanse our hearts by the light of the Holy Spirit. Through Our Lord . . . in the unity of the same Holy Spirit, God, etc. *Turn to* ⑬ *on page 47.*

COMMUNION VERSE ⑭

SUDDENLY THERE CAME a sound from heaven, as of a violent wind coming, where they were sitting, alleluia; and they were *all filled with the Holy Spirit,* speaking the wonderful works of God, alleluia, alleluia. *Turn to* ⑮ *on page 62.*

POST-COMMUNION ⑯

MAY THE OUTPOURING of the Holy Spirit purify our hearts, O Lord, and so sprinkle them with the dew of His *interior* grace that they may be fruitful in *good works.* Through Our Lord . . . in the unity of the same Holy Spirit, God, etc. *Turn to* ⑰ *on page 63.*

⑱ ***Review** "Mass Vestments, a Symbol", **page 26.***

PICTURE AND MASS THEME EXPLAINED

"Blessed be the Holy Trinity" (INTROIT), *"in the name of the Father, and of the Son, and of the Holy Spirit"* (GOSPEL).

The Most Adorable Trinity! *"All things"* good, in nature and grace, flow from and return to the Trinity; *"from Him,"* God the Father, our Creator; *"through Him,"* God the Son, our Redeemer; *"unto Him,"* God the Holy Spirit, our Sanctifier (EPISTLE).

May we ever be "on the alert" to the presence of the Trinity in our souls! At Baptism we became the adopted "sons of the Father," "co-heirs with Christ," "temples of the Holy Spirit!"

In our offering of Holy Mass, *"we will give glory to"* the Trinity (INTROIT), and God will show *"mercy to us"* (OFFERTORY, COMMUNION). On this Feast we should also renew our baptismal vows (page 331), that this *"profession of our faith . . . may be of profit to our health, in body and soul"* (POSTCOMMUNION).

NOW BEGIN MASS AT 1 ON PAGE 35.

INTROIT *Tob. 12* ❷

BLESSED be the Holy Trinity, and undivided Unity: we will give glory to Him, because He hath shown His mercy to us.* O Lord our Lord, how wonderful is Thy Name in all the earth. Glory be, etc. *Turn to* ❸ *on page 38.*

PRAYER ❹

O ALMIGHTY, Everlasting God, Who hast given Thy servants the grace to proclaim the glory of the Eternal Trinity in the professing of the true faith and to adore Thy Unity in the power of Thy Majesty, grant that by *steadfastness in the same faith,* we may evermore be *defended from all misfortune.* Through Our Lord, etc. *Continue below.*

« *The Prayer from the First Sunday after Pentecost is also said* »

O GOD, the strength of all those who put their trust in Thee, kindly hear our prayers, and because our mortal weakness can do nothing without Thee, grant us the help of Thy grace, so that, in keeping Thy commandments, we may please Thee both in will and in deed. Through Our Lord, etc. *Continue below.*

EPISTLE *Rom. 11* ❺

OH, THE DEPTH of the riches of the wisdom and of the knowledge of God! How incomprehensible are His judgments and how unsearchable His ways! For "Who has known the mind of the Lord, or who has been His counsellor? Or who has first given to Him, that recompense should be made him?" For *from Him* and *through Him* and *unto Him* are *all things.* To Him be the glory forever, amen. THANKS BE TO GOD. *Continue below.*

GRADUAL *Dan. 3* ⑥

BLESSED ART THOU, O Lord, Who beholdest the depths, and sittest upon the cherubim. Blessed art Thou, O Lord, in the firmament of heaven, and worthy of praise for ever. Alleluia, alleluia. Blessed art Thou, O Lord God of our fathers, and worthy of praise for ever. Alleluia. *Turn to ⑦ on page 40.*

GOSPEL *Matt. 28* ⑧

AT THAT TIME, Jesus said to His disciples, "All power in heaven and on earth has been given to Me. Go, therefore, and make disciples of all nations, *baptizing them in the name of the Father, and of the Son, and of the Holy Spirit,* teaching them to observe all that I have commanded you; and behold, *I am with you* all days, even unto the consummation of the world." *Turn to ⑨ on page 41.*

OFFERTORY *Tob. 12* ⑩

BLESSED BE GOD the Father, and the only-begotten Son of God, and also the Holy Spirit; because He hath shown His mercy toward us. *Turn to ⑪ on page 43.*

SECRET ⑫

HAVING CALLED upon Thy holy Name, we pray Thee, O Lord, our God, to sanctify the victim of this offering and, as a result of it, *make of us an eternal offering to Thee.* Through Our Lord, etc. *Continue on next page.*

« The Secret from the First Sunday after Pentecost is also said »

BE PLEASED, we implore Thee, O Lord, to accept the offerings we dedicate to Thee, and grant that they may become unto us a means of perpetual help. Through Our Lord, etc. *Turn to* ⑬ *on page 47.*

COMMUNION VERSE ⑭

WE BLESS the God of heaven, and *before all living we will praise Him;* because He has shown His mercy to us. *Turn to* ⑮ *on page 62.*

POST-COMMUNION ⑯

MAY OUR receiving of this Sacrament, O Lord, our God, and the *profession of our faith* in the eternal, Holy Trinity and of Its undivided Unity be of profit to our health, *in body and soul.* Through Our Lord, etc. *Continue below.*

« The Postcommunion from the First Sunday after Pentecost is also said »

NOW that we have been filled with Thy great gift, we pray Thee, O Lord, that we may receive it unto our salvation and never cease from praising Thee. Through Our Lord, etc. *Turn to* ⑰ *on page 63.*

« The following Gospel (Luke 6, 36-42) is recited instead of the usual last Gospel on page 63 »

AT THAT TIME, Jesus said to His disciples, "Be merciful, therefore, even as your Father is merciful. Do not judge, and you shall not be judged; do not condemn, and you shall not be condemned. Forgive, and you shall be forgiven; give, and it shall be given to you; good measure, pressed down, shaken together, running over, shall they pour into your lap. For with what measure you measure, it shall be measured to you." And He spoke a parable also to them, "Can a blind man guide a blind man? Will not both fall into a pit? No disciple is above his teacher; but when perfected, everyone will be like his teacher. But why dost thou see the speck in thy brother's eye, and yet dost not consider the beam in thy own eye? And how canst thou say to thy brother, 'Brother, let me cast out the speck from thy eye,' while thou thyself dost not see the beam in thy own eye? Thou hypocrite, first cast out the beam from thy own eye, and then thou wilt see clearly to cast out the speck from thy brother's eye." THANKS BE TO GOD. *Turn back to page 65.*

⑱ *AFTER MASS, REVIEW YOUR CATECHISM.*

I believe that the chief means for obtaining God's grace are *prayer,* whereby we ask for it, and the *use of the Sacraments,* which contain it and apply it to the soul.

I believe that actual or personal sin is any *violation of God's law* by thought, word, deed, whether of omission or commission, against God Himself, ourselves or our neighbor; that *repeating* the same actual sin forms a *dangerous habit* of sin leading to the sin against the Holy Spirit.

I believe that we must also give an account to God for the *sins of others* in so far as *we may have been the cause* by command, counsel, consent or failing to prevent them when we could and should have done so.

I believe that *MORTAL SIN* is a *deliberate* and *wilful* offence against God's law in an *important* matter.

Sunday within Octave of Corpus Christi

PICTURE AND MASS THEME EXPLAINED

"Bring in here the poor, and the crippled" (GOSPEL).

Last Thursday was the Feast of Corpus Christi. This Mass sets forth the *social graces* flowing from the "Body of Christ" into the *"large place"* (INTROIT) of everyday life; how Divine Providence will *"never fail to govern"* (PRAYER) and direct the social order.

We can learn to *"love the brethren"* when *"we have come to know His love"* (EPISTLE), in His Sacrament and Sacrifice of Love. This is the one true guarantee of unity amongst men. Then, and only then, will they recognize neighbor as *"brother."*

The GOSPEL, in story form, illustrates the attitude of different individuals towards the *"great supper"* of this Divine Bread. All are invited; some stay away, offering the *"excuse"* of business or pleasure, like the man with his *"oxen"* (seen in the distance through the window). The above picture represents all the suffering masses and classes, ready to commune with one another because they have communed at the *"supper"* altar rail. Frequently must we commune (POSTCOMMUNION).

NOW BEGIN MASS AT 1 ON PAGE 35.

INTROIT *Ps. 17* ❷

THE LORD became my protector, and He brought me forth *into a large place*: He saved me, because He was well pleased with me.* I will love Thee, O Lord my strength: the Lord is my firmament, and my refuge, and my deliverer. Glory be, etc. *Turn to* ❸ *on page 38.*

PRAYER ❹

GRANT, O LORD, that we may always have both a love and fear of Thy holy Name, since Thou never failest to *govern* those whom Thou dost bring up in the *firmness* of Thy love. Through Our Lord, etc. *Continue below.*

« The Prayer from last Thursday's "Feast of Corpus Christi" is also said »

O GOD, Who in this wonderful Sacrament, hast left us a memorial of Thy Passion, grant us, we beseech Thee, so to venerate the sacred Mysteries of Thy Body and Blood, that we may ever experience within us the fruit of Thy Redemption. Who livest, etc. *Continue below.*

EPISTLE *1 John 3* ❺

DEARLY BELOVED, do not be surprised if the world hates you. We know that we have passed from death to life, because we *love* the brethren. He who does not love abides in death. Everyone who hates his brother is a murderer. And you know that no murderer has eternal life abiding in him. In this *we have come to know His love,* that He laid down His life for us; and *we* likewise *ought to lay down our life for the brethren.* He who has the goods of this world and *sees his brother in need* and closes his heart to him, *how does the love of God abide in him?* My dear children, let us not love in word, neither with the tongue, but *in deed* and in truth. THANKS BE TO GOD. *Continue below.*

GRADUAL
Ps. 119 ⑥

IN MY TROUBLE I cried to the Lord, and He heard me. O Lord, deliver my soul from wicked lips and a deceitful tongue. Alleluia, alleluia. O Lord my God, in Thee have I put my trust: save me from all them that persecute me, and deliver me. Alleluia. *Turn to* ⑦ *on page 40.*

GOSPEL
Luke 14 ⑧

AT THAT TIME, Jesus spoke to the Pharisees this parable, "A certain man gave a great supper, and he invited many. And he sent his servant at supper time to tell those invited to come, for everything is now ready. And *they all with one accord began to excuse themselves.* The first said to him, 'I have bought a farm, and I must go out and see it; I pray thee hold me excused.' And another said, 'I have bought five yoke of oxen, and I am on my way to try them; I pray thee hold me excused.' And another said, 'I have married a wife, and therefore I cannot come.' and the servant returned, and reported these things to his master. Then the master of the house was angry and said to his servant, 'Go out quickly into the streets and lanes of the city, and *bring in here the poor, and the crippled,* and the blind, and the lame.' And the servant said, 'Sir, thy order has been carried out, and still there is room.' Then the master said to the servant, *'Go out into the highways and hedges,* and make them come in, so that *my house may be filled.* For I tell you that none of those who were invited shall taste of *my supper.'"* *Turn to* ⑨ *on page 41.*

OFFERTORY *Ps. 6* ⑩

TURN TO ME, O Lord, and deliver my soul: O save me for Thy mercy's sake. *Turn to* ⑪ *on page 43.*

SECRET ⑫

MAY THIS OFFERING, O Lord, about to be dedicated to Thy holy Name, purify us and make us advance day by day in the practice of a heavenly life. Through Our Lord, etc. *Continue below.*

« The Secret from last Thursday's "Feast of Corpus Christi" is also said »

WE PLEAD with Thee, O Lord, mercifully grant to Thy Church the gifts of unity and peace, which are mystically symbolized under the gifts we offer. Through Our Lord, etc. *Turn to* ⑬ *on page 47.*

COMMUNION VERSE ⑭

I WILL SING to the Lord, Who giveth me good things: and I will sing to the Name of the Lord the most high. *Turn to* ⑮ *on page 62.*

POST-COMMUNION (16)

We who have received Thy sacred gifts, pray Thee, O Lord, *that the more often we receive this Sacrament,* the more surely may its salutary effects increase within us. Through Our Lord, etc. *Continue below.*

« The Postcommunion from last Thursday's "Feast of Corpus Christi" is also said »

Grant us, we beseech Thee, O Lord, to be filled with the everlasting enjoyment of Thy Divinity, which is prefigured by the present receiving of Thy precious Body and Blood. Who livest, etc. *Turn to* (17) *on page 63.*

(18) *AFTER MASS, REVIEW YOUR CATECHISM.*

I believe that *MORTAL SIN* is the *greatest evil* that can happen to us; that it is the *source* of all other misery in this world; that it *deprives* the soul of sharing in the Divine Nature and *condemns* it to eternal death in hell.

I believe that we should be ready to suffer the *loss of all earthly joys,* even to *welcome death* itself, rather than commit one mortal sin; that when tempted, I should immediately think of *hell* on the one hand and of *Christ crucified* on the other; and that mortal sin tramples on His Wounds and Precious Blood.

I believe that *VENIAL SIN* is a violation of God's law either in a *small* matter or even in an important matter but without *sufficient thought* or *full consent* of the will.

I believe that *VENIAL SIN lessens our love* for God, *weakens our will* and makes it *easier to commit mortal sin;* that we thereby incur a debt of *temporal* punishment that must be paid either in this world or in the next.

PICTURE AND MASS THEME EXPLAINED

"'Rejoice with me, because I have found my sheep that was lost' ... There will be joy in heaven over one sinner who repents, more than over ninety-nine just who have no need of repentance" (GOSPEL).

"The Sacred Heart for the world, the world for the Sacred Heart," was the theme of last Friday's Feast. Today we witness the *mutual search* between the Divine Heart and our heart.

In the INTROIT the sinner voices his sense of being *"alone"* in his inner struggles, so often beyond all human aid. This life is a warfare against *"your adversary the devil;"* nevertheless be *"steadfast in the faith;"* hear the call to *"resist."* Ultimate victory is *"in Christ Jesus"* (EPISTLE).

Who of us could ever doubt the Love of the Sacred Heart after reading this GOSPEL? Who of us on earth would not add to His joy in heaven by leading some soul back to His Sacred Heart?

NOW BEGIN MASS AT ❶ ON PAGE 35.

INTROIT *Ps. 24* ❷

LOOK THOU upon me, O Lord, and have mercy on me; for I am *alone* and poor. See my abjection and my labor; and forgive me all my sins, O my God.* To Thee, O Lord, have I lifted up my soul: in Thee, my God, I put my trust; let me not be ashamed. Glory be, etc.
Turn to ❸ *on page 38.*

PRAYER ❹

O GOD, the protector of all who hope in Thee, without Whom nothing is strong, nothing is holy, multiply Thy mercy upon us, that, with Thee as our ruler and leader, we may so pass through *the good things of the present* as not to lose those of eternity. Through Our Lord, etc.
Continue below.

« The Prayer from last Friday's "Feast of the Sacred Heart" is also said »

O GOD, Who, in the Heart of Thy Son, wounded by our sins, dost mercifully condescend to enrich us with the infinite wealth of Thy Love, grant, we beg of Thee, that we, who now offer to His Heart the reverence of our devotion, may also make a worthy reparation for our sins. Through the same Lord, etc.
Continue below.

EPISTLE *1 Peter 5* ❺

DEARLY BELOVED, humble yourselves, therefore, under the mighty hand of God, that He may exalt you in the time of visitation; cast all your anxiety upon Him, because He cares for you. Be sober, be watchful! *For your adversary the devil,* as a roaring lion, goes about *seeking someone to devour.* Resist him, *steadfast in the faith,* knowing that the same suffering befalls your brethren all over the world. But the God of all grace, Who has called us unto His eternal glory *in Christ Jesus,* will Himself, after we have suffered a little while, perfect, strengthen and establish us. To Him is the dominion forever and ever. Amen. THANKS BE TO GOD. *Continue below.*

GRADUAL *Ps. 54* ❻

CAST THY CARE upon the Lord and He shall sustain thee. When I cried to the Lord He heard my voice, from them that draw near to me. Alleluia, alleluia. God is a just judge, strong and patient; is He angry every day? Alleluia. *Turn to* ❼ *on page 40.*

GOSPEL *Luke 15* ❽

AT THAT TIME, the publicans and sinners were drawing near to Him to listen to Him. And the Pharisees and the Scribes murmured, saying, "This man welcomes sinners and eats with them." But he spoke to them this parable, saying, "What man of you having a hundred sheep, and losing one of them, does not leave the ninety-nine in the desert, and *go after that which is lost, until he finds it?* And when he has found it, he lays it upon his shoulders rejoicing. And on coming home he calls together his friends and neighbors, saying to them, 'Rejoice with me, because I have found my sheep that was lost.' I say to you that, even so, there will be joy in heaven over *one sinner who repents,* more than over ninety-nine just who have no need of repentance. Or what woman, having ten drachman, if she loses one drachma, does not light a lamp and sweep the house and search carefully until she finds it? And when she has found it, she calls together her friends and neighbors, saying, 'Rejoice with me, for I have found the drachma that I had lost.' Even so, I say to you, there will be joy among the angels of God over *one sinner who repents." Turn to ⑨ on page 41.*

OFFERTORY *Ps. 9* ⑩

LET THEM trust in Thee who know Thy Name, O Lord: for Thou hast not forsaken them that seek Thee: sing ye to the Lord, Who dwelleth in Sion: for He hath not forgotten the cry of the poor. *Turn to ⑪ on page 43.*

SECRET ⑫

LOOK UPON the offerings of Thy praying Church and grant that they may ever be received unto the perpetual sanctification and salvation of those who believe. Through Our Lord, etc. *Continue below.*

« The Secret from last Friday's "Feast of the Sacred Heart" is also said »

LOOK, we beg of Thee, O Lord, on the Heart of Thy beloved Son, Whose Love no words can describe, that what we offer may be an acceptable gift and a reparation for our sins. Through the same Lord, etc. *Turn to ⑬ on page 47.*

COMMUNION VERSE ⑭

I SAY TO YOU, *there will be joy among the angels* of God over *one sinner who repents." Turn to ⑮ on page 62.*

POST-COMMUNION ⑯

May Thy Sacrament, which we have received, give us life, and having cleansed us from sin, prepare us for Thine everlasting mercies. Through Our Lord, etc. *Continue below.*

« *The Postcommunion from last Friday's "Feast of the Sacred Heart" is also said* »

May Thy Sacrament, O Lord Jesus, produce in us a Divine fervor whereby we may learn, after tasting the sweetness of Thy most tender Heart, to spurn the things of earth and to love those of heaven. Who livest, etc.
Turn to ⑰ *on page 63.*

⑱ *AFTER MASS, REVIEW YOUR CATECHISM.*

I believe that PRAYER is the devout raising up of the soul to God, to *adore* Him in His Infinite excellence, to *thank* Him for benefits received, to *beg His pardon* for our sins and to *ask Him* for other things necessary or useful for ourselves or for others.

I believe that adoration and thanksgiving become a *frequent duty to God,* while petition becomes a necessary *source of pardon and grace to us.*

I believe that our prayers to be acceptable to the Trinity should be offered *in the name of Jesus* as is done at the end of all the "Prayers, Secrets and Postcommunions" of this Missal.

I believe that God regards our prayers, not for how *elegant* they are, but how *sincere* they are, i.e., praying with *confidence, contrition, perseverance and resignation.*

I believe that the ideal prayer is the "*Our Father*" taught by Jesus (explained on page 57).

PICTURE AND MASS THEME EXPLAINED

"Put out into the deep . . . lower your nets for a catch . . . Henceforth thou shalt catch men" (GOSPEL).

Simon Peter received the "call to action." How did he respond? *"At Thy word I will lower the net."* What was his reward? *"All . . . were amazed at the catch."* The call to Catholic Action has been repeated by the Popes in our day. *"They* (have) *beckoned to their comrades . . . to come and help them"* (GOSPEL).

More than ever in this age of global war, *"all creation groans . . . in pain,"* waiting for *"redemption"* from life-killing sin; waiting for its *"adoption"* into Divine Life *"as sons"* of God (EPISTLE). For their sake we must act as members of a Church Militant, not of a Church "pacifist" or sleeping. *"Enlighten my eyes, that I never sleep in death"* (OFFERTORY).

Do not be afraid to answer this call for Catholic Action; *"put out into the deep!" "Lower your nets!"* even though *"armies in camp should stand together against"* you (INTROIT).

NOW BEGIN MASS AT 1 ON PAGE 35.

INTROIT *Ps. 26* ❷

THE LORD is my light and my salvation: whom shall I fear? The Lord is the protector of my life: of whom shall I be afraid? My *enemies that trouble* me have themselves been weakened and have *fallen.** If armies in camp should stand together against me, my heart shall not fear. Glory be, etc. *Turn to* ❸ *on page 38.*

PRAYER ❹

GRANT, we beseech Thee, O Lord, that the *affairs of this world may be directed in Thy peace* and order and that Thy Church may serve Thee in joy and *peaceful* devotion. Through Our Lord, etc. *Continue below.*

EPISTLE *Rom. 8* ❺

BRETHREN, I reckon that the *sufferings of the present time are not worthy to be compared with the glory to come* that will be revealed in us. For the eager longing of creation awaits the revelation of the sons of God. For creation was made subject to vanity—not by its own will but by reason of Him who made it subject—in hope, because creation itself also will be delivered from its slavery to corruption into the freedom of the glory of the sons of God. For we know that all creation groans and travails in pain until now. And not only it, but we ourselves also who have the first-fruits of the Spirit—we ourselves groan within ourselves, *waiting for the adoption as sons,* the redemption of our body; in Christ Jesus our Lord. THANKS BE TO GOD. *Continue on next page.*

GRADUAL *Ps. 78* 6

FORGIVE US our sins, O Lord, lest the Gentiles should at any time say: Where is their God? Help us, O God, our Savior; and for the honor of Thy Name, O Lord, deliver us. Alleluia, alleluia. O God, Who sittest upon the throne, and judgest justice, be Thou the refuge of the poor in tribulation. Alleluia. *Turn to* 7 *on page 40.*

GOSPEL *Luke 5* 8

AT THAT TIME, while the crowds were pressing upon Jesus to hear the word of God, He was standing by Lake Genesareth. And He saw two boats moored by the lake, but the fishermen had gotten out of them and were washing their nets. And *getting into one of the boats, the one that was Simon's,* He asked him to *put out a little from the land.* And sitting down, He began to teach the crowds from the boat. But when He had ceased speaking, He said to Simon, *"Put out into the deep,* and lower your nets for a catch." And Simon answered and said to Him, "Master, the whole night through we have toiled and have taken nothing; but *at Thy word* I will lower the net." And when they had done so, they enclosed a great number of fishes, but their net was breaking. And they beckoned to their comrades in the other boat to come and help them. And they came and filled both the boats, so that they began to sink. But when Simon Peter saw this, he fell down at Jesus' knees, saying, *"Depart from me, for I am a sinful man, O Lord."* For he and all who were with him were amazed at the catch of fish they had made; and so were also James and John, the sons of Zebedee, who were partners with Simon. And Jesus said to Simon, *"Do not be afraid; henceforth thou shalt catch men."* And when they had brought their boats to land, they left all and followed Him. *Turn to* 9 *on page 41.*

OFFERTORY *Ps. 12* 10

ENLIGHTEN MY EYES, that *I never sleep* in death; lest at any time my enemy say: I have prevailed against him. *Turn to* 11 *on page 43.*

SECRET 12

WE PRAY THEE, O Lord, be pleased to accept these our offerings, and in Thy mercy compel our rebellious wills to turn unto Thee. Through Our Lord, etc. *Turn to* 13 *on page 47.*

COMMUNION VERSE 14

THE LORD is my firmament, and my refuge, and my deliverer; my God is my helper. *Turn to* 15 *on page 62.*

POST-COMMUNION 16

MAY THE SACRAMENT we have received purify us, we beseech Thee, O Lord, and may its gift *defend us.* Through Our Lord, etc. *Turn to* 17 *on page 63.*

18 *AFTER MASS, REVIEW YOUR CATECHISM.*

I believe that there are *seven Sacraments,* namely: Baptism, Penance, Confirmation, Holy Eucharist, Extreme Unction, Holy Orders and Matrimony.

I believe that *Sacraments* are *outward signs* instituted by Christ to *give grace.*

I believe that the *Sacraments* are the *channels* through which the life of God comes into my soul.

PICTURE AND MASS THEME EXPLAINED

"Go first to be reconciled to thy brother, and then come and offer thy gift" (GOSPEL).

This is Brotherhood Sunday! Human experience confirms the need of this Divine teaching. Only when the *Fatherhood of God* is recognized, will the *Brotherhood of Man* be realized. Returning good for evil is possible only to those who love God (EPISTLE). Oh, how much our hate-torn world needs this prayer: *"Pour into our hearts . . . an experience of Thy Love"* (PRAYER).

In the practice of the Golden Rule, we plead with the Divine *"Helper"* against *worldly persecution* (INTROIT) and *diabolical "enemies"* (POSTCOMMUNION).

How can one who harbors anger, envy, bitterness, indifference, aversion of any kind against his neighbor, have part in the Sacrifice of Him Who offers Himself for His enemies? The sacrifice of our selfish or even wounded feelings for Christ's sake, is a most acceptable *"gift"* to *"leave ... before the altar"* (GOSPEL).

NOW BEGIN MASS AT 1 ON PAGE 35.

INTROIT *Ps. 26* ❷

HEAR, O LORD, my voice with which I have cried to Thee: be Thou my helper, forsake me not, nor do Thou despise me, O God my Savior.* The Lord is my light, and my salvation: whom shall I fear? Glory be, etc. *Turn to* ❸ *on page 38.*

PRAYER ❹

O GOD, SINCE Thou hast prepared for those who love Thee such good things as human eye hath never seen, pour into our hearts such *an experience of Thy Love* that we may obtain these Thy promises which surpass all desire, by loving Thee in all things and above all things. Through Our Lord, etc. *Continue below.*

EPISTLE *1 Peter 3* ❺

DEARLY BELOVED, be all like-minded, compassionate, *lovers of the brethren,* merciful, humble; *not rendering evil for evil,* or abuse for abuse, but contrariwise, blessing; for unto this were you called that you might inherit a blessing. For, "He who would love life, and see good days, let him refrain his tongue from evil, and his lips that they speak no deceit. Let him turn away from evil and do good, let him seek after peace and pursue it. For the eyes of the Lord are upon the just, and His ears unto their prayers; but the face of the Lord is against those who do evil." And who is there to harm you, if you are zealous for what is good? But *even if you suffer anything for justice' sake, blessed are you.* So have no fear of their fear and do not be troubled. But hallow the Lord Christ in your hearts. THANKS BE TO GOD. *Continue on next page.*

GRADUAL *Ps. 83* ⑥

BEHOLD, O GOD our protector, and look on Thy servants. O Lord God of hosts, give ear to the prayers of Thy servants. Alleluia, alleluia. In Thy strength, O Lord, the king shall joy; and in Thy salvation he shall rejoice exceedingly. Alleluia. *Turn to* ⑦ *on page 40.*

GOSPEL *Matt. 5* ⑧

AT THAT TIME, Jesus said to His disciples, "*Unless your justice exceeds* that of the Scribes and Pharisees, you shall not enter the kingdom of heaven. You have heard that it was said to the ancients, 'Thou shalt not kill'; and that whoever shall murder shall be liable to judgment. But I say to you that everyone who is angry with his brother shall be liable to judgment; and whoever says to his brother, 'Raca,' shall be liable to the Sanhedrin; and whoever says, 'Thou fool!', shall be liable to the fire of Gehenna. Therefore, if thou art offering thy gift at the altar, and there rememberest that thy brother has anything against thee, *leave thy gift before the altar* and go first to *be reconciled to thy brother,* and then come and offer thy gift." *Turn to* ⑨ *on page 41.*

OFFERTORY *Ps. 15* ⑩

I WILL BLESS the Lord, Who hath given me understanding: I set God always in my sight; for He is at my right hand, that I be not moved. *Turn to* ⑪ *on page 43.*

SECRET ⑫

BE MERCIFUL, O Lord, to our humble pleading, and receive kindly these offerings of Thy servants, both men and women, that what they have each *offered for the glory of Thy Name* may be of profit to the salvation of all. Through Our Lord, etc. *Turn to* ⑬ *on page 47.*

COMMUNION VERSE ⑭

ONE THING I have asked of the Lord, this will I seek after; that I may dwell in the house of the Lord all the days of my life. *Turn to* ⑮ *on page 62.*

POST-COMMUNION ⑯

SINCE THOU hast fed us with Thy heavenly gift, grant, we beg of Thee, O Lord, that we may be cleansed from our hidden sins and *delivered from the snares* of our enemies. Through Our Lord, etc. *Turn to* ⑰ *on page 63.*

⑱ *AFTER MASS, REVIEW YOUR CATECHISM.*

I believe that BAPTISM *cleanses us* from original sin, makes us *Christians, children* of God and *heirs* of heaven.

I believe that I am a Christian because I have been christened.

I believe that by *Baptism* I became a *member* of Christ's Mystical Body, the Church.

I believe that by *Baptism* I am *born again,* this time spiritually into another world, the world of grace.

I believe that, because of the sacrament of *Baptism,* I am a *"lay priest"* with the *privilege and duty* of uniting with the ordained priest in offering Christ to His Heavenly Father in the Holy Mass.

I believe that, as one of the baptized citizens of the Church I take an oath of allegiance to *serve under Christ,* the King of all life, of all interior and social justice.

PICTURE AND MASS THEME EXPLAINED

"Taking the seven loaves, He gave thanks, broke them and gave them to His disciples to distribute; and they set them before the crowd . . . (about four thousand) . . . And they ate and were satisfied" **(GOSPEL).**

"*I have compassion on the crowd.*" Some of us may "*have* (had to) *come from a distance*" in our wanderings from God. But this sentiment of His Heart, so Divine, so human, inspires our plea to "*save*" us from eternal hunger in "*the pit*" of hell (INTROIT).

At Baptism we were reborn to a new life, to be "*dead to sin, but alive to God*" (EPISTLE). Daily with Christ we must die to sin and evil. Daily with Him we must rise to God and good works. Daily we would "*faint on the way,*" famished with hunger, crying out: "*How will anyone be able to satisfy* (us) *in* (the) *desert*" of life (GOSPEL)?

At the altar of sacrifice God *will not allow the hopes of anyone to be "in vain"* (SECRET). Only at the altar will our instinctive hunger for God be really "*filled*" (POSTCOMMUNION).

NOW BEGIN MASS AT 1 ON PAGE 35.

INTROIT *Ps. 27* ❷

THE LORD is the strength of His people, and the protector of the salvation of His anointed: save, O Lord, Thy people, and bless Thy inheritance, and rule them for ever.* Unto Thee will I cry, O Lord: *O my God, be not Thou silent to me,* lest if Thou be silent to me, I become like them that go down into the pit. Glory be, etc. *Turn to* ❸ *on page 38.*

PRAYER ❹

O GOD OF ALL POWER and might, Thou Who art the source of everything that is best, implant in our hearts *the love of Thy Name,* and grant us an increase of religion, promoting such things as are good, and by Thy watchful care, guarding what Thou hast promoted. Through Our Lord, etc. *Continue below.*

EPISTLE *Rom. 6* ❺

BRETHREN, *all we who have been baptized into Christ Jesus* have been baptized into His death. For we were buried with Him by means of Baptism into death, in order that, just as Christ has arisen from the dead through the glory of the Father, so we also may walk in *newness of life.* For if we have been united with Him in the likeness of His death, we shall be so in the likeness of His resurrection also. For we know that our old self has been crucified with Him, in order that the body of sin may be destroyed, that we may no longer be slaves to sin; for he who is dead is acquitted of sin. But if we have died with Christ, we believe that we shall also live together with Christ; for we know that Christ, having risen from the dead, dies now no more, death shall no longer have dominion over Him. For the death that He died, He died to sin once for all, but the life that He lives, He lives unto God. Thus do you consider yourselves also as *dead to sin, but alive to God* in Christ Jesus our Lord. THANKS BE TO GOD. *Continue below.*

GRADUAL *Ps. 89* **6**

RETURN, O LORD, a little; and be entreated in favor of Thy servants. Lord, Thou hast been our refuge from generation to generation. Alleluia, alleluia. In Thee, O Lord, have I hoped, let me never be confounded: deliver me in Thy justice, and release me; bow down Thy ear to me, make haste to deliver me. Alleluia. *Turn to* **7** *on page 40.*

GOSPEL *Mark 8* **8**

AT THAT TIME, when there was a great crowd with Jesus and they had nothing to eat, He called His disciples together and said to them, *"I have compassion on the crowd,* for behold, they have now been with Me three days, and have nothing to eat; and if I send them away to their homes fasting, they will faint on the way, for some of them have come from a distance." And His disciples answered Him, *"How will anyone be able to satisfy these with bread, here in a desert?"* And He asked them, "How many loaves have you?" And they said, "Seven." And He bade the crowd recline on the ground. Then taking the seven loaves, He gave thanks, broke them and gave them to His disciples to distribute; and they set them before the crowd. And they had a few little fishes; and He blessed them, and ordered them to be distributed. And *they ate and were satisfied;* and *they took up what was left of the fragments, seven baskets.* Now those who had eaten were about four thousand. And He dismissed them. *Turn to* ⑨ *on page 41.*

OFFERTORY *Ps. 16* ⑩

PERFECT THOU my goings in Thy paths, that my footsteps be not moved: incline Thy ear, and hear my words: show forth Thy wonderful mercies, Thou Who savest them that trust in Thee, O Lord. *Turn to* ⑪ *on page 43.*

SECRET ⑫

BE APPEASED by our humble pleadings, O Lord, and please accept these offerings of Thy people; and *that no one's prayer go in vain,* no one's petition go unheard, grant that we may actually obtain what we ask in lively faith. Through Our Lord, etc. *Turn to* ⑬ *on page 47.*

COMMUNION VERSE ⑭

I WILL go round, and offer up in His tabernacle a sacrifice of jubilation; I will sing, and recite a psalm to the Lord. *Turn to* ⑮ *on page 62.*

POST-COMMUNION ⑯

GRANT, we entreat Thee, O Lord, that *we who have been filled with Thy gifts* may be cleansed by their effects and strengthened by their help. Through Our Lord, etc. *Turn to* ⑰ *on page 63.*

⑱ *AFTER MASS, REVIEW YOUR CATECHISM.*

I believe that through CONFIRMATION we *receive the Holy Ghost* to make us strong and perfect Christians and *soldiers of Jesus Christ.*

I believe that if Baptism makes me a child in God's own family, Confirmation *enrolls me as a soldier* to fight Antichrist within and without.

PICTURE AND MASS THEME EXPLAINED

"Every tree that does not bear good fruit is cut down and thrown into the fire ... Not everyone who says to Me, 'Lord, Lord,' ... but he who does the will of my Father ... shall enter the kingdom of heaven" (GOSPEL).

The INTROIT is a call to the tongue to pray in a *"voice of joy;"* a call also to action: *"Clap your hands."* In early ages this signified not only to praise a person by the tongue, but to work for him with the hands. If all the tree's life goes into "wagging" leaves, how can there be any fruit?

Not so much what one *"says"* about the Lord, but how he *"does"* His *"Will,"* is what brings forth *"good fruit"* (GOSPEL). Deeds, not mere words, are acceptable to God; acceptable to neighbor also. Example is the best precept.

The final fruit of sin is *"death;"* the fruit of *"justice"* is *"life everlasting"* (EPISTLE). The Holy Eucharist is the *"health-giving"* (POSTCOMMUNION) Fruit of Calvary, our antidote against the poison-laden "Dead-Sea" fruit of the world, the flesh and the devil.

NOW BEGIN MASS AT 1 ON PAGE 35.

INTROIT *Ps. 46* ❷

O CLAP YOUR *hands,* all ye nations: shout unto God with *the voice of joy.** For the Lord is most high, He is terrible; He is a great King over all the earth. Glory be, etc. *Turn to* ❸ *on page 38.*

PRAYER ❹

O GOD, Whose Providence never fails in its plans, we humbly plead for ourselves that Thou remove whatever may be harmful and grant whatever may be useful. Through Our Lord, etc. *Continue below.*

EPISTLE *Rom. 6* ❺

BRETHREN, I speak in a human way because of the weakness of your flesh; for as you yielded your members as slaves of uncleanness and iniquity unto iniquity, so now yield your members as slaves of justice unto sanctification. For when you were the slaves of sin, you were free as regards justice. But what fruit had you then from those things of which you are now ashamed? For the end of these things is death. But now set free from sin and become slaves to God, you have *your fruit unto sanctification,* and as your end, life everlasting. For the *wages of sin is death,* but the gift of God is life everlasting in Christ Jesus our Lord. THANKS BE TO GOD. *Continue below.*

GRADUAL *Ps. 33* ❻

COME, CHILDREN, harken to me; I will teach you the fear of the Lord. Come ye to Him and be enlightened; and your faces shall not be confounded. Alleluia, alleluia. O clap your hands, all ye nations; shout unto God with the voice of joy. Alleluia. *Turn to* 7 *on page 40.*

GOSPEL *Matt. 7* 8

AT THAT TIME, Jesus said to His disciples, "Beware of false prophets, who come to you in sheep's clothing, but inwardly are ravenous wolves. *By their fruits you will know them.* Do men gather grapes from thorns, or figs from thistles? Even so, every good tree bears good fruit, but the bad tree bears bad fruit. A good tree cannot bear bad fruit, nor can a bad tree bear good fruit. Every tree that does not bear good fruit is cut down and thrown into the fire. Therefore, by their fruits you will know them. Not everyone who *says to Me, 'Lord, Lord,'* shall enter the kingdom of heaven; but he who *does the will of My Father* in heaven shall enter the kingdom of heaven." *Turn to* 9 *on page 41.*

OFFERTORY *Dan. 3* 10

AS IN HOLOCAUSTS of rams and bullocks, and as in thousands of fat lambs; so let our sacrifice be made in Thy sight this day, that it may please Thee: for there is no confusion to them that trust in Thee, O Lord. *Turn to* 11 *on page 43.*

SECRET 12

O GOD, Who didst permit a variety of sacrifices under the Old Law awaiting the One Perfect Sacrifice, receive this Sacrifice from Thy devoted servants and sanctify it, as Thou didst sanctify the gifts of Abel, so that what each one has brought here to the glory of Thy Majesty may be of profit to all of us. Through Our Lord, etc. *Turn to* ⑬ *on page 47.*

COMMUNION VERSE ⑭

BOW DOWN Thy ear, make haste to deliver me. *Turn to* ⑮ *on page 62.*

POST-COMMUNION ⑯

MAY THY *health-giving* grace, O Lord, both lead us from our wrong ways and lead us unto Thy right way. Through Our Lord, etc. *Turn to* ⑰ *on page 63.*

⑱ *AFTER MASS, REVIEW YOUR CATECHISM.*

I believe that while Baptism gives me a passive share in Christ's Priesthood, Confirmation gives me an active share; that in Confirmation the Holy Spirit confirms me as a *co-worker with Christ* in every form of Catholic Action.

I believe that Jesus instituted PENANCE for the purpose of forgiving sins committed after Baptism (see page 337).

I believe that the *repentant sinner,* with his sins removed by absolution *again becomes a living member* of the Mystical Body of Christ.

I believe that by prayer, penance, acts of piety and the practice of the spiritual and corporal works of mercy one may also be *cleared of venial sin and the temporal punishment* due to sin.

I believe that one should *examine* his conscience beforehand, then make a *full* confession, *at least of all mortal* sins: that the most important part is a *genuine sorrow* for sin together with a *determination* to sin no more.

PICTURE AND MASS THEME EXPLAINED

'There was a certain rich man who had a steward, . . . 'eported . . . as squandering his possessions. And he 'alled him and said to him, 'What is this that I hear of 'hee? Make an accounting of thy stewardship, . . . hou canst be steward no longer' " (GOSPEL).

As children we have access to our Father's *"possessions"* (GOSPEL). *"By virtue"* of our Baptism, *"we* all) *cry, . . . Father!"* unto our God. No longer are ve to be *"debtors . . . to the flesh,"* by which we *'will die;"* but *"sons of God, . . . joint heirs with Christ,"* by Whom we shall *"live"* (EPISTLE).

In the business of salvation the Father has appointed s as *"stewards"* over human goods and Divine races, to use, not to abuse them. The INTROIT recalls hat even though we now receive *"mercy,"* yet one lay we must stand before *"Justice."*

The meaning of this Gospel story is: *"Act prudently,"* you children of God; use material treasures o as to make eternal friends; exercise your talents in he spiritual and corporal works of mercy. Those whom you help to save, will help save you.

NOW BEGIN MASS AT 1 ON PAGE 35.

INTROIT *Ps. 47* ❷

We have received *Thy mercy,* O God, in the midst of Thy temple; according to Thy Name O God, so also is Thy praise unto the ends o the earth: Thy right hand is *full of justice.* Great is the Lord and exceedingly to be praised in the city of our God, in His holy mountain Glory be, etc. *Turn to* ❸ *on page 38.*

PRAYER ❹

We pray Thee, O Lord, in Thy mercy to grant us the spirit of *always thinking and doing wha is right,* so that we who cannot exist withou Thee, may be able to live according to Thy wil Through Our Lord, etc. *Continue below.*

EPISTLE *Rom. 8* ❺

Brethren, *we are debtors, not to the flesh,* that we should live according to the flesh, for if you liv according to the flesh *you will die;* but if by th spirit you put to death the deeds of the flesh *you will live.* For whoever are led by the Spiri of God, they are the *sons of God.* Now you hav not received a spirit of bondage so as to be agai in fear, but you have received a spirit of adoptio as sons, by virtue of which we cry, "Abba Father!" The Spirit Himself gives testimony t our spirit that we are sons of God. But if we ar sons, we are heirs also: heirs indeed of God an *joint heirs with Christ.* Thanks be to Go *Continue below.*

GRADUAL *Ps. 30* ❻

Be Thou unto me a God, a protector, and a place of refuge, to save me. In Thee, O God, have hoped: O Lord, let me never be confounded. Alleluia, alleluia. Great is the Lord, and exceedingly to be praised; in the city of our God, in His holy mountain. Alleluia. *Turn to* 7 *on page 40.*

GOSPEL
Luke 16 8

AT THAT TIME, Jesus spoke to His disciples this parable: "There was a certain rich man who had a steward, who was reported to him as squandering his *possessions.* And he called him and said to him, 'What is this that I hear of thee? *Make an accounting of thy stewardship,* for thou canst be steward no longer.' And the steward said within himself, 'What shall I do, seeing that my master is taking away the stewardship from me? To dig I am not able; to beg I am ashamed. I know what I shall do, that when I am removed from my stewardship they may receive me into their houses.' And he summoned each of his master's debtors and said to the first, 'How much dost thou owe my master?' And he said, 'A hundred jars of oil.' He said to him, 'Take thy bond and sit down at once and write fifty.' Then he said to another, 'How much dost thou owe?' He said, 'A hundred kors of wheat.' He said to him, 'Take thy bond and write eighty.' And the master commended the unjust steward, in that *he had acted prudently*; for the children of this world are in relation to their own generation more prudent than are the children of the light. And I say to you, *make friends for yourselves with the mammon of wickedness,* so that when you fail they may receive you into the everlasting dwellings." *Turn to* 9 *on page 41.*

OFFERTORY *Ps. 17* ⑩

THOU WILT *save the humble people,* O Lord, and *wilt bring down* the eyes of the *proud;* for who is God but Thee, O Lord? *Turn to* ⑪ *on page 43.*

SECRET ⑫

RECEIVE, we beseech Thee, O Lord, *these gifts,* which, *out of Thine own generosity, we bring unto Thee,* that these most holy Mysteries, by the working power of Thy grace, may sanctify our conduct in this life and bring us to joys without end. Through Our Lord, etc. *Turn to* ⑬ *on page 47.*

COMMUNION VERSE ⑭

TASTE AND SEE that the Lord is sweet: blessed is the man that hopeth in Him. *Turn to* ⑮ *on page 62.*

POST-COMMUNION ⑯

MAY THIS heavenly Sacrament be to us, O Lord, a renewal of *both mind and body,* so that as we perform this act of worship we may also feel its effect. Through Our Lord, etc. *Turn to* ⑰ *on page 63.*

⑱ *AFTER MASS, REVIEW YOUR CATECHISM.*

I believe that the HOLY EUCHARIST *contains Christ Himself,* the Second Person of the Blessed Trinity, His Body and Blood, His Soul and Divinity—all *under the appearances* of bread and wine.

I believe that in the Holy Eucharist as a SACRAMENT, Jesus satisfies man's hunger for a *personal union with God;* and also *unites men together* in a real social and mystical union to work for one another.

PICTURE AND MASS THEME EXPLAINED

"He . . . began to cast out those who were selling and buying in (the temple), *saying to them, . . . 'My house is a house of prayer,' but you have made it a den of thieves"* (GOSPEL).

The tears of Jesus! The lashes of His righteous anger! Why does Jesus still weep? Why must He still *"cast out?"* Because amongst us there are those who desecrate what is consecrate—their baptized, Christened souls! even as Jerusalem, chosen by God, rejected his Christ (GOSPEL).

What is the great lesson of history? It is that men do not profit by its lessons! Consider what happened to *"idolaters,"* rejecting God; to materialists who lived merely *"to eat and drink, and . . . play."* War, disease, famine, depression were the penalty. *"There fell in one day twenty-three thousand"* (EPISTLE).

Yet you must not go through life with a fear complex. *"God . . . will not permit you to be tempted beyond your strength."* God is within me (COMMUNION VERSE) to *"defend me"* (GRADUAL).

NOW BEGIN MASS AT 1 ON PAGE 35.

INTROIT *Ps. 53* ❷

BEHOLD, *God is my helper,* and the Lord is the protector of my soul: turn back the evils upon my enemies, and cut them off in Thy truth, O Lord my protector.* Save me, O God, by Thy Name, and deliver me in Thy strength. Glory be, etc. *Turn to* ❸ *on page 38.*

PRAYER ❹

LET THY merciful ears, O Lord, be open to the prayers of Thy lowly petitioners and in order to satisfy their desires, make them *ask only such things as are pleasing to Thee.* Through Our Lord, etc. *Continue below.*

EPISTLE *1 Cor. 10* ❺

BRETHREN, we should not lust after evil things even as they lusted. And do not become *idolaters,* even as some of them were, as it is written, "The people sat down to eat and drink, and rose up to play." Neither let us commit fornication, even as some of them committed fornication, and there fell in one day twenty-three thousand. *Neither let us tempt Christ,* as some of them tempted, and perished by the serpents. Neither murmur, as some of them murmured, and perished at the hands of the destroyer. Now all these things happened to them as a type, and they were *written for our correction,* upon whom the final age of the world has come. Therefore let him who thinks he stands take heed lest he fall. May no temptation take hold of you but such as man is equal to. God is faithful and *will not permit you to be tempted beyond your strength,* but with the temptation will also give you a way out that you may be able to bear it. THANKS BE TO GOD. *Continue below.*

GRADUAL *Ps. 8* (6)

O LORD, our Lord, how admirable is *Thy Name in the whole earth!* For Thy magnificence is elevated above the heavens. Alleluia, alleluia. Deliver me from my enemies, O my God: and defend me from them that rise up against me. Alleluia. *Turn to* (7) *on page 40.*

GOSPEL *Luke 19* (8)

AT THAT TIME, when Jesus drew near and saw Jerusalem, He wept over it, saying, *"If thou hadst known,* in this thy day, even thou, the things that are for thy peace! But now they are hidden from thy eyes. For days will come upon thee when thy enemies will throw up a rampart about thee, and surround thee and shut thee in on every side, and will dash thee to the ground and thy children within thee, and will not leave in thee one stone upon another, because *thou hast not known the time of thy visitation."* And He entered the temple, and *began to cast out those who were selling* and buying in it, saying to them, "It is written, 'My house is a house of prayer,' but you have made it a den of thieves." And He was *teaching daily* in the temple. *Turn to* (9) *on page 41.*

OFFERTORY *Ps. 18* (10)

THE JUSTICES of the Lord are right, rejoicing hearts, and His *judgments sweeter* than honey and the honeycomb: for Thy servant keepeth them. *Turn to* (11) *on page 43.*

SECRET ⑫

We beseech Thee, O Lord, for the grace of worthily frequenting these Mysteries, because every time this memorial Sacrifice is offered up, the work of our redemption is carried on. Through Our Lord, etc. *Turn to* ⑬ *on page 47.*

COMMUNION VERSE ⑭

"He who *eats* My flesh, and drinks My blood, abides in Me, and I in him," said the Lord. *Turn to* ⑮ *on page 62.*

POST-COMMUNION ⑯

May the reception of Thy Sacrament, O Lord, obtain for us both a purity of heart and a unity with one another. Through Our Lord, etc. *Turn to* ⑰ *on page 63.*

⑱ *AFTER MASS, REVIEW YOUR CATECHISM*

I believe that in the Holy Eucharist as a *SACRIFICE,* I unite my sacrifices with the Sacrifice of Jesus and thus my *offering becomes acceptable* to God.

I believe that Mass is offered up to adore, thank, atone and implore God; that the best way to assist at Mass and to *receive the Fruit* of the Sacrifice is to *use this Missal* as explained on page 14.

I believe that EXTREME UNCTION, through the *anointing and prayer* of the priest gives *health and strength to the soul* and *sometimes to the body* when one is in danger of death from sickness, accident or old age.

I believe that every Catholic home should have a *sick-call set;* that it is *sinfully neglectful* to wait until the sick person has lost consciousness before calling the priest.

PICTURE AND MASS THEME EXPLAINED

"The Pharisee stood and began to pray . . . 'O God . . . I am not like the rest of men . . .' But the publican . . . kept striking his breast, saying, 'O God, be merciful to me the sinner'" (GOSPEL).

Pride is the curse of our day! The Pharisee, self-sufficient, self-righteous, wants the applause of men, while pretending to honor God. A hypocrite! Yes, he does refrain from some misdeeds but he neglects the essence of religion, love for God and neighbor. And he measures himself not by the All-Perfect God, but by imperfect men.

Humility is our salvation! The publican confesses his misuse of grace, appeals for pardon, shows a willingness to atone. For him God will *"multiply . . . mercy"* (PRAYER). From him He will *"accept the sacrifice . . . upon* (the) *altar"* (COMMUNION VERSE).

God is the source of all *"gifts,"* intended to lead us and others back to Himself, not to *"dumb idols"* (EPISTLE).

NOW BEGIN MASS AT 1 ON PAGE 35.

INTROIT 2
Ps. 54

WHEN I CRIED to the Lord He heard my voice, from them that draw near to me; and He humbled them, *Who is before all ages,* and remains forever: cast thy care upon the Lord, and He shall sustain thee.* Hear, O God, my prayer, and despise not my supplication; be attentive to me and hear me. Glory be, etc. *Turn to* ③ *on page 38.*

PRAYER ④

O God, since Thou dost display Thy power mainly by showing pardon and pity, *multiply Thy mercy* upon us, so that, hastening on to Thy promises, we may gain a share in Thy heavenly treasures. Through Our Lord, etc. *Continue below.*

EPISTLE *1 Cor. 12* ⑤

Brethren, you know that when you were Gentiles, you went to *dumb idols* according as you were led. Wherefore I give you to understand that no one speaking in the Spirit of God says "Anathema" to Jesus. And no one can say "Jesus is Lord," except in the Holy Spirit. Now there are *varieties of gifts,* but the same Spirit; and there are varieties of ministries, but the same Lord; and there are varieties of workings, but the same God, who works all things in all. Now the manifestation of the Spirit is given to everyone for profit. To one through the Spirit is given the utterance of wisdom; and to another the utterance of knowledge, according to the same Spirit; to another faith, in the same Spirit; to another the gift of healing, in the one Spirit; to another the working of miracles; to another prophecy; to another the distinguishing of spirits; to another various kinds of tongues; to another interpretation of tongues. But all these things are the work of one and the same Spirit, who divides to everyone according as He will. Thanks be to God. *Continue on next page.*

GRADUAL *Ps. 16* ⑥

KEEP ME, O Lord, as the apple of Thy eye: protect me under the shadow of Thy wings. Let my judgment come forth from Thy countenance: let Thy eyes behold the things that are equitable. Alleluia, alleluia. A hymn, O God, becometh Thee in Sion: and a vow shall be paid to Thee in Jerusalem. Alleluia. *Turn to* ⑦ *on page 40.*

GOSPEL *Luke 18* ⑧

AT THAT TIME, Jesus spoke this parable to some who *trusted in themselves* as being just and despised others. "Two men went up to the temple to pray, the one a Pharisee and the other a publican. The Pharisee stood and began to pray thus within himself: 'O God, I thank Thee that *I am not* like the rest of men, robbers, dishonest, adulterers, or even *like this publican.* I fast twice a week; I pay tithes of all that I possess.' But the publican, standing afar off, would not so much as lift up his eyes to heaven, but kept striking his breast, saying, *'O God, be merciful to me the sinner!'* I tell you, this man went back to his home *justified* rather than the other; for everyone who exalts himself shall be humbled, and he who humbles himself shall be exalted." *Turn to* ⑨ *on page 41.*

OFFERTORY *Ps. 24* ⑩

TO THEE, O Lord, have I lifted up my soul: in Thee, O my God, I put my trust, let me not be ashamed: neither let my enemies laugh at me: for none of them that wait on Thee shall be confounded. *Turn to* ⑪ *on page 43.*

SECRET ⑫

LET THESE appointed sacrifices be paid back unto Thee, O Lord, since Thou hast given them to be offered for the honor of Thy Name, so that at the same time they might become a *remedy for all our ills*. Through Our Lord, etc. *Turn to* ⑬ *on page 47*.

COMMUNION VERSE ⑭

THOU WILT ACCEPT the sacrifice of justice, oblations, and holocausts, upon Thy altar, O Lord. *Turn to* ⑮ *on page 62.*

POST-COMMUNION ⑯

O LORD, OUR GOD, we pray Thee that Thy help may not be lacking to those whom Thou dost never cease to *renew* with Thy divine Sacraments. Through Our Lord, etc. *Turn to* ⑰ *on page 63.*

⑱ *AFTER MASS, REVIEW YOUR CATECHISM.*

I believe that Extreme Unction gives us strength to bear our sufferings and enlivens our trust in a merciful welcome at the gates of heaven.

I believe that by HOLY ORDERS bishops, priests and other ministers of the Church are ordained and *receive the power and grace* to perform their sacred duties.

I believe that priests have the mission of *teaching and governing* in the truth and law of Christ for the sake of sanctifying members in the Mystical Body of Christ; that they are *messengers* of God's truth and *dispensers* of the Sacraments.

I believe that we should have the deepest *respect and reverence* for their high office; that we should *pray often* for priestly laborers in Christ's vineyard.

PICTURE AND MASS THEME EXPLAINED

"They brought to Him one deaf and dumb . . . And his ears were at once opened, and . . . his tongue was loosed, and he began to speak correctly" (GOSPEL).

May your ears tune in on God (symbolized by kneeling figures at left). May your tongue broadcast His Gospel (indicated by figure of "speaker" to the right), in the *"holy place"* of your parish activities, in the *"house"* of your family, among the *"people"* of your acquaintance (INTROIT).

Before curing the man *"deaf and dumb,"* Jesus took him apart. If we are *"to hear"* His Voice, we must go *"aside from the crowd"* at our Sunday Mass, for at least one uninterrupted hour. Only then, like the cured deaf-mute, shall we return and gladly *"publish"* the truth (GOSPEL).

St. Paul relates how he received *"the gospel"*; how he then passed it on to others. *"Hold it fast as I preached it to you"* (EPISTLE).

NOW BEGIN MASS AT 1 ON PAGE 35.

INTROIT *Ps. 67* ❷

GOD IN HIS *holy place;* God Who maketh men of one mind to dwell in a *house;* He shall give power and strength to His *people.** Let God arise, and let His enemies be scattered: and let them that hate Him flee from before His face. Glory be, etc.

Turn to ❸ *on page 38.*

PRAYER ❹

O ALMIGHTY and Eternal God, since, in the abundance of Thy loving kindness, Thou dost *usually go beyond the merits and desires* of Thy lowly petitioners, pour forth Thy mercy upon us both to forgive what our conscience fears and to give what our prayer would not presume to ask. Through Our Lord, etc. *Continue below.*

EPISTLE *1 Cor. 15* ❺

BRETHREN, I *recall to your minds,* the gospel that I preached to you, which also you received, wherein also you stand, through which also you are being saved, if you hold it fast, as I preached it to you—unless you have believed to no purpose. For I delivered to you first of all, what I also received, that Christ died for our sins according to the Scriptures, and that He was buried, and that He rose again the third day, according to the Scriptures, and that He appeared to Cephas, and after that to the Eleven. Then He was seen by more than five hundred brethren at one time, many of whom are with us still, but some have fallen asleep. After that He was seen by James, then by all the apostles. And last of all, as by one born out of due time, *He was seen also by me.* For I am the least of the apostles, and am not worthy to be called an apostle, because I persecuted the Church of God. But *by the grace of God I am what I am,* and His grace in me has not been fruitless. THANKS BE TO GOD. *Continue below.*

GRADUAL *Ps. 27* 6

IN GOD hath my heart confided, and I have been helped; and my flesh hath flourished again; and with my will I will give praise to Him. Unto Thee will I cry, O Lord: *O my God, be not Thou silent;* depart not from me. Alleluia, alleluia. Rejoice to God our helper; sing aloud to the God of Jacob: take a pleasant psalm with the harp. Alleluia. *Turn to 7 on page 40.*

GOSPEL *Mark 7* 8

AT THAT TIME, Jesus departing again from the district of Tyre, came by way of Sidon to the sea of Galilee, through the midst of the district of Decapolis. And they brought to Him one *deaf and dumb,* and entreated Him to lay His hand upon him. And taking him *aside* from the *crowd,* He put His fingers into the man's ears, and spitting, He touched his tongue. And looking up to heaven, He sighed, and said to him, *"Ephpheta," that is, "Be thou opened."* And his ears were at once opened, and the bond of his tongue was loosed, and he began to speak correctly. And He charged them to tell no one. But the more He charged them, so much the more did they continue to *publish* it. And so much the more did they wonder, saying, "He has done all things well. He has made both the *deaf to hear* and the *dumb to speak." Turn to 9 on page 41.*

OFFERTORY *Ps. 29* ⑩

I WILL EXTOL THEE, O Lord, for Thou hast upheld me; and hast not made my enemies to rejoice over me: O Lord, I have cried to Thee, and Thou hast healed me. *Turn to ⑪ on page 43.*

SECRET ⑫

LOOK DOWN graciously upon our service, we plead with Thee, O Lord, that our offering may be a gift acceptable to Thee and a *support to us in our weakness.* Through Our Lord, etc. *Turn to ⑬ on page 47.*

COMMUNION VERSE ⑭

HONOR THE LORD with thy substance, and with the first of all thy fruits: and thy barns shall be filled with abundance, and thy presses shall run over with wine. *Turn to ⑮ on page 62.*

POST-COMMUNION ⑯

BY THE RECEPTION of Thy Sacrament, we implore Thee, O Lord, that we may find *help for soul and body*; and, having been saved in both, that we may glory in the fulness of this heavenly remedy. Through Our Lord, etc. *Turn to ⑰ on page 63.*

⑱ *AFTER MASS, REVIEW YOUR CATECHISM.*

I believe that MATRIMONY is also a sacrament which *unites* a Christian man and woman in lawful marriage.

I believe that the sacrament of Matrimony is a symbol of the union of Christ's *Divinity* with His *Humanity;* that it is a symbol furthermore of the union between *Christ* the Bridegroom, and the *Church* His Bride.

PICTURE AND MASS THEME EXPLAINED

"A Samaritan (seeing the robbers' victim) *was moved with compassion, bound up his wounds, pouring on oil and wine, and took care of him. And Jesus said, 'Go and do thou also in like manner'"* (GOSPEL).

St. Bede suggests that this victim is Adam and the human race robbed by Satan (pictured at left). Jesus, our Divine Rescuer (pictured at right), comes to pour *"wine and oil"* into our *"wounds:"* the *"life"*-giving Wine of His Precious Blood (POSTCOMMUNION), the *"cheerful . . . oil"* of all His Sacraments (COMMUNION VERSE).

Otherwise, having left the *"Jerusalem"* of Divine Life, how could we *"run without stumbling"* (PRAYER) lifeless into the Dead Sea next to *"Jericho"*? *"We are not sufficient of ourselves . . . our sufficiency is from God."* Without Jesus the Ten Commandments would be dead *"letters upon stones"* (EPISTLE).

What Christ does for us, we *"in like manner"* are to do unto others, to Jew and Gentile, friend and foe. "Samaritan-charity" is Christ's own teaching.

NOW BEGIN MASS AT 1 ON PAGE 35.

INTROIT *Ps. 69* 2

INCLINE UNTO MY AID, O God: O Lord, *make haste to help me:* let my enemies be confounded and ashamed, who seek my soul.* Let them be turned backward and blush for shame, who desire evils to me. Glory be, etc. *Turn to* ❸ *on page 38.*

PRAYER ❹

O ALMIGHTY and Eternal God, by Whose gift Thy faithful are able to serve Thee worthily and praiseworthily, grant, we pray Thee, that we may run without stumbling to the fulfilment of Thy promises. Through Our Lord, etc. *Continue below.*

EPISTLE *2 Cor. 3* ❺

BRETHREN, such is the assurance I have through Christ towards God. Not that we are sufficient of ourselves to think anything, as from ourselves, but our sufficiency is from God. He also it is who has made us fit ministers of the new covenant, not of the letter but of the spirit; for the letter kills, but the spirit gives life. Now if the *ministration of death,* which was engraved in *letters upon stones,* was inaugurated in such glory that the children of Israel could not look steadfastly upon the face of Moses on account of the transient glory that shone upon it, shall not the ministration of the spirit be still more glorious? For if there is glory in the ministration that condemned, much more does the ministration that justifies abound in glory. THANKS BE TO GOD. *Continue below.*

GRADUAL *Ps. 33* ❻

I WILL BLESS the Lord *at all times;* His praise shall be ever in my mouth. In the Lord, shall my soul be praised: let the meek hear, and rejoice. Alleluia, alleluia. O Lord, the God of my salvation, I have cried in the day, and in the night before Thee. Alleluia. *Turn to* ❼ *on page 40.*

GOSPEL 8
Luke 10

AT THAT TIME, Jesus said to His disciples: "Blessed are the eyes that see what you see! For I say to you, many prophets and kings have desired to see *what you see, and they have not seen it;* and to *hear what you hear, and they have not heard it.*" And behold, a certain lawyer got up to test Him, saying, "Master, what must I do to gain eternal life?" But He said to him, "What is written in the Law? How dost thou read?" He answered and said, "Thou shalt love the Lord thy God with thy whole heart, and with thy whole soul, and with thy whole strength, and with thy whole mind; and *thy neighbor* as thyself." And He said to him, "Thou hast answered rightly; do this and thou shalt live." But he, wishing to justify himself, said to Jesus, "And who is my neighbor?" Jesus took him up and said, "A certain man was going down from Jerusalem to Jericho, and he fell in with robbers, who after both stripping him and beating him went their way, leaving him half-dead. But, as it happened, a certain priest was going down the same way; and when he saw him, he passed by. And likewise a Levite also, when he was near the place and saw him, passed by. But a certain Samaritan as he journeyed came upon him, and seeing him, was moved with compassion. And he went up to him and bound up his wounds, pouring on oil and wine. And setting him on his own beast, he brought him to an inn and took care of him. And the next day he took out two denarii and gave them to the innkeeper and said, 'Take care of him; and whatever more thou spendest, I, on my way back, will repay thee.'

Which of these three, in thy opinion, proved himself neighbor to him who fell among the robbers?" And he said, *"He who took pity on him."* And Jesus said to him, *"Go and do thou also in like manner."* *Turn to* 9 *on page 41.*

OFFERTORY *Ex. 32* 10

MOSES prayed in the sight of the Lord his God, and said: Why, O Lord, is Thy indignation enkindled against Thy people? Let the anger of Thy mind cease; remember Abraham, Isaac, and Jacob, to whom Thou didst swear to give a land flowing with milk and honey: and *the Lord was appeased* from doing the evil, which He had spoken of doing against the people. *Turn to* 11 *on page 43.*

SECRET 12

IN THY MERCY, we beseech Thee, O Lord, to behold the sacrifices which we lay upon Thy sacred altars, so that while they obtain pardon for us, they may also give honor to Thy Name. Through Our Lord, etc. *Turn to* 13 *on page 47.*

COMMUNION VERSE 14

THE EARTH *shall be filled* with the fruit of Thy works, O Lord, that Thou mayest bring bread out of the earth, and that wine may cheer the heart of man; that he may make the face cheerful with oil; and that bread may strengthen man's heart. *Turn to* 15 *on page 62.*

POST-COMMUNION 16

MAY THE HOLY RECEPTION of this Sacrament, we pray Thee, O Lord, give us life and may it also be our atonement and protection. Through Our Lord, etc. *Turn to* 17 *on page 63.*

18 *Review "Midsummer", page 33.*

PICTURE AND MASS THEME EXPLAINED

"*Were not the ten* (lepers) *made clean? Where are the* (other) *nine*" (GOSPEL)?

Leprosy, dread disease, meant exile "*afar off*" as a castout from home and city. Mankind, rejecting Divine Life, became leprous, cast out from Eden here, from heaven hereafter.

How amazing, then, that God should make a "*covenant*" with man as though he were His equal (EPISTLE)!

What is this "*covenant?*" By it God bestows on all "*those who believe*" in Jesus the right to inherit His Life, promised to Abraham; not to those who look merely to "*the Law*" of Moses.

Today let us not be content, as were "*the nine,*" with mere health of body but with the "*increase of faith, hope and charity*" (PRAYER). As with the lepers, so our opening prayer is: "*Have regard, O Lord, to Thy covenant, and forsake not . . . Thy poor . . .*(do not) *cast us off*" (INTROIT).

NOW BEGIN MASS AT ❶ ON PAGE 35.

INTROIT *Ps. 73* ❷

HAVE REGARD, O Lord, *to Thy covenant,* and forsake not to the end the souls of Thy poor: arise, O Lord, and judge Thy cause, and forget not the voices of them that seek Thee.* O God, why hast Thou cast us off unto the end: why is Thy wrath enkindled against the sheep of Thy pasture? Glory be, etc. *Turn to* ❸ *on page 38.*

PRAYER ❹

O ALMIGHTY and Eternal God, grant us an increase of *faith, hope* and *charity;* and that we may deserve to obtain what Thou dost promise, make us love what Thou dost command. Through Our Lord, etc. *Continue below.*

EPISTLE *Gal. 3* ❺

BRETHREN, the *promises* were made to Abraham and to his offspring. He does not say, "And to his offsprings," as of many; but as of one, "And to thy offspring," who is Christ. Now I mean this: The Law which was made four hundred and thirty years later does not annul the covenant which was ratified by God, so as to make the promise void. For if the right to inherit be from the Law, it is no longer from a promise. But God gave it to Abraham by promise. What then was the Law? It was *enacted* on account of transgressions, being delivered by angels through a mediator, *until the offspring should come* to whom the promise was made. Now there is no intermediary where there is only one; but God is one. Is the Law then contrary to the promises of God? By no means. For if a law had been given that could *give life,* justice would truly be from the Law. But the Scripture shut up all things under *sin,* that by the faith of Jesus Christ the promise might be given to those who believe. THANKS BE TO GOD. *Continue below.*

GRADUAL *Ps. 73* (6)

HAVE REGARD, O Lord, to Thy covenant, and forsake not to the end the souls of Thy poor. Arise, O Lord, and judge Thy cause: remember the reproach of Thy servants. Alleluia, alleluia. Lord, Thou hast been our refuge, from generation to generation. Alleluia. *Turn to* (7) *on page 40.*

GOSPEL *Luke 17* (8)

AT THAT TIME, as Jesus was going to Jerusalem, He was passing between Samaria and Galilee. And as He was entering a certain village, there met Him ten lepers, who stood afar off and lifted up their voice, crying, "Jesus, master, have pity on us." And when He saw them He said, "Go, show yourselves to the priests." And it came to pass as they were on their way, that they were made clean. But one of them, seeing that he was *made clean,* returned, with a loud voice glorifying God, and he fell on his face at His feet, giving thanks; and he was a Samaritan. But Jesus answered and said, "Were not the *ten made clean?* But where are the nine? Has no one been found to return and give glory to God except this *foreigner?*" And He said to him, "Arise, *go thy way, for thy faith has saved thee.*" *Turn to* (9) *on page 41.*

OFFERTORY *Ps. 30* (10)

IN THEE, O Lord, *have I hoped:* I said, Thou art my God, my times are in Thy hands. *Turn to* (11) *on page 43.*

SECRET ⑫

LOOK WITH FAVOR upon Thy people, O Lord; look with favor upon their gifts and, being appeased by this offering, mercifully grant us pardon of our sins and the blessings that we ask. Through Our Lord, etc. *Turn to* ⑬ *on page 47.*

COMMUNION VERSE ⑭

THOU HAST GIVEN US, O Lord, bread from heaven, having in it all that is delicious, and the sweetness of every taste. *Turn to* ⑮ *on page 62.*

POST-COMMUNION ⑯

HAVING RECEIVED Thy heavenly Sacrament, O Lord, we pray Thee that it may advance us more and more towards our eternal salvation. Through Our Lord, etc. *Turn to* ⑰ *on page 63.*

⑱ *AFTER MASS, REVIEW YOUR CATECHISM.*

I believe that because of natural ana supernatural reasons Christ has forbidden divorce, although for grave reasons there may be separation.

I believe that *mixed marriages* most frequently lead to *indifference, loss of faith* and *neglect of the religious education* of children.

I believe that young people should realize, during courtship, that they are *preparing to receive a Sacrament,* consequently they should have the greatest respect for each other; that before engagement they should consult their elders, *pray for light* and *receive the Sacraments* frequently.

I believe that the sacrament of Matrimony *sanctifies* the love between husband and wife, and *saves* marriage from *mere physical lust;* that it *gives them God's grace* in every physical or temperamental crisis; that it enables them to bring up their children in the fear and love of God.

PICTURE AND MASS THEME EXPLAINED

"Seek first the kingdom of God and His justice, and all these things shall be given you besides" (GOSPEL).

The castle (at the left) symbolizes earthly goods, about which some are too *"anxious."* The symbol of the Trinity (at the right) represents *"the kingdom of God."* We must serve either *"the Spirit"* or *"the flesh"* (EPISTLE), *"God"* or *"mammon"* (GOSPEL).

In the EPISTLE is a vivid account of the struggle between *"the spirit,"* reborn in Baptism, enlightened by faith, sanctified by grace; and *"the flesh"* with its evil passions of the body, idolatrous outrages against God, crimes against one's neighbor.

The GOSPEL should be read and re-read, as the antidote to our twentieth-century cult of the body. To those who *"seek first the kingdom of God,"* and who use material goods as a means of obtaining spiritual graces, Jesus promises that *"all these* (material) *things shall be given . . . besides."*

NOW BEGIN MASS AT 1 ON PAGE 35.

INTROIT
Ps. 83 ❷

BEHOLD, O God, our protector, and look on the face of Thy Christ: for *better is one day in Thy courts* above thousands.* How lovely are Thy tabernacles, O Lord of hosts! My soul *longeth* and fainteth for the courts of the Lord. Glory be, etc. *Turn to* ❸ *on page 38.*

PRAYER ❹

GUARD THY CHURCH, we implore Thee, O Lord, with Thy perpetual mercy and, since without Thee our human weakness is ever ready to fall, by Thy help always keep it from all things harmful and lead it to all things helpful to our salvation. Through Our Lord, etc. *Continue below.*

EPISTLE
Gal. 5 ❺

BRETHREN, walk in the *Spirit,* and you will not fulfill the lusts of the *flesh.* For the *flesh* lusts against the *spirit,* and the spirit against the flesh; for these are opposed to each other, so that you do not do what you would. But if you are led by the Spirit, you are not under the Law. Now the *works of the flesh are manifest,* which are immorality, uncleanness, licentiousness, idolatry, witchcrafts, enmities, contentions, jealousies, anger, quarrels, factions, parties, envies, murders, drunkenness, carousings, and suchlike. And concerning these I warn you, as I have warned you, that they who do such things will not attain the kingdom of God. But *the fruit of the Spirit is:* charity, joy, peace, patience, kindness, goodness, faith, modesty, continency. Against such things there is no law. And they who belong to Christ have crucified their flesh with its passions and desires. THANKS BE TO GOD. *Continue below.*

GRADUAL
Ps. 117 ⑥

IT IS GOOD to *confide in the Lord,* rather than to have *confidence in man.* It is good to trust in the Lord, rather than to trust in princes. Alleluia, alleluia. Come, let us praise the Lord with joy; let us joyfully sing to God our Savior. Alleluia. *Turn to* ⑦ *on page 40.*

GOSPEL
Matt. 6 ⑧

AT THAT TIME, Jesus said to His disciples: "No man can serve two masters; for either he will hate the one and love the other, or else he will stand by the one and despise the other. You cannot serve *God* and *mammon.* Therefore I say to you, *do not be anxious* for your life, what you shall eat; nor yet for your body, what you shall put on. Is not the life a greater thing than the food, and the body than the clothing? Look at the birds of the air: they do not sow, or reap, or gather into barns; yet your heavenly Father feeds them. Are not you of much more value than they? But which of you by being anxious about it can add to his stature a single cubit? And as for clothing, why are you anxious? See how the lilies of the field grow; they neither toil nor spin, yet I say to you that *not even Solomon in all his glory was arrayed like one of these.*

But if God so clothes the grass of the field, which today is alive and tomorrow is thrown into the oven, how much more you, *O you of little faith!* Therefore do not be anxious, saying, 'What shall we eat?' or, 'What shall we drink?', or, 'What are we to put on?' (for after all these things the Gentiles seek); for your Father knows that you need all these things. But seek *first the kingdom of God* and His justice, and *all these things shall be given you besides." Turn to ⑨ on page 41.*

OFFERTORY *Ps. 33* ⑩

THE ANGEL of the Lord shall encamp round about them that fear Him, and shall deliver them: O taste and see that the Lord is sweet! *Turn to ⑪ on page 43.*

SECRET ⑫

GRANT, we plead with Thee, O Lord, that this saving Victim may both cleanse our sins and appease Thy Power. Through Our Lord, etc. *Turn to ⑬ on page 47.*

COMMUNION VERSE ⑭

"SEEK *first* the kingdom of God and all things shall be *given* you besides," says the Lord. *Turn to ⑮ on page 62.*

POST-COMMUNION ⑯

MAY THY SACRAMENTS, O God, purify and strengthen us at all times and lead us to the fruit of everlasting salvation. Through Our Lord, etc. *Turn to ⑰ on page 63.*

⑱ ***Review "Pray the Mass", page 33.***

PICTURE AND MASS THEME EXPLAINED

"'Young man, I say to thee, arise.' And he who was dead . . . began to speak. And (Jesus) *gave him to his mother"* (GOSPEL).

Holy Mother Church, like unto *"a widow,"* weeps for the return of every sinner (figure in background) as if for an *"only child;"* that the Christ-Life might return to the godless, to the apostate.

"I say to thee, arise." Though alive we may be dead! Go to Him in prayer, *"morning"* and *"night"* (GRADUAL); and in the Sacraments also, that His Life-giving *"graces"* may save us from our death-dealing *"inclinations"* (POSTCOMMUNION).

"While we have time, let us do good to all men," that they, too, may be reborn, renewed in this Christ-Life. *"Instruct . . .* (one who is) *doing something wrong . . . Bear one another's burdens, and so you will fulfill the law of Christ"* (EPISTLE).

NOW BEGIN MASS AT 1 ON PAGE 35.

INTROIT *Ps. 85* ❷

BOW DOWN Thy ear, O Lord, to me, and hear me: save Thy servant, O my God, that trusteth in Thee: have mercy on me, O Lord, for I have cried to Thee all day.* Give joy to the soul of Thy servant; for to Thee, O Lord, have I lifted up my soul. Glory be, etc. *Turn to* ❸ *on page 38.*

PRAYER ❹

LET THY *continual* pity, O Lord, cleanse and protect Thy Church; and since it cannot continue in safety without Thee, govern it evermore by Thy help. Through Our Lord, etc. *Continue below.*

EPISTLE *Gal. 5* ❺

BRETHREN, if we *live by the Spirit,* by the Spirit let us also walk. Let us not become desirous of vainglory, provoking one another, envying one another. Brethren, even if a person is caught doing something wrong, you who are spiritual *instruct such a one* in a spirit of meekness, considering thyself, lest thou also be tempted. *Bear one another's burdens, and so you will fulfill the law of Christ.* For if anyone thinks himself to be something, whereas he is nothing, he deceives himself. But let everyone test his own work, and so he will have glory in himself only, and not in comparison with another. For each one will bear his own burden. And let him who is instructed in the word share all good things with his teacher. Be not deceived, God is not mocked. For what a man sows, that he will also reap. For he who sows in the flesh, from the flesh also he will reap corruption. But he who sows in the spirit, from the spirit he will reap life everlasting.

And in doing good let us not grow tired; for in due time we shall reap if we do not relax. Therefore, while we have time, *let us do good to all men,* but especially to those who are of the household of faith. THANKS BE TO GOD. *Continue below.*

GRADUAL *Ps. 91* (6)

IT IS GOOD to give praise to the Lord; and to sing to Thy Name, O Most High. To show forth Thy mercy in the morning, and Thy truth in the night. Alleluia, alleluia. For the Lord is a great God, and a great *King above all the earth.* Alleluia. *Turn to* (7) *on page 40.*

GOSPEL *Luke 7* (8)

AT THAT TIME, Jesus went to a town called Naim; and His disciples and a large crowd went with Him. And as He drew near the gate of the town, behold, a dead man was being carried out, the only son of his mother, and she was a widow; and a large gathering from the town was with her. And the Lord, seeing her, had compassion on her, and said to her, *"Do not weep."* And He went up and touched the stretcher; and the bearers stood still. And He said, *"Young man, I say to thee, arise."* And he who was dead, sat up, and began to speak. And He gave him to his mother. But fear seized upon all, and they began to glorify God, saying, "A great Prophet has risen among us," and *"God has visited his people."* *Turn to* (9) *on page 41.*

OFFERTORY *Ps. 39* (10)

WITH EXPECTATION I have waited for the Lord, and He had regard to me; and He heard my prayer, and He put a new canticle into my mouth, a song to our God. *Turn to* ⑪ *on page 43.*

SECRET ⑫

MAY THY SACRAMENTS *be our safeguard,* O Lord, and ever defend us against the attacks of the evil spirit. Through Our Lord, etc. *Turn to* ⑬ *on page 47.*

COMMUNION VERSE ⑭

"THE BREAD that I will give is My flesh for the life of the world." *Turn to* ⑮ *on page 62.*

POST-COMMUNION ⑯

MAY THE ACTION of this heavenly gift *control our bodies and souls* completely, so that, not our own inclinations, but rather its graces may ever prevail in us. Through Our Lord, etc. *Turn to* ⑰ *on page 63.*

⑱ *AFTER MASS, REVIEW YOUR CATECHISM.*

I believe that there is *no contradiction* and never can be any contradiction between *true* science and *true* religion, because God, Who is all truthful, cannot reveal one truth through religion and a contrary truth through science.

I believe that as a Catholic I can and should accept all the truths of science.

I believe that there is nothing to hinder me from accepting all the *established* truths of science and leading a *devout* Catholic life.

I believe that many of the so-called truths of science are *not proved;* that therefore I act as a reasonable man when I refuse to accept them or suspend judgment.

PICTURE AND MASS THEME EXPLAINED

"For everyone who exalts himself shall be humbled, and he who humbles himself shall be exalted" (GOSPEL).

Jesus reveals His Love by curing the victim of *"dropsy"* (pictured at the left). Love overcomes all human obstacles. The humble man does not, of course, expose his talents to the contempt of others. But he does recognize that "every best gift is from above," loaned not for himself alone, but for his less favored neighbor as well.

"For this reason I bend my knees to the Father" (EPISTLE), exclaims St. Paul, as he reflects on *"His glorious riches:"* how Divine love PURGES us by strength *"through His Spirit,"* ILLUMINATES us *"through"* our *"faith"* and then UNITES us in *"Christ's love . . . unto . . . the fullness of God."* Humbly must we recognize *"the power that is at work in us."*

NOW BEGIN MASS AT 1 ON PAGE 35.

INTROIT 2
Ps. 85

HAVE MERCY *on me,* O Lord, for I have cried to Thee all the day; for Thou, O Lord, art sweet and mild, and *plenteous in mercy to all* that call upon Thee.* Bow down Thy ear to me, O Lord, and hear me; for I am needy and poor. Glory be, etc. *Turn to* ❸ *on page 38.*

PRAYER ❹

LET THY GRACE, we beg of Thee, O Lord, ever *precede* and *follow* us, and may it stir up a never-failing zeal for good works. Through Our Lord, etc. *Continue below.*

EPISTLE *Eph. 3* ❺

BRETHREN, I pray you not to be disheartened at my tribulations for you, for they are your glory. For this reason I bend my knees to the Father of our Lord Jesus Christ, from Whom all fatherhood in heaven and on earth receives its name, that He may grant you from His glorious riches to be *strengthened* with power *through His Spirit* unto the progress of the inner man; and to have Christ dwelling through *faith* in your hearts: so that, being rooted and grounded in love, you may be able to comprehend with all the saints what is the breadth and length and height and depth, and to know Christ's *love* which surpasses knowledge, in order that you may be filled unto all the fullness of God. Now, to him who is able to accomplish all things in a measure far beyond what we ask or conceive, in keeping with the power that is at work in us—to him be glory in the Church and in Christ Jesus down through all the ages of time without end. Amen. THANKS BE TO GOD. *Continue below.*

GRADUAL *Ps. 101* ❻

THE GENTILES shall fear Thy Name, O Lord, and all the kings of the earth Thy glory. For the

Lord hath built up Sion, and He shall be seen in His Majesty. Alleluia, alleluia. Sing ye to the Lord a new canticle, because the Lord hath done wonderful things. Alleluia. *Turn to* 7 *on page 40.*

GOSPEL
Luke 14 8

AT THAT TIME, when Jesus entered the house of one of the rulers of the Pharisees on the Sabbath to take food, they were watching Him. And behold, there was a certain man before Him who had the dropsy. And Jesus asked the lawyers and Pharisees, saying, "Is it lawful to *cure on the Sabbath?*" But they remained silent. And He took and healed him and let him go. Then addressing them, He said, "Which of you shall have an ass or an ox fall into a pit, and will not immediately draw him up on the Sabbath?" And they could give Him no answer to these things. But He also spoke a parable to those invited, observing how they were choosing the first places at table, and He said to them, "When thou art invited to a wedding feast, do not recline in the first place, lest perhaps one more distinguished than thou have been invited by him, and he who invited thee and him come and say to thee, 'Make room for this man'; and then thou begin with shame to take the last place. But when thou art invited, go and recline in the last place; that when he who invited thee comes in, he may say to thee, 'Friend, go up higher!' Then thou wilt be honored in the presence of all who are at table with thee. For everyone who *exalts* himself shall be *humbled,* and he who *humbles himself* shall be *exalted.*" *Turn to* 9 *on page 41.*

OFFERTORY ⑩
Ps. 39

LOOK DOWN, O Lord, to *help me;* let them be confounded and ashamed that seek after my soul to take it away; look down, O Lord, to *help me.* *Turn to ⑪ on page 43.*

SECRET ⑫

CLEANSE US, we implore Thee, O Lord, by the effect of the sacrifice here present, and in Thy mercy make us worthy to share in it. Through Our Lord, etc. *Turn to ⑬ on page 47.*

COMMUNION VERSE ⑭

O LORD, I will be mindful of Thy justice alone: Thou hast taught me, O God, *from my youth,* and unto old age and gray hairs, O God, forsake me not. *Turn to ⑮ on page 62.*

POST-COMMUNION ⑯

WE BESEECH THEE, O Lord, in Thy loving kindness to purify and renew our minds with this heavenly Sacrament, so that even our bodies may also obtain help both in the present and future. Through Our Lord, etc. *Turn to ⑰ on page 63.*

⑱ *AFTER MASS, REVIEW YOUR CATECHISM.*

I believe that after death my *body will return to the dust* from which God made it.

I believe that at the end of the world my *body shall rise to life* for the General Judgment.

I believe that my *soul will never die.*

I believe that at death my soul will separate from my body and appear *before the judgment seat of* God.

I believe that I shall be sent to *Heaven,* to *Hell,* or temporarily to *Purgatory* according to my conduct in this life.

PICTURE AND MASS THEME EXPLAINED

"Love . . . thy God . . . and . . . thy neighbor as thyself" (GOSPEL).

"On these two (loves) *depend the whole"* code and creed. Each time we *"walk in* (this) *law"* (INTROIT), we not only *"avoid . . . contact with the devil"* (PRAYER), but we answer the question: *"What do you think of . . . Christ?"* By deeds we profess our faith that He is *"My Lord"* (GOSPEL). We bear *"with one another in love,"* because through Baptism God becomes the *"Father of all"* (EPISTLE).

NOW BEGIN MASS AT 1 ON PAGE 35.

INTROIT *Ps. 118* 2

THOU ART JUST, O Lord, and Thy judgment is right; deal with Thy servant according to Thy mercy.* Blessed are the undefiled in the way: who walk in *the law of the Lord*. Glory be, etc. *Turn to 3 on page 38.*

PRAYER 4

GRANT to Thy people, we pray Thee, O Lord, to avoid every contact with the devil and with a pure mind to *follow only Thee,* O God. Through Our Lord, etc. *Continue on next page.*

EPISTLE *Eph. 4* ❺

BRETHREN, I, the prisoner in the Lord, exhort you to walk in a manner worthy of the calling with which you were called, with all humility and meekness, with patience, bearing with *one another in love,* careful to preserve the *unity* of the Spirit in the bond of peace: one body and one Spirit, even as you were called in one hope of your calling; one Lord, *one faith, one Baptism; one God and Father of all,* who is above all, and throughout all, *and in us all,* Who is blessed for ever and ever. Amen. THANKS BE TO GOD. *Continue below.*

GRADUAL *Ps. 32* ❻

BLESSED IS THE NATION whose God is the Lord: the people whom He hath chosen for His inheritance. By the word of the Lord the heavens were established; and all the power of them by the Spirit of His mouth. Alleluia, alleluia. O Lord, hear my prayer; and let me cry come to Thee. Alleluia. *Turn to* ❼ *on page 40.*

GOSPEL *Matt. 22* ❽

AT THAT TIME, the Pharisees came to Jesus, and one of them, a doctor of the Law, putting Him to the test, asked Him, "Master, which is the great commandment in the Law?" Jesus said to him, " 'Thou shalt *love the Lord thy God* with thy whole heart, and with thy whole soul, and with thy whole mind.' This is the greatest and the first commandment. And the second is like it, *'Thou shalt love thy neighbor as thyself.'* On these two commandments depend the whole Law and the Prophets." Now while the Pharisees were gathered together, Jesus questioned them, saying, "What do you think of the Christ?

Whose son is He?" They said to Him, "David's." He said to them, "How then does David in the Spirit call Him Lord, saying, 'The Lord said to My Lord: Sit thou at My right hand, till I make Thy enemies the footstool of Thy feet'? If David, therefore, calls Him 'Lord,' how is He his son?" And no one could answer Him a word; neither did anyone dare from that day forth to ask Him any more questions. *Turn to* ⑨ *on page 41.*

OFFERTORY ⑩
Dan. 9

I DANIEL, prayed to my God, saying: Hear, O Lord, the prayers of Thy servant; show Thy face upon Thy sanctuary, and favorably look down upon this people upon whom Thy Name is invoked, O God. *Turn to* ⑪ *on page 43.*

SECRET ⑫

WE HUMBLY implore Thy Majesty, O Lord, that the holy Mysteries which we are celebrating may free us from past sins and keep us from future sins. Through Our Lord, etc. *Turn to* ⑬ *on page 47.*

COMMUNION VERSE ⑭

VOW YE, and pay to the Lord your God, all you that round about Him bring presents: to Him that is terrible, even to Him Who taketh away the spirit of princes; to the terrible with all the kings of the earth. *Turn to* ⑮ *on page 62.*

POST COMMUNION ⑯

BY THY sanctifying Sacrament, O Almighty God, may our sinful passions be healed and Thy eternal remedies be provided. Through Our Lord, etc. *Turn to* ⑰ *on page 63.*

⑱ ***Review "Amice and Alb", page 27.***

PICTURE AND MASS THEME EXPLAINED

"Jesus, seeing (the) *faith* (of those who brought the paralytic) *said ... 'Take courage son; thy sins are forgiven thee.'* (Because of those who criticized this absolution), *then He said to the paralytic, 'Arise, take up thy pallet and go to thy house.' ... The crowds ... glorified God Who had given such power to men"* (GOSPEL).

We approach the end of the Church's year. We, too, have grown to maturity. In our youth we regarded perfection an easy accomplishment. Now we plead for Redemption. Our plea today is: *"Give peace, O Lord."* What is the condition for peace with neighbor, peace amongst nations? It is peace with God. Our prayer for peace is a call to set ourselves right with God!

We implore His Mercy to *"direct our hearts"* (PRAYER) in the *"evening"* of our life (OFFERTORY), so that *"sacrifice,"* ours with His, may bring us *"into His courts"* (COMMUNION VERSE). We *"patiently wait for"* God (INTROIT). But how to wait? Not by accumulating material things but by being *"enriched in Him"* (EPISTLE).

Are we ambassadors of peace to others? The *"paralytic"* was unable to do anything for himself. Did not Jesus cure him, absolve him, only when his friends *"brought"* him and He saw *"their faith?"*

NOW BEGIN MASS AT 1 ON PAGE 35.

INTROIT *Ecclus. 36* **2**

GIVE PEACE, O Lord, to them that *patiently wait for Thee,* that Thy prophets may be found faithful: hear the prayers of Thy servant, and of Thy people Israel.* I rejoiced at the things that were said to me: We shall go into the house of the Lord. Glory be, etc. *Turn to* 3 *on page 38.*

PRAYER **4**

LET THE EXERCISE of Thy mercy direct our hearts, we beg of Thee, O Lord, since without Thee, we are not able to please Thee. Through Our Lord, etc. *Continue below.*

EPISTLE *1 Cor. 1* **5**

BRETHREN, I give thanks to my God always concerning you for the grace of God which was given you in Christ Jesus, because in everything you have been *enriched in Him,* in all utterance and in all knowledge; even as the witness to the Christ has been made so firm in you that you lack no grace, while awaiting the appearance of our Lord Jesus Christ, who will also keep you secure unto the end, unimpeachable in the day of the coming of our Lord Jesus Christ. THANKS BE TO GOD. *Continue on next page.*

GRADUAL *Ps. 121* 6

I REJOICED at the things that were said to me: We shall go *into the house of the Lord.* Let peace be in thy strength, and abundance in thy towers. Alleluia, alleluia. The Gentiles shall fear Thy Name, O Lord: and all the kings of the earth Thy glory. Alleluia. *Turn to* 7 *on page 40.*

GOSPEL *Matt. 9* 8

AT THAT TIME, Jesus getting into a boat, crossed over and came to His own town. And behold, they brought to Him a *paralytic* lying on a pallet. And Jesus, seeing their faith, said to the paralytic, *"Take courage, son; thy sins are forgiven thee."* And behold, some of the Scribes said within themselves, "This Man blasphemes." And Jesus, knowing their thoughts, said, "Why do you harbor evil thoughts in your hearts? For which is easier, to say, 'Thy sins are forgiven thee,' or to say, 'Arise, and walk'? But that you may know that the Son of Man has power on earth to forgive sins," then He said to the paralytic, "Arise, take up thy pallet and go to thy house." And he arose, and went away to his house. But when the crowds saw it, they were struck with fear, and glorified God who had given such power to men. *Turn to* 9 *on page 41.*

OFFERTORY *Ex. 24* 10

MOSES CONSECRATED an altar to the Lord, offering upon it holocausts, and sacrificing victims: he made an evening *sacrifice to the Lord* God for an odor of sweetness, *in the sight of the children* of Israel. *Turn to* 11 *on page 43.*

SECRET ⑫

O God, Who dost make us *partakers* of Thy Supreme Godhead by means of the communion in this adorable Sacrifice, grant, we pray Thee, that since we know Thy truth, we may live up to it by a worthy life. Through Our Lord, etc. *Turn to* ⑬ *on page 47.*

COMMUNION VERSE ⑭

Bring up sacrifices, and *come into* His courts: adore ye the Lord in His holy court. *Turn to* ⑮ *on page 62.*

POST-COMMUNION ⑯

We give Thee thanks, O Lord, for having been nourished by Thy sacred gift, beseeching Thy mercy that Thou make us worthy to receive it. Through Our Lord, etc. *Turn to* ⑰ *on page 63.*

⑱ *AFTER MASS, REVIEW YOUR CATECHISM.*

I believe that HEAVEN is a state of *perfect* and *never failing* happiness, without the presence or fear of any evil, that "Eye has not seen nor ear heard what things God has prepared for those" who enter into the *Vision of and Union with the Three Divine Persons.*

I believe that any true happiness or pleasure on this earth comes from God and is but a *finite* fraction of the *infinite* Real Thing in heaven.

I believe that there is a PURGATORY; that this is a *consoling* and *reasonable* doctrine.

I believe that since *nothing defiled* can enter heaven and since many die with the guilt of venial sins on their souls, without having *sufficiently* atoned for sins forgiven, thereby having rendered themselves *unworthy* to enter into the presence of God, yet *not guilty* enough to suffer the punishment of hell, — there is a Purgatory where these souls are cleansed.

PICTURE AND MASS THEME EXPLAINED

"*'Go therefore to the crossroads, and invite* (to the marriage feast) *whomever you shall find.' . . . The . . . feast was filled with guests . . . And he said* (to one of them), *'Friend, how didst thou come in here without a wedding garment'* " (GOSPEL)?

Under this symbol of a wedding feast Jesus indicates that all, Jew and Gentile, are called. He alone is *"the salvation of the people"* from their self-begotten misery. What folly to decline when He implores us to *"incline . . . to"* His invitation (INTROIT).

Of those first invited, His own chosen people, some refused on mere pretexts. Then did He ask His followers to *"declare His deeds among the Gentiles"* (GRADUAL).

May our *"ways be directed"* (COMMUNION VERSE) to this banquet hall. But to receive Jesus worthily, a wedding garment is necessary. St. Paul describes the warp and woof of this garment: *"put on"* Christ and *"put away"* the spirit of Antichrist in our own soul and in dealings with our neighbor (EPISTLE).

NOW BEGIN MASS AT 1 ON PAGE 35.

INTROIT *Ps. 77* ②

I AM THE *salvation of the people,* saith the Lord: in whatever tribulation they shall cry to Me, I will hear them, and I will be their Lord for ever.* Attend, O My people, to My law; *incline your ears to the words* of My mouth. Glory be, etc. *Turn to ③ on page 38.*

PRAYER ④

O ALMIGHTY and Merciful God, do Thou kindly keep us from all things that war against us, so that after being freed both in mind and body, we may with ready souls do the works that are Thine. Through Our Lord, etc. *Continue below.*

EPISTLE *Eph. 4* ⑤

BRETHREN, be renewed in the spirit of your mind, and *put on the new man,* which has been created according to God in justice and holiness of truth. Wherefore, *put away* lying and speak truth each one with his neighbor, because we are members of one another. "Be angry and do not sin": do not let the sun go down upon your anger: do not give place to the devil. He who was wont to steal, let him steal no longer; but rather let him labor, working with his hands at what is good, that he may have something to share with him who suffers need. THANKS BE TO GOD. *Continue below.*

GRADUAL *Ps. 140* ⑥

LET MY PRAYER be directed as incense in Thy sight, O Lord. The lifting up of my hands as evening sacrifice. Alleluia, alleluia. Give glory to the Lord, and call upon His Name: *declare His deeds among the Gentiles.* Alleluia. *Turn to* 7 *on page 40.*

GOSPEL *Matt. 22* 8

AT THAT TIME, Jesus spoke to the chief priests and the Pharisees in parables, saying: "The kingdom of heaven is like a king who made a marriage feast for his son. And he sent his servants to call in those invited to the marriage feast, but they would not come. Again he sent out other servants, saying, 'Tell those who are invited, Behold, I have prepared my dinner; my oxen and fatlings are killed, and everything is ready; come to the marriage feast.' But they made light of it, and went off, one to his farm, and another to his business; and the rest laid hold of his servants, treated them shamefully, and killed them. But when the king heard of it, he was angry; and he sent his armies and destroyed those murderers, and burnt their city. Then he said to his servants, 'The marriage feast indeed is ready, but those who were invited were not worthy; go therefore to the crossroads, and invite to the marriage feast whomever you shall find.' And his servants went out into the roads, and gathered all whom they found, both good and bad; and the marriage feast was filled with guests. Now the king went in to see the guests, and he saw there a man who had not on a wedding garment. And he said to him, 'Friend, *how didst thou come in here without a wedding garment?'* But he was speechless. Then the king said to the attendants, 'Bind his hands and feet and cast him forth into the darkness outside, where there will be the weeping, and the gnashing of teeth.' For many are called, but few are chosen." *Turn to* ⑨ *on page 41.*

OFFERTORY ⑩
Ps. 137

IF I SHALL WALK in the midst of tribulation, Thou wilt quicken me, O Lord; and Thou wilt stretch forth Thy hand against the wrath of my enemies; and Thy right hand shall save me. *Turn to* ⑪ *on page 43.*

SECRET ⑫

GRANT, we implore Thee, O Lord, that these gifts which we offer up in the sight of Thy Majesty may be helpful to our salvation. Through Our Lord, etc. *Turn to* ⑬ *on page 47.*

COMMUNON VERSE ⑭

THOU HAST COMMANDED Thy commandments *to be kept most diligently:* O that my ways may be directed to keep Thy justifications. *Turn to* ⑮ *on page 62.*

POST-COMMUNION ⑯

MAY THY healing grace, O Lord of mercy, deliver us from all wickedness of heart and make us ever hold fast to Thy commandments. Through Our Lord, etc. *Turn to* ⑰ *on page 63.*

⑱ AFTER MASS, REVIEW YOUR CATECHISM.

I believe that there is a HELL of everlasting fire, because Christ has said so.

I believe that if I die in the state of mortal sin, I shall be *lost forever;* that out of hell there is *no redemption;* that the chief punishment of hell consists in the pain of *losing* the Vision of and Union with God Who is the *source of all joy, peace and happiness.*

PICTURE AND MASS THEME EXPLAINED

" 'Go thy way, thy son lives.' The man believed . . . As he was . . . going down, his servants met him and brought word saying that his son lived" (GOSPEL).

The weakened condition of the ruler's son reminds us of our own world. It is worn out by the fever of passion. It is unable to help itself until faith in God returns.

A humble confession of sin is the secret of obtaining God's *"mercy"* (INTROIT) and *"pardon"* (PRAYER).

"Be filled with the Spirit" during the *"psalms and hymns"* of Mass; *"be subject to one another"* in public life (EPISTLE).

Liturgy and Catholic Action are twins!

When the *"official's"* faith was rewarded, he immediately spread the faith in his *"whole household,"* his relatives and employees.

Gratitude should prompt you also to be lay

apostles, ever ready to "speak religion" in and outside your house.

NOW BEGIN MASS AT 1 ON PAGE 35.

INTROIT *Dan. 3* 2

ALL THAT THOU hast done to us, O Lord, Thou has done in true judgment; because we have sinned against Thee, and we have not obeyed Thy commandments: but give glory to Thy Name, and deal with us according to the multitude of *Thy mercy.** Blessed are the undefiled in the way; who walk in the law of the Lord. Glory be, etc. *Turn to* 3 *on page 38.*

PRAYER 4

BE APPEASED, O generous God, and to Thy faithful people grant peace and *pardon,* so that after being cleansed from all their sins, they may serve Thee with a secure mind. Through Our Lord, etc. *Continue below.*

EPISTLE *Eph. 5* 5

BRETHREN, see to it therefore, that you walk with care: not as unwise but as wise, *making the most of your time,* because the days are evil. Therefore do not become foolish, but understand what the will of the Lord is. And do not be drunk with wine, for in that is debauchery; but be filled with the Spirit, speaking to one another in psalms and hymns and spiritual songs, singing and making melody in your hearts to the Lord, giving thanks always for all things in the name of our Lord Jesus Christ to God the Father. Be subject to one another in the fear of Christ. THANKS BE TO GOD. *Continue on next page.*

GRADUAL
Ps. 144 ⑥

THE EYES OF *all hope* in Thee, O Lord; and Thou givest them meat *in due season.* Thou openest Thy hand, and fillest every living creature with Thy *blessing.* Alleluia, alleluia. My heart is ready, O God, my heart is ready: I will sing, and will give praise to Thee, my glory. Alleluia. *Turn to* ⑦ *on page 40.*

GOSPEL
John 4 ⑧

AT THAT TIME, there was a certain royal official whose son was lying sick at Capharnaum. When he heard that Jesus had come from Judea into Galilee, he went to Him and besought Him to come down and heal his son, for he was *at the point of death.* Jesus therefore said to him, "Unless you see signs and wonders, you do not believe." The royal official said to Him, "Sir, come down before my child dies." Jesus said to him, *"Go thy way, thy son lives."* The man believed the word that Jesus spoke to him, and departed. But even as he was now going down, his servants met him and brought word saying that his son lived. He asked of them therefore the hour in which he had got better. And they told him, "Yesterday, at the seventh hour, the fever left him." The father knew then that it was at that very hour in which Jesus had said to him, "Thy son lives." And he himself believed, and his *whole household.* *Turn to* ⑨ *on page 41.*

OFFERTORY
Ps. 136 ⑩

UPON THE RIVERS of Babylon, there we sat and wept; when we remembered Thee, O Sion. *Turn to* ⑪ *on page 43.*

SECRET ⑫

LET THESE MYSTERIES, we beseech Thee, O Lord, be our heavenly medicine and root out all vice from our hearts. Through Our Lord, etc. *Turn to ⑬ on page 47.*

COMMUNION VERSE ⑭

BE THOU MINDFUL of Thy word to Thy servant, O Lord, in which Thou hast given me hope: this hath comforted me in my humiliation. *Turn to ⑮ on page 62.*

POST-COMMUNION ⑯

THAT WE MAY be made worthy of Thy sacred gifts, O Lord, make us, we pray Thee, ever ready *to obey Thy commandments.* Through Our Lord, etc. *Turn to ⑰ on page 63.*

⑱ *AFTER MASS, REVIEW YOUR CATECHISM.*

I believe that my *Catholic Faith* is my most precious inheritance, my proudest boast, my *"pearl of great price"*, something more precious to me than all the honors and riches of this world.

I believe that by living up to the dictates of my Catholic Faith I shall obtain peace and contentment of soul *in this world* and eternal happiness *in the life to come.*

HOW a LAY PERSON is to BAPTIZE in CASE of NECESSITY

Pour common water on the head or face of the person to be baptized, and say while pouring it: *"I baptize thee in the name of the Father, and of the Son, and of the Holy Ghost."*

N. B.—Any person of either sex who has reached the use of reason can baptize in case of necessity.

PICTURE AND MASS THEME EXPLAINED

"Wicked servant! I forgave thee all the debt ... Shouldst not thou also have had pity on thy fellow-servant" (GOSPEL)?

Life is indeed a warfare! Yet mercy must now be our weapon in dealing with others. Otherwise stern justice will be our eternal downfall (as symbolized by small figures at the right). Divine Mercy is angry with those who fail in mercy.

The well-equipped Christian soldier must wear *"the shield of faith, . . . the breastplate of justice, . . . the sword of the spirit,"* in *"wrestling . . . against the world-rulers of . . . darkness"* and their un-Christian blackouts (EPISTLE).

O Christian woman, admire the ancient "valiant woman," Esther! By her confident prayer and strong virtue she saved herself and her people (INTROIT). O Christian man, behold the example of Job (OFFERTORY). His faith never wavered until it was crowned in victory.

NOW BEGIN MASS AT 1 ON PAGE 35.

INTROIT *Esther 13* 2

ALL THINGS are in Thy will, O Lord; and there

is none that can resist Thy will: for Thou hast made all things, heaven and earth, and all things that are under the cope of heaven: Thou art Lord of all.* Blessed are the undefiled in the way; who walk in the law of the Lord. Glory be, etc. *Turn to* ❸ *on page 38.*

PRAYER ❹

WE IMPLORE THEE, O Lord, to keep Thy family, the Church, in religious perseverance, so that through Thy protection it may be free from all misfortune and devoted in good works to the glory of Thy Name. Through Our Lord, etc. *Continue below.*

EPISTLE *Eph. 6* ❺

BRETHREN, be strengthened in the Lord and in the might of His power. Put on the armor of God, that you may be able to stand against *the wiles of the devil.* For our wrestling is not *against flesh and blood,* but against the Principalities and the Powers, against the world-rulers of this darkness, against the spiritual forces of wickedness on high. Therefore take up the armor of God, that you may be able to resist in the evil day, and stand in all things perfect. Stand, therefore, having girded your loins with truth, and having put on the breastplate of justice, and having your feet shod with the readiness of the gospel of peace, in all things taking up the shield of faith, with which you may be able to quench all the fiery darts of the most wicked one. And take unto you the helmet of salvation and the sword of the spirit, that is, the word of God. THANKS BE TO GOD. *Continue on next page.*

GRADUAL *Ps. 89* ⑥

LORD, Thou hast been *our refuge*, from generation to generation. Before the mountains were made, or the earth and the world was formed; from eternity and to eternity Thou art God. Alleluia, alleluia. When Israel went out of Egypt, the house of Jacob from a barbarous people. Alleluia.
Turn to ⑦ *on page 40.*

GOSPEL *Matt. 18* ⑧

AT THAT TIME, Jesus spoke to His disciples this parable: "The kingdom of heaven is likened to a king who desired to settle accounts with his servants. And when he had begun the settlement, one was brought to him who owed him ten thousand talents. And as he had no means of paying, his master ordered him to be sold, with his wife and children and all that he had, and payment to be made. But the servant fell down and besought him, saying, 'Have patience with me and I will pay thee all!' And moved with compassion, the master of that servant released him, and forgave him the debt. But as that servant went out, he met one of his fellow-servants who owed him a hundred denarii, and he laid hold of him and throttled him, saying, '*Pay what thou owest.*' His fellow-servant therefore fell down and began to entreat him, saying, 'Have patience with me and I will pay thee all.' But he would not; but went away and cast him into prison until he should pay what was due. His fellow-servants therefore, seeing what had happened, were very much saddened, and they went and informed their master of all that had happened. Then his master called him, and said to him, 'Wicked servant! *I forgave thee all the debt, because thou didst entreat me.* Shouldst not thou also have had pity on thy fellow-servant, even as I had pity on thee?' And his master, being angry, *handed him over to the torturers* until he should pay all that was due to him. So also my heavenly Father will do to you, *if you do not* each *forgive* your brothers from your hearts." *Turn to* ⑨ *on page 41.*

OFFERTORY ⑩
Job 1

THERE WAS A MAN in the land of Hus, whose name was Job, simple, and upright, and fearing God: whom Satan besought that he might tempt: and power was given him from the Lord over his possessions and his flesh; and he destroyed all his substance and his children; and wounded his flesh also with a grievous ulcer. *Turn to* ⑪ *on page 43.*

SECRET ⑫

MERCIFULLY ACCEPT these victim-offerings by which in Thy mighty love Thou hast willed that atonement be made unto Thee and salvation restored unto us. Through Our Lord, etc. *Turn to* ⑬ *on page 47.*

COMMUNION VERSE ⑭

MY SOUL is in Thy salvation, and in Thy word have I hoped: when wilt Thou execute judgment on them that persecute me? The wicked have persecuted me: help me, O Lord my God. *Turn to* ⑮ *on page 62.*

POST-COMMUNION ⑯

AFTER BEING NOURISHED with the food of immortality, we ask of Thee, O Lord, that what we received on the tongue we may follow up with a pure mind. Through Our Lord, etc. *Turn to* ⑰ *on page 63.*

⑱ **Review "Cincture", page 28.**

PICTURE AND MASS THEME EXPLAINED

"Render . . . to Caesar the things that are Caesar's, and to God the things that are God's" (GOSPEL).

We now approach the end of the ecclesiastical year. In today's Mass the Church bids us prepare *"without offense unto the day of Christ,"* that is, the day of Final Judgment (EPISTLE). Hence St. Paul prays with us today that our *"charity may . . . abound in . . . discernment."*

Yes, *"discernment!"* lest we be deceived by the tricky questions of Pharisee friends and foes, or even the Pharisee spirit in our own conscience. Jesus gives the answer: *"Render . . . to Caesar the things that are Caesar's"* (symbolized by small figures at right), *"and to God the things that are God's"* (symbolized by small figures at left).

Then will citizens *"dwell together in unity."* Then will rulers have God as their *"helper and protector"* (GRADUAL). On this Sunday, officials and citizens alike may well cry out *"from the depths"* (INTROIT) for forgiveness of their failure to prepare.

NOW BEGIN MASS AT 1 ON PAGE 35.

INTROIT *Ps. 129* 2

IF THOU SHALT observe iniquities, O Lord, Lord, who shall endure it? For with Thee is propitiation, O God of Israel.* *From the depths* I have cried to Thee, O Lord: Lord, hear my voice. Glory be, etc. *Turn to* 3 *on page 38.*

PRAYER 4

O GOD, our refuge and our strength, Thou Who art the source of all devotion, give ear to the devout prayers of Thy Church, and grant that what we ask in faith, we may obtain in fact. Through Our Lord, etc. *Continue below.*

EPISTLE *Philip. 1* 5

BRETHREN, we are convinced of this, that He who has begun a good work in you will bring it to perfection until *the day of Christ Jesus.* And I have the right to feel so about you all, because I have you in my heart, all of you, alike in my *chains* and in the defense and confirmation of the gospel, as *sharers in my joy.* For God is my witness how I long for you all in the heart of Christ Jesus. And this I pray, that your *charity* may *more and more abound in knowledge* and all discernment, so that you may approve the better things, that you may be upright and *without offense unto the day of Christ, filled with the fruit of justice,* through Jesus Christ, to the glory and praise of God. THANKS BE TO GOD. *Continue below.*

GRADUAL *Ps. 132* 6

BEHOLD how good and how pleasant it is for brethren to dwell together in unity. It is like the precious ointment on the head, that ran down upon the beard, the beard of Aaron. Alleluia, alleluia.

They that fear the Lord, let them hope in Him: He is their helper and protector. Alleluia. *Turn to* 7 *on page 40.*

GOSPEL *Matt. 22* 8

AT THAT TIME, the Pharisees went and took counsel how they might entrap Jesus in His talk. And they sent to Him their disciples with the Herodians, saying, "Master, we know that Thou art truthful, and that Thou teachest the way of God in truth and that Thou carest naught for any man; for Thou dost not regard the person of men. Tell us, therefore, what dost Thou think: Is it lawful to give tribute to Cæsar, or not?" But Jesus, knowing their wickedness, said, "Why do you test Me, you hypocrites? Show Me the coin of the tribute." So they offered Him a denarius. Then Jesus said to them, "Whose are this image and the inscription?" They said to Him, "Cæsar's." Then He said to them, *"Render,* therefore, *to Cæsar the things that are Cæsar's, and to God the things that are God's."* *Turn to* 9 *on page 41.*

OFFERTORY *Esther 14* 10

REMEMBER ME, O Lord, Thou Who rulest above all power; and give a well-ordered speech in my mouth, that my words may be pleasing in the sight of the prince. *Turn to* 11 *on page 43.*

SECRET 12

GRANT UNTO US, O God of mercy, that this saving sacrifice may forever free us from our guilty deeds and shield us from all harm. Through Our Lord, etc. *Turn to* 13 *on page 47.*

COMMUNION VERSE 14

I HAVE CRIED, for Thou, O God, hast heard me: O

incline Thy ear unto me, and hear my words. *Turn to* ⑮ *on page 62.*

POST-COMMUNION ⑯

WE HAVE RECEIVED, O Lord, the gifts of Thy sacred mystery, humbly praying that what Thou hast commanded us to do in remembrance of Thee may be of help to our weakness. Who livest, etc. *Turn to* ⑰ *on page 63.*

⑱ *AFTER MASS, REVIEW YOUR CATECHISM.*

The TEN COMMANDMENTS

1. I am the Lord thy God; thou shalt not have strange gods before Me.
2. Thou shalt not take the Name of the Lord thy God in vain.
3. Remember that thou keep holy the Sabbath day.
4. Honor thy father and thy mother.
5. Thou shalt not kill.
6. Thou shalt not commit adultery.
7. Thou shalt not steal.
8. Thou shalt not bear false witness against thy neighbor.
9. Thou shalt not covet thy neighbor's wife.
10. Thou shalt not covet thy neighbor's goods.

The SIX PRECEPTS of the CHURCH

1. To hear Mass on Sundays and Holydays of Obligation. 2. To fast and abstain on the days appointed. 3. To confess at least once a year. 4. To receive the Holy Eucharist during the Easter-time. 5. To contribute to the support of our pastors. 6. Not to marry persons who are not Catholics, or who are related to us within the third degree of kindred, nor privately without witnesses, nor to solemnize marriage at forbidden times.

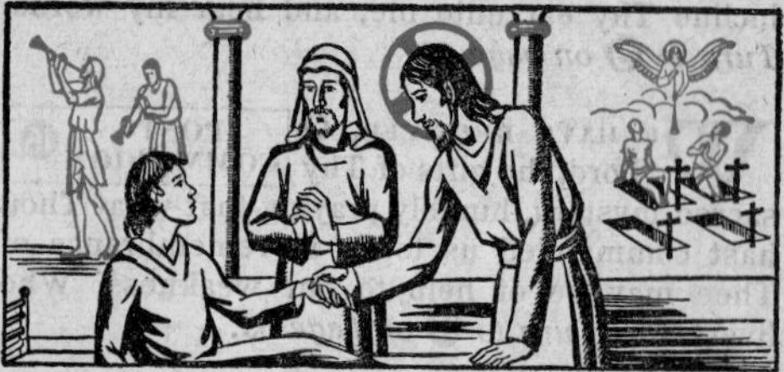

PICTURE AND MASS THEME EXPLAINED

"When Jesus came to the ruler's house, and saw the flute players and the crowd making a din, He said, 'Begone, the girl is asleep, not dead.' And they laughed Him to scorn. But when the crowd had been put out, He went in and took her by the hand; and the girl arose" (GOSPEL).

Notice the small flute-playing figures at the left. They represent *"the crowd"* of people who laugh their Creator *"to scorn."*

Yet how often we move among them, enjoying what we call "life," even though we may be spiritually dead.

The trumpet-blowing angel at the right, summoning the dead to life, represents how Jesus, after *"the crowd has been put out"* by us, raises His *"Hand"* over us in absolution, extends His *"Hand"* to us in Holy Communion.

St. Paul, too, warns us against these *"enemies of the cross of Christ"* whose *"end is ruin,"* whose *"god is the belly."*

Since *"our citizenship is in heaven,"* let us plead with Jesus to *"refashion the body of our lowliness,"* that we may *"stand fast . . . in the Lord"* and *"be of one mind"* with our brother citizens (EPISTLE).

NOW BEGIN MASS AT 1 ON PAGE 35.

INTROIT *Jer. 29* 2

THE LORD SAITH: I think thoughts of *peace,* and *not of affliction:* you shall call upon Me, and I will hear you; and I will bring back your captivity from all places.* Lord, Thou hast *blessed Thy land,* Thou hast turned away the *captivity* of Jacob. Glory be, etc. *Turn to* 3 *on page 38.*

PRAYER 4

O LORD, we beg of Thee, absolve the sins of Thy people, so that by Thy kind forgiveness we may be set free from the chains of our sins *in which our weakness had entangled* us. Through Our Lord, etc. *Continue below.*

EPISTLE *Phillip 3* 5

BRETHREN, be imitators of me, and mark those who walk after the pattern you have in us. For many walk, of whom I have told you often and now tell you even weeping, that they are *enemies of the cross* of Christ. *Their end is ruin,* their god is the belly, their glory is in their shame, they mind the things of earth. But our citizenship is in heaven from which also we eagerly await a Savior, our Lord Jesus Christ, Who will *refashion the body of our lowliness,* conforming it to the body of His glory by exerting the power by which He is able also to subject all things to Himself.

So then, my brethren, beloved and longed for, my joy and my crown, *stand fast thus in the Lord,* beloved. I entreat Evodia and I exhort Syntyche to *be of one mind in the Lord.* And I beseech thee also, my loyal comrade, help them, for they have toiled with me in the gospel, as have Clement and the rest of my fellow-workers whose names are in the book of life. THANKS BE TO GOD. *Continue below.*

GRADUAL *Ps. 43* ⑥

THOU hast delivered us, O Lord, from them that afflict us: and hast put them to shame that hate us. In God we will glory all the day: and in Thy Name we will give praise forever. Alleluia, alleluia. From the *depths* I have cried to Thee, O Lord: Lord, hear my prayer. Alleluia. *Turn to* ⑦ *on page 40.*

GOSPEL *Matt. 9* ⑧

AT THAT TIME, as Jesus was speaking to the crowds, behold, a ruler came up and worshipped Him, saying, "My daughter has just now died; but come and lay Thy hand upon her, and she will return to life." And Jesus arose and followed him, and so did His disciples. Now a woman who for twelve years had been suffering from hemorrhage, came up behind Him and *touched the tassel of His cloak,* saying to herself, "If I touch but His cloak I shall be saved." But Jesus, turning and seeing her, said, "Take courage, daughter; thy faith has saved thee." And the woman was restored to health from that moment. And when Jesus came to the ruler's house, and saw the flute players and the crowd *making a din,* He said, "Begone, the girl is asleep, not dead." And they laughed Him to scorn. But when the crowd had been put out, *He* went in and *took her by the hand; and the girl arose.* And the report of this spread throughout all that district. *Turn to* ⑨ *on page 41.*

OFFERTORY ⑩
Ps. 129

FROM THE DEPTHS I have cried out to Thee, O Lord; Lord, hear my prayer: from the depths I have cried out to Thee, O Lord. *Turn to* ⑪ *on page 43.*

SECRET ⑫

WE OFFER THEE, O Lord, this sacrifice of praise for the sake of *increasing our service* and of mercifully completing in us what Thou hast begun without any merit of ours. Through Our Lord, etc. *Turn to* ⑬ *on page 47.*

COMMUNION VERSE ⑭

"THEREFORE I say to you, all things whatever you ask for in prayer, believe that you shall receive, and they shall come to you." *Turn to* ⑮ *on page 62.*

POST-COMMUNION ⑯

WE PRAY THEE, O Almighty God, that Thou wilt not allow us to be *overcome* by *human dangers* since Thou hast gladdened us with a share in *Divine* life. Through Our Lord, etc. *Turn to* ⑰ *on page 63.*

⑱ **Study Morning and Evening Prayers.**

A practical Christian begins and ends the day with God. By reading each day the Morning and Evening Prayers on Pages 330-333, you will soon memorize them.

Calendar, page 1, indicates other Sundays after Pentecost are taken from Sundays after Epiphany

PICTURE AND MASS THEME EXPLAINED

"... Then will appear the sign of the Son of Man in heaven ... And He will send forth His angels with a trumpet, ... and they will gather His elect from the four winds" (GOSPEL).

The world is coming to its end! Such an announcement would make *"all tribes of the earth mourn,"* especially him who clings to earthly things and now realizes he must *"not turn back to take his cloak."* Let us be realists: the world will dissolve, disappear in ruin!

The liturgical year comes to an end today. For those who have watched with Christ in His physical life as Man, and the coming of the Holy Spirit in the birth, growth and triumph of His Mystical Body, it is the symbol of the final assumption of His Mystical Body into heaven, the last act in an eternal drama.

An old year ends! a new begins, *"even at the door." "The leaves break forth"* (GOSPEL). Let us *"seek the fruit of ... divine service"* from His *"tender mercy"* as *"remedies"* for ourselves (PRAYER), *"bearing fruit in every good work"* towards our neighbor (EPISTLE).

May we flee from the *"false christs"* who *"lead astray . . . even the elect"* (GOSPEL), enslaving, misleading, corrupting their minds, especially in the press and "over" the radio.

NOW BEGIN MASS AT ❶ ON PAGE 35.

INTROIT *Jer. 29* ❷

THE LORD SAITH: I think thoughts of peace, and not of affliction; you shall call upon Me and I will hear you; and I will bring back your captivity from all places.* Lord, Thou hast blessed Thy land: Thou hast turned away the captivity of Jacob. Glory be, etc. *Turn to ❸ on page 38.*

PRAYER ❹

STIR UP THE *wills* of Thy faithful people, we entreat Thee, O Lord, so that the more earnestly they seek the fruit of Thy *divine service,* the more abundantly will they receive the remedies of Thy tender mercy. Through Our Lord, etc. *Continue below.*

EPISTLE *Col. 1* ❺

BRETHREN, we too have been praying for you unceasingly, since the day we heard this, and asking that you may be filled with knowledge of His will, in all spiritual wisdom and understanding. May you walk worthily of God and please Him in all things, *bearing fruit in every good work* and growing in the *knowledge of God.* May you be completely strengthened through His glorious power unto perfect patience and long-suffering; joyfully rendering thanks to the Father, Who has made us worthy to share the lot of the *saints* in light. He has rescued us from the power of darkness and transferred us into the kingdom of His beloved Son, in Whom we have our redemption (through *His blood*), the remission of our sins. THANKS BE TO GOD. *Continue below.*

GRADUAL *Ps. 43* 6

THOU HAST delivered us, O Lord, from them that afflict us: and hast put them to shame that hate us. In God we will glory all the day: and in Thy Name we will give praise for ever. Alleluia, alleluia. From the depths I have cried to Thee, O Lord: Lord, hear my prayer. Alleluia. *Turn to* 7 *on page 40.*

GOSPEL *Matt. 24* 8

AT THAT TIME, Jesus said to His disciples, "When you see the abomination of desolation, which was spoken of by Daniel the prophet, standing in the holy place—let him who reads understand—then let those who are in Judea *flee to the mountains;* and let him who is on the housetop not go down to take anything from his house; and let him who is in the field not turn back to take his cloak. But woe to those who are with child, or have infants at the breast in those days! But pray that your flight may not be in the winter, or on the Sabbath. For then there will be great tribulation, such as has not been from the beginning of the world until now, nor will be. And unless those days had been shortened, no living creature would have been saved. But for the sake of the elect those days will be shortened. Then if any-one say to you, 'Behold, here is the Christ,' or, 'There He is,' do not believe it. For *false christs* and false prophets will arise, and will show great signs and wonders, so as *to lead astray,* (if possible), *even the elect.* Behold, I have told it to you beforehand. If therefore they say to you, 'Behold, He is in the desert,' do not go forth; 'Behold, He is in the inner chambers,' do not believe it. For as the lightning comes forth from the east and shines even to the west, so also will the coming of the Son of Man be. Wherever the body is, there will the eagles be gathered together. But immediately after the tribulation of those days, the sun will be darkened, and the moon will not give her light, and the stars will fall from heaven, and the powers of heaven will be shaken. And *then will appear the sign of the Son of Man in heaven;* and then will all tribes of the earth mourn, and they will see the Son of Man coming upon the clouds of heaven with great power and majesty. And He will send forth His angels with a trumpet and a great sound, and they will gather His elect from the four winds, from end to end of the heavens. Now from the fig tree learn this parable. When its branch is now tender, and the leaves break forth, you know that summer is near. Even so, when you see all these things, know that it is near, even at the door. Amen I say to you, this generation will not pass away till all these things have been accomplished. Heaven and earth will pass away, but My words will not pass away." *Turn to* (9) *on page 41.*

OFFERTORY
Ps. 129 (10)

FROM THE DEPTHS I have cried out to Thee, O Lord: Lord, hear my prayer; from the depths I have cried out to Thee, O Lord. *Turn to* (11) *on page 43.*

SECRET ⑫

BE THOU GRACIOUS, O Lord, to our humble appeals and, after receiving the prayers and offerings of Thy people, convert the *hearts of us all* to Thyself, so that, having been set free from the greed of earthly pleasures, we may pass on to the desire of heavenly treasures. Through Our Lord, etc. *Turn to* ⑬ *on page 47.*

COMMUNION VERSE ⑭

"THEREFORE, I say to you, all things whatever you ask for in prayer, believe that you shall receive, and they shall come to you. *Turn to* ⑮ *on page 62.*

POST-COMMUNION ⑯

GRANT, we beseech Thee, O Lord, through this Sacrament which we have received, that whatever is *diseased in our hearts* may be cured by the gift of its healing power. Through Our Lord, etc. *Turn to* ⑰ *on page 63.*

⑱ ***Sanctify your Daily Work.***

¶ ***How monotonous daily life must have seemed to Jesus in the carpenter shop of Joseph! Yet He put His Heart into His work. And loved it, even though it was lowly. And loved it, because it was His Father's Will; loved it, for love of us. Therefore, O Christian man and woman, frequently throughout the day, let your prayer be:***

All for Thee, O most Sacred Heart of Jesus. « 300 days »

PICTURE AND MASS THEME EXPLAINED

"Hail, full of grace, the Lord is with thee. Blessed art thou among women" (GOSPEL).

"Eva" (Latin name for Eve) by her sin brought terrible effects on us, her children. "Ave," first word of the "Ave Maria," is the reverse of "Eva." Through Mary, Jesus came to reverse us back to God.

Mary's conception and subsequent life were *"immaculate"* (PRAYER), because she was to be the living ciborium out of which Jesus was to take His Body, the living chalice out of which He was to take His Blood.

We behold a truly beautiful picture of Mary (EPISTLE) as she appeared to the Spirit of God even before her creation; as she should appear to us now in the present, watching *"daily at* (her) *gates"* to receive *"instruction"* in the *"life"* of her Jesus.

Let us frequently recite the "Hail Mary" (GOSPEL); invoke *"her intercession"* (PRAYER); offer the same sacrifice that *"preserved"* her (SECRET); receive the

Sacraments which *"heal in us the wounds of* (original) *sin"* (POSTCOMMUNION).

NOW BEGIN MASS AT ❶ ON PAGE 35.

INTROIT *Is. 61* ❷

I WILL GREATLY REJOICE in the Lord, and my soul shall be joyful in my God; for He hath clothed me with the garments of salvation, and with the robe of justice He hath covered me, as a bride adorned with her jewels.* I will extol Thee, O Lord, for Thou hast upheld me: and hast not made my enemies to rejoice over me. Glory be, etc. *Turn to ❸ on page 38.*

PRAYER ❹

O GOD, Who by the *Immaculate* Conception of the Virgin didst prepare a worthy dwelling-place for Thy Son and didst preserve her from every stain by foreseeing the future death of Thy same Son, we pray that Thou wilt permit us to come to Thee, after being purified by her *intercession.* Through the same Lord, etc. *Continue below.*

EPISTLE *Prov. 8* ❺

THE LORD possessed me in the beginning of His ways, before He made anything, from the beginning. I was set up from eternity, and of old, before the earth was made. The depths were not as yet, and I was already conceived: neither had the fountains of waters as yet sprung out; the mountains with their huge bulk had not as yet been established: before the hills I was brought forth; He had not yet made the earth, nor the rivers, nor the poles of the world. When He prepared the heavens, I was there; when with a certain law and compass He enclosed the depths; when He established the sky above, and poised the fountains of waters; when He compassed the sea with its bounds, and set a law to the waters that they should not pass their limits; when He balanced the foundations of the earth, I was with Him, forming all things, and was delighted every day, playing before Him at all times, playing in the world: and my delight is to be with the children of men. Now, therefore, ye children, hear me: blessed are they that keep my ways. *Hear instruction,* and be wise, and refuse it not. Blessed is the man that heareth me, and that watcheth *daily at my gates,* and waiteth at the posts of my doors. He that shall find me shall find life, and shall have salvation from the Lord. THANKS BE TO GOD. *Continue below.*

GRADUAL *Judith 13* ⑥

BLESSED ART THOU, O Virgin Mary, by the Lord, the Most High God, above all women, upon the earth. Thou art the glory of Jerusalem, thou art the joy of Israel, thou art the *honor of our people.* Alleluia, alleluia. Thou art all fair, O Mary, and there is in thee no stain of original sin. Alleluia. *Turn to* ⑦ *on page 40.*

GOSPEL *Luke 1* ⑧

THE ANGEL GABRIEL was sent from God to a town of Galilee called Nazareth, to a virgin betrothed to a man named Joseph, of the house of David, and the virgin's name was Mary. And when the angel had come to her, he said, *"Hail, full of grace,* the Lord is with thee. Blessed art thou among women." *Turn to* ⑨ *on page 41.*

"HAIL, MARY, full of grace, the *Lord is with thee.* Blessed art thou among women." Alleluia. *Turn to* ⑪ *on page 43.*

OFFERTORY *Luke 1* ⑩

RECEIVE, O LORD, this saving Victim which we offer to Thee on this feast of the Immaculate Conception of the Blessed Virgin Mary, and grant that, even as we proclaim her to have been *preserved* by Thy grace from all stain, so we may be delivered by her intercession from all our sins. Through Our Lord, etc. *Turn to* ⑬ *on page 47.*

SECRET ⑫

GLORIOUS THINGS are spoken of thee, O Mary; for He that is mighty hath done great things *unto thee. Turn to* ⑮ *on page 62.*

COMMUNION VERSE ⑭

MAY THE SACRAMENT which we have received, O Lord our God, *heal in us the wounds* of that sin from which Thou didst preserve one alone, Our Blessed Lady, in her Immaculate Conception. Through Our Lord, etc. *Turn to* ⑰ *on page 63.*

POST-COMMUNION ⑯

⑱ *Crusade for Purity.*

BY THINE Immaculate Conception O Mary, make my body pure and my soul holy. « *Three times, followed each time by a Hail Mary, 300 days Indulgence* »
O Mary, pray that I may live in God, with God and for God. « *300 days Ind.* »
My Mother, keep me this day from mortal sin. Hail Mary, *three times.* « *200 days Ind.* »

PICTURE AND MASS THEME EXPLAINED

"Mary has been taken into heaven and the entire host of angels rejoices" (ALLELUIA V.)

Mary could well say: *"He Who is mighty has done great things for me"* (GOSPEL). Jesus would not allow her immaculate body to corrupt in the grave.

We on earth rejoice because the immaculate Virgin Mother of God was taken into the glory of heaven in body and soul (PRAYER); and because through the merits and intercession of the Blessed Virgin Mary we hope to be brought to a glorious resurrection (POSTCOMMUNION).

We rejoice with Mary on her Assumption. We rely on Mary through her intercession.

NOW BEGIN MASS AT 1 ON PAGE 35.

INTROIT *Ps. 97* 2

AND a great sign appeared in heaven: a woman clothed with the sun, and the moon was under her feet, and upon her head a crown of twelve stars.* Sing to the Lord a new song, because he has done wonderful things. Glory be, etc.
Turn to 3 *on page 38.*

PRAYER 4

ALMIGHTY God of eternal life by Whom Mary, the immaculate Virgin Mother of Thy Son, was taken into the glory of heaven in body and soul, grant, we beseech Thee, that by keeping our minds ever fixed on heavenly things, we may become worthy to share her glory. Through the same Lord, etc. *Continue below.*

EPISTLE *Judith 13* 5

THE LORD hath blessed thee by His power, because by thee He hath brought our enemies to naught. Blessed art thou, O daughter, by the Lord the most high God, above all women upon the earth. Blessed by the Lord Who made heaven and earth, Who hath directed thee to cutting off the head of the prince of our enemies, because He hath so magnified thy name this day, that thy praise shall not depart out of the mouth of men who shall be mindful of the power of the Lord forever; for that thou hast not spared thy life, by reason of the distress and tribulation of thy people, but hast prevented our ruin in the presence of our God. Thou art the glory of Jerusalem, thou art the joy of Israel, thou art the honor of our people. THANKS BE TO GOD. *Continue below.*

GRADUAL *Ps. 44* 6

HEARKEN, O daughter, and see and incline thy ear. The King shall greatly desire thy beauty. The daughter of the King enters all adorned; of cloth of gold is her raiment. Alleluia, alleluia. Mary has been taken into heaven, and the entire host of angels rejoices. Alleluia. *Turn to* 7 *on page 40.*

GOSPEL *Luke 1* 8

AT THAT TIME Elizabeth was filled with the Holy Spirit, and cried out with a loud voice, saying, "Blessed art thou among women and blessed is the fruit of thy womb! And how have I deserved that the mother of my Lord should come to me? For behold, the moment that the sound of thy greeting came to my ears, the babe in my womb leapt for joy. And blessed is she who has believed, because the things promised her by the Lord shall be accomplished." And Mary said, "My soul magnifies the Lord, and my spirit rejoices in God my saviour; because He has regarded the lowliness of his handmaid; for behold, henceforth all generations shall call me blessed; because He Who is mighty has done great things for me, and holy is His name; and His mercy is from generation to generation on those who fear Him." *Turn to* 9 *on page 41.*

OFFERTORY *Gen. 3* 10

I WILL put enmities between thee and the woman, and thy seed and her seed. *Turn to* 11 *on page 43.*

SECRET 12

MAY THE OFFERING of our devoted service ascend unto Thee, O Lord; and may the ever blessed Virgin Mary, who was taken into Heaven by Thee, so assist us with her prayers, that our hearts, inflamed with love, may ever more yearn after Thee. Through our Lord, etc. *Turn to* 13 *on page 47.*

COMMUNION VERSE 14

ALL generations shall call me blessed; because He Who is mighty has done great things for me. *Turn to* 15 *on page 62.*

POST-COMMUNION 16

WE BESEECH THEE, O Lord, grant us who have partaken of the Sacrament of Life, that through the merits and intercession of that

Blessed Virgin Mary whom Thou hast taken into Heaven we may be brought to a glorious resurrection. Through our Lord, etc. *Turn to* ⑰ *on page 63.*

⑱ Study Perfect Contrition.

¶ ***Perfect Contrition becomes easy by meditating on a Crucifix: "Who" is suffering? "What" is He suffering? "Why?" To feel sorry is not necessary. It is sufficient if the will turns from sin to the love of God.***

¶ ***Perfect Contrition immediately washes away even mortal sin, but in such a case it is necessary to go to Confession before Holy Communion. Hence, there is no reason for ever remaining in sin, « a condition which leads to habits of sinning. Teach the Act of Perfect Contrition to non-Catholics, » especially to one in danger of death. Get the habit of making it yourself. It can save your soul at death if no priest is near for the last Sacraments.***

O MY GOD, I am heartily sorry and beg pardon for all my sins, NOT SO MUCH because these sins bring suffering and hell to me, » but because they have crucified my loving Savior Jesus Christ and offended Thy Infinite Goodness. I firmly resolve, with the help of Thy grace, to confess my sins, to do penance and to amend my life. Amen.

« as ejaculation say frequently »

« in emergency say always »

O MY GOD, I am sorry for having offended Thee, because I love Thee.

PICTURE AND MASS THEME EXPLAINED

"He shall rule . . . unto the ends of the earth . . . All kings . . . shall adore Him, all nations shall serve Him" (GRADUAL).

The "modern" man acts as "monarch of all he surveys" in the study of science, the enjoyment of pleasure, the worship of the State.

Yet we are not the creators of our resources but only the beneficiaries of the Creator. This Feast reaffirms that the *"wounds"* in *"the families of nations"* are caused by sin, namely, the abuse of these borrowed gifts; that *"all things* (must be) *restored in* (Christ)" (PRAYER).

Jesus alone has the right, well earned, as the Redeeming *"Lamb Who was slain"* (INTROIT), to be King over all *"the earth"* (GRADUAL); to be King of *"Truth"* in our minds (GOSPEL); to be King of our wills under the *"standard"* of His Law (POST-COMMUNION); to be King of Love in our hearts (EPISTLE).

"The Lord will bless His people with peace" (COMMUNION VERSE) only when they accept Him as King.

NOW BEGIN MASS AT 1 ON PAGE 35.

INTROIT *Apoc. 5* ②

WORTHY *is the Lamb Who was slain to receive power* and Divinity and wisdom and strength and honor. To Him belong glory and dominion forever and ever.* Give to the King Thy judgment, O God: and to the King's Son Thy justice. Glory be, etc. *Turn to* ③ *on page 38.*

PRAYER ④

O ALMIGHTY, EVERLASTING God, Who hast willed to *restore all things in Thy beloved Son,* King of all the world, grant in Thy mercy that all the *families* of nations, torn asunder by the *wound* of sin, may place themselves under His most gentle rule. Who with Thee liveth, etc. *Continue below.*

EPISTLE *Col. 1* ⑤

BRETHREN, we render thanks to the Father, Who has made us worthy to share the lot of the saints in light. He has rescued us from the power of darkness and transferred us into the kingdom of His beloved Son, in Whom we have our redemption (*through His blood*), the remission of our sins. He is the image of the invisible God, the firstborn of every creature. For in Him were created all things in the heavens and on the earth, things visible and things invisible, whether Thrones, or Dominations, or Principalities, or Powers. All things have been created through and unto Him, and He is before all creatures, and in Him all things hold together. Again, He is the head of His body, the Church; He, Who is the beginning, the firstborn from the dead, that in all things He may have the first place. For it has pleased God the Father that in Him all His fulness should dwell, and that through Him he should reconcile to Himself all things, whether on the earth or in the heavens, making peace through the blood of His cross, in Christ Jesus Our Lord. THANKS BE TO GOD. *Continue below.*

GRADUAL *Ps. 71* ⑥

HE SHALL RULE from sea to sea, and from the river unto the ends of the earth. And all kings of the earth shall adore Him, all nations shall serve Him. Alleluia, alleluia. His power is an everlasting power that shall not be taken away: and His kingdom, a kingdom that shall not be destroyed. Alleluia. *Turn to* ⑦ *on page 40.*

GOSPEL *John 18* ⑧

AT THAT TIME, Pilate said to Jesus: "Art Thou the King of the Jews?" Jesus answered, "Dost thou say this of thyself, or have others told thee of Me?" Pilate answered, "Am I a Jew? Thy own people and the chief priests have delivered Thee to me. What hast Thou done?" Jesus answered, "My kingdom is not of this world. If My kingdom were of this world, My followers would have fought that I might not be delivered to the Jews. But, as it is, My kingdom is not from here." Pilate therefore said to him, "Thou art then a king?" Jesus answered, "Thou sayest it; I am a King. This is why I was born, and why I have come into the world, to bear witness *to the truth.* Everyone who is of the truth hears My voice." *Turn to* ⑨ *on page 41.*

OFFERTORY *Ps. 2* ⑩

ASK OF ME, and I will give Thee the Gentiles for Thy inheritance, and the utmost parts of the earth for Thy possession. *Turn to* ⑪ *on page 43.*

SECRET ⑫

WE OFFER unto Thee, O Lord, this Victim of man's reconciliation to God, imploring this same Jesus Christ, Thy Son and our God, Whom we now immolate in this sacrifice, to grant unto all nations the gifts of His unity and peace. Who with Thee liveth, etc. *Turn to* ⑬ *on page 47.*

COMMUNION VERSE ⑭

THE LORD shall sit a King for ever. The Lord will *bless His people with peace.* *Turn to* ⑮ *on page 62.*

POST-COMMUNION ⑯

HAVING RECEIVED the food of immortality, we pray Thee, O Lord, that we who now glory in striving earnestly under the *standard* of Christ the King, may one day glory in reigning forever with Him in His heavenly court. Who with Thee liveth, etc. *Turn to* ⑰ *on page 63.*

⑱ *Gratitude for Daily Food.*

BEFORE MEALS. Bless us, O Lord, and these Thy gifts, which we are about to receive from Thy bounty, and be Thou the eternal food of our souls, through Christ our Lord. Amen.

AFTER MEALS. We give Thee thanks, O Almighty God, for all Thy benefits, « Who livest and reignest now and forever. Amen. May the souls of the faithful departed, through the mercy of God, rest in peace. Amen.

Feast of All Saints

PICTURE AND MASS THEME EXPLAINED

"Rejoice, . . . your reward is great in heaven" (GOSPEL).

The center emblem, pictured in the Catacombs, represents Christ enthroned. Beneath is the ship of the Church, sailing through the seas of time and eternity. The Martyr holds a cross; the Evangelist, a book; the Virgin, a palm; the Confessor, a sword; the Apostle, a key; the Holy Woman, a scroll.

The EPISTLE lifts the veil, beholding *"a great multitude which no man could number"* entering heaven. Oh, the comforting thought that it is a great multitude!

What are the *laws of entrance?* The Eight Beatitudes (GOSPEL), which clearly indicate that the Christian life is not so much a *"giving up"* but rather an "exchange" of natural "things" for supernatural graces, the prelude to the glory of the Beatific Vision and Union, eternal, without end.

Read, re-read, and memorize this GOSPEL!

NOW BEGIN MASS AT 1 ON PAGE 35.

INTROIT *Ps. 32* **2**

LET US ALL REJOICE in the Lord, celebrating a feast in honor of all the Saints, in whose solemnity the angels rejoice and join in praising the Son of God.* Rejoice in the Lord, ye just: praise becometh the upright. Glory be, etc. *Turn to* ❸ *on page 38.*

PRAYER ❹

O ALMIGHTY and Eternal God, Who hast granted us the favor of honoring the merits of all the Saints on this one Feastday, we beseech Thee, through the intercession of so many Saints, to enrich us with the fulness of Thy much-desired mercy. Through Our Lord, etc. *Continue below.*

EPISTLE ❺
Apoc. 7

IN THOSE DAYS, behold, I, John, saw another angel ascending from the rising of the sun, having the seal of the living God; and he cried with a loud voice to the four angels, who had it in their power to harm the earth and the sea, saying, "Do not harm the earth or the sea or the trees, till we have sealed the servants of our God on their foreheads." And I heard the number of those who were sealed, a hundred and forty-four thousand sealed, out of every tribe of the children of Israel; of the tribe of Juda, twelve thousand sealed; of the tribe of Ruben, twelve thousand; of the tribe of Gad, twelve thousand; of the tribe of Aser, twelve thousand; of the tribe of Nephthali, twelve thousand; of the tribe of Manasses, twelve thousand; of the tribe of Simeon, twelve thousand; of the tribe of Levi, twelve thousand; of the tribe of Issachar, twelve thousand; of the tribe of Zabulon, twelve thousand; of the tribe of Joseph, twelve thousand; of the tribe of Benjamin, twelve thousand sealed. After this I saw a *great multitude which no man could number,* out of all nations and tribes and peoples and tongues, standing before the throne and before the Lamb, clothed in white robes, and with palms in their hands. And they cried with a loud voice, saying, "Salvation belongs to our God Who sits upon the throne, and to the Lamb." And all the angels were standing round about the throne, and the elders and the four living creatures; and they fell on their faces before the throne and worshipped God, saying, "Amen. Blessing and glory and wisdom and thanksgiving and honor and power and strength to our God forever and ever. Amen." THANKS BE TO GOD. *Continue below.*

GRADUAL *Ps. 33* ⑥

FEAR THE LORD, all ye His saints: for there is no want to them that fear Him. But they that seek the Lord shall not be deprived of any good. Alleluia, alleluia. "Come to Me, all you who labor and are burdened, and I will give you rest." Alleluia. *Turn to ⑦ on page 40.*

GOSPEL *Matt. 5* ⑧

AT THAT TIME, Jesus seeing the crowds, went up the mountain. And when He was seated, His disciples came to Him. And opening His mouth He taught them, saying, "Blessed are the *poor in spirit,* for theirs is the kingdom of heaven. Blessed are the *meek,* for they shall possess the earth. Blessed are they who *mourn,* for they shall be comforted. Blessed are they who *hunger* and *thirst for justice,* for they shall be satisfied. Blessed are the *merciful,* for they shall obtain mercy. Blessed are the *pure* of heart, for they shall see God. Blessed are the *peacemakers,* for they shall be called children of God. Blessed are they who *suffer persecution* for justice' sake, for theirs is the kingdom of heaven. Blessed are you when men reproach you, and persecute you, and, speaking falsely, say all manner of evil against you, for my sake. *Rejoice and exult, because your reward is great in heaven." Turn to ⑨ on page 41.*

OFFERTORY *Wis. 3* ⑩

THE SOULS of the just are in the hand of God, and the torment of malice shall not touch them: in the sight of the unwise they seemed to die, but they are in peace. Alleluia. *Turn to ⑪ on page 43.*

SECRET ⑫

WE OFFER TO THEE, O Lord, the gifts of our devotion, that they may be pleasing to Thee in honor of all Thy Saints and also helpful to our salvation by Thy mercy. Through Our Lord, etc. *Turn to ⑬ on page 47.*

COMMUNION VERSE ⑭

"BLESSED are the pure of heart, for they shall see God. Blessed are the peacemakers, for they shall be called children of God. Blessed are they who suffer persecution for justice' sake, for theirs is the kingdom of heaven." *Turn to ⑮ on page 62.*

POST-COMMUNION ⑯

GRANT, we pray Thee, O Lord, that Thy faithful people may ever rejoice in the veneration of all Thy Saints and may they ever be guarded by their perpetual intercession. Through Our Lord, etc. *Turn to ⑰ on page 63.*

⑱ *Pray for Souls in Purgatory,* **page 345.**

† Cross in margin of Ordinary (pages 35, 36, 39, 40, 45, 58, 59, 63), indicates paragraph is omitted in Mass for Dead.

« Use this Mass on All Souls Day, November 2nd; also on any weekday »

INTROIT *Ps. 64* ❷

ETERNAL REST give to them, O Lord; and let perpetual light shine upon them.† A hymn, O God, becometh Thee in Sion; and a vow shall be paid to Thee in Jerusalem: O Lord, hear my prayer; all flesh shall come to Thee. Eternal rest, etc. *Turn to* ❸ *on page 38.*

PRAYER ❹

O GOD, the bestower of pardon and lover of man's salvation, we beseech Thy Clemency, through the intercession of Blessed Mary, ever a Virgin, and all Thy Saints, so that the brethren of our congregation, our relatives and benefactors who have passed out of this world, may together enjoy everlasting happiness. Through our Lord Jesus Christ, Thy Son, Who lives and reigns with Thee in the unity of the Holy Spirit, God, world without end. [R] Amen. *Continue below.*

O GOD, Who art ever inclined to pity and to spare, have mercy on the souls of Thy servants and handmaids, and forgive them all their sins, so that after their departure from this life, they may enter life eternal. *Continue below.*

O GOD, the Creator and Redeemer of all the faithful, grant to the souls of Thy servants and handmaids the remission of all their sins, so that by devout prayers they may obtain the pardon which they ever desired. Who lives and reigns with God the Father, in the unity of the

Holy Spirit, God, world without end. [R] Amen. *Continue below.*

EPISTLE *Apoc. 14* ⑤

IN THOSE DAYS, I heard a voice from heaven saying, "Write: Blessed are the dead who die in the Lord henceforth. Yes, says the Spirit, let them rest from their labors, for their works follow them." [R] THANKS BE TO GOD. *Continue:*

GRADUAL *Ps. 111* ⑥

ETERNAL REST give to them, O Lord; and let perpetual light shine upon them. The just shall be in everlasting remembrance; he shall not fear the evil hearing. [*Tract*] Absolve, O Lord, the souls of all the faithful departed from every bond of sin. And by the help of Thy grace let them be found worthy to escape the sentence of vengeance, and to enjoy the full beatitude of the light eternal. *Turn to* ⑦ *on page 40.*

GOSPEL *John 6* ⑧

AT THAT TIME Jesus said to the crowds of Jews, "I am the living bread that has come down from heaven. If anyone eat of this bread he shall live forever; and the bread that I will give is my flesh for the life of the world." The Jews on that account argued with one another, saying, "How can this man give us his flesh to eat?" Jesus therefore said to them, "Amen, amen, I say to you, unless you eat the flesh of the Son of Man, and drink his blood, you shall not have life in you. He who eats my flesh and drinks my blood has life everlasting and I will raise him up on the last day." *Turn to* ⑨ *on page 41.*

OFFERTORY ⑩

O LORD JESUS CHRIST, the King of glory, deliver

the souls of all the faithful departed from the pains of hell and from the deep pit; deliver them from the lion's mouth, that hell engulf them not, that they fall not into the darkness; but let Michael, the holy standard-bearer, bring them into the holy light which Thou didst promise of old to Abraham and his seed. We offer Thee sacrifices and prayers of praise, O Lord; do Thou accept them for those souls of whom we this day make commemoration; cause them, O Lord, to pass from death to the life which of old Thou didst promise to Abraham and his seed. *Turn to* (11) *on page 43.*

SECRET (12)

O God, Whose Mercy is boundless, mercifully receive our lowly prayers and, through these Sacraments of our salvation, grant the forgiveness of all sin in our brethren, relatives and benefactors who from Thee received the grace of praising Thy Name. Through our Lord Jesus Christ, Thy Son, Who lives and reigns with Thee in the unity of the Holy Spirit, God, world without end. ℟ Amen. *Continue below.*

Consent, we beseech Thee, O Lord, that this sacrifice benefit the souls of Thy servants and handmaids, as Thou has granted so that, by the offering of it, the sins of all the world should be forgiven. *Continue below.*

Mercifully look down, we beseech Thee, O Lord, upon the Sacrifice which we offer Thee for the souls of Thy servants and handmaids, that, to those on whom Thou didst confer the gift of Christian Faith, Thou mayest also grant its reward. Through our Lord Jesus Christ,

Thy Son, Who lives and reigns with Thee in the unity of the Holy Spirit, God. *Turn to* ⑬ *page 47.*

COMMUNION VERSE ⑭

MAY ETERNAL LIGHT shine upon them, O Lord, with Thy Saints forever, because Thou art kind. Grant them everlasting rest, O Lord, and let perpetual light shine upon them, with Thy Saints, for Thou art merciful. *Turn to* ⑮ *page 62.*

POST-COMMUNION ⑯

GRANT, we beseech Thee, O Almighty and Merciful God, that the souls of our brethren, kindred and benefactors, for whom we have offered this Sacrifice of praise to Thy Majesty, being purified of all sins by the virtue of this Sacrament, may, by Thy Mercy, receive the happiness of perpetual light. Through Our Lord Jesus Christ, Thy Son, Who lives and reigns with Thee in the Unity of the Holy Spirit, God, world without end. [R] Amen. *Continue below.*

O GOD, Who alone art competent to administer healing remedies after death, grant, we beseech Thee, that the souls of Thy servants and handmaids, rid of earthly contagion, may be numbered among those whom Thou hast redeemed. *Continue below.*

MAY OUR PRAYERS of petition help the souls of Thy servants and handmaids, we beseech Thee, O Lord, so that Thou mayest free them from all sin and give them a share in Thy Redemption. Who lives and reigns, with God the Father, in the unity of the Holy Spirit, God, world without end. *Turn to* ⑰ *on page 63.*

⑱ ***Read "Souls in Purgatory", page 345.***

PRAYERS to be MEMORIZED

THE LORD'S PRAYER — See Page 57.

THE ANGEL'S SALUTE TO MARY. HAIL Mary, full of grace! The Lord is with thee: blessed art thou amongst women, and blessed is the fruit of thy womb, Jesus. Holy Mary, Mother of God, pray for us sinners, now and at the hour of our death. Amen.

THE APOSTLES' CREED. I BELIEVE IN GOD, the Father Almighty, Creator of heaven and earth; and in Jesus Christ, His only Son, our Lord; Who was conceived by the Holy Ghost, born of the Virgin Mary, suffered under Pontius Pilate, was crucified, died, and was buried. He descended into hell; the third day He arose again from the dead: He ascended into heaven, sitteth at the right hand of God, the Father Almighty: from thence He shall come to judge the living and the dead. I believe in the Holy Ghost, the holy Catholic Church, the communion of saints, the forgiveness of sins, the resurrection of the body, and life everlasting. Amen.

AN ACT of FAITH. O MY GOD, I firmly believe that Thou art one God in three Divine Persons, Father, Son, and Holy Ghost; I believe that Thy Divine Son became man, and died for our sins, and that He will come to judge the living and the dead. I believe these and all the truths which the Holy Catholic Church teaches, because Thou hast revealed them, Who canst neither deceive nor be deceived.

AN ACT of HOPE. O MY GOD, relying on Thy infinite goodness and promises, I hope to obtain pardon of my sins, the help of Thy grace, and life everlasting, through the merits of Jesus Christ, my Lord and Redeemer.

AN ACT of LOVE. O MY GOD, I love Thee above all things, with my whole heart and soul, because Thou art all-good and worthy of all love. I love my neighbor as myself for the love of Thee. I forgive all who have injured me, and ask pardon of all whom I have injured.

MEMORIZE "COMMANDMENTS," page 299, and "Examination of Conscience," page 337.

MORNING PRAYERS

BAPTISM. The Sacrament by which I began a new day, receiving God's own Life, when I was born again as a member of Christ's Mystical Body, the Church! cleansed from original sin, made a Christian, a child of God and an heir of heaven! The new day when I took an oath of allegiance to serve under Christ, the King of all life.

✠ In the Name of the Father, and of the Son, and of the Holy Ghost. Amen. (Always bless yourself on rising). Our Father, etc.; Hail, Mary, etc.; Glory be, etc.

O LORD GOD ALMIGHTY, Who hast safely brought us to the beginning of a new day, defend us this day by Thy Power, so that we may not only turn away from all sin, but also that our every thought, word and deed may proceed from and be directed according to Thy Will. Through our Lord Jesus Christ, Thy Son, Who lives and reigns with Thee in the unity of the Holy Spirit, God, world without end. Amen.

RENEWAL of BAPTISMAL VOWS

I RENEW my baptismal vows, I renounce Satan and all his works and all his pomps, I take JESUS CHRIST for my Model and my Guide and I promise to be faithful to Him unto the end of my life. Amen.

CONFIRMATION. *The Sacrament by which I received the Holy Spirit to make me a strong, perfect Christian and soldier of Jesus Christ; to fight Antichrist inside and outside myself; to be a co-worker with Christ in every form of Catholic Action.*

RENEWAL of CONFIRMATION GRACES

O MY GOD, I thank Thee for all Thy infinite Goodness in sending down upon my soul Thy Holy Spirit with all His Gifts and graces. O, may He take full possession of me forever. May His heavenly Wisdom reign in my heart; His Understanding enlighten my darkness; His Counsel guide me; His Fortitude strengthen me; His Knowledge instruct me; His Piety make me fervent; His divine Fear keep me from all evil. Give me grace to be Thy faithful soldier, so that by fighting the good fight of faith, I may be brought to the crown of eternal life by the merits of Thy Son and our Savior, Jesus Christ. Amen.

EVENING PRAYERS

PENANCE. *The Sacrament by which, as a repentant sinner, I receive forgiveness even of mortal sin, and thus become again a living member of Christ's Mystical Body. Tonight, therefore, I shall examine my conscience in preparation for a full Confession, realizing that I must have a genuine sorrow for sin, together with a determination to sin no more.*

ETERNAL FATHER, I offer Thee the Sacred Heart of Jesus, with all Its Love, all Its sufferings and all Its merits: TO EXPIATE all the sins I have committed this day, and during all my life. Glory be to the Father, etc.

TO PURIFY the good I have done in my poor way this day, and during all my life. Glory be to the Father, etc.

TO MAKE UP for the good I ought to have done and that I have neglected this day, and during all my life. Glory be to the Father, etc.

Recite Acts of Faith, Hope, Love (page 329), Contrition (page 338).

EXTREME UNCTION. *Each night I should pray for this "Last Anointing" (however near or distant it may be). This Sacrament, received worthily, will insure my death in Christ's friendship. It is the greatest grace we can ask of God! A happy death means a heaven of eternal happiness. A bad death means a hell of eternal misery.*

An ACT of RESIGNATION

MY LORD GOD, even now I accept at Thy hands, cheerfully and willingly, with all its anxieties, pains and sufferings, whatever kind of death it shall please Thee to be mine. Amen. (*7 years ind. each time*). *(Plenary Indulgence, under the usual conditions, the Our Father, the Hail Mary and Glory Be to the Father once for our Holy Father's intentions; to be applied at death, if recited the next time you go to the Sacraments.)*

JESUS, MARY, JOSEPH, I give you my heart and my soul. JESUS, MARY, JOSEPH, assist me in my last agony. JESUS, MARY, JOSEPH, may I breathe forth my soul in peace with You. Amen. (*7 years indulgence*).

PROTECTION DURING the NIGHT

VISIT, we beseech Thee, O Lord, this house, and drive far from it all snares of the enemy. May Thy holy Angels dwell herein to keep us in peace, and may Thy blessing be on us always. Amen.

COMMUNE with GOD DURING the DAY

HOLY EUCHARIST. ***Every one of us frequently thinks, speaks of God during each day, sometimes even taking His Name in vain. Develop the good habit of silent ejaculatory prayer. In such spiritual communing with God or by any simple aspiration of the soul, even a "prayer without words" while at work, during a temptation or while carrying a cross, you will thereby prepare for sacramental Communion. By this Sacrament of His very Body and Blood, His Soul and Divinity, Jesus satisfies man's instinctive hunger for a personal union with his God.***

(*Memorize, recite frequently during the day*).

MY JESUS, mercy! (*300 days Ind.*) . . . All for Thee, O most Sacred Heart of Jesus (*300 days Ind.*) . . . Blessed be God! (*50 days Ind., if recited upon hearing a blasphemy*) . . . Grant, O Lord, that I may know Thy Will and do it (*300 days Ind.*) . . . My God, I love Thee (*300 days Ind.*) . . . O Jesus, save me (*300 days Ind.*) . . . Sacred Heart of Jesus, I put my trust in Thee (*300 days Ind.*) . . . Mother of Mercy, pray for us (*300 days Ind.*) . . . Merciful Lord Jesus, give them (him, her) everlasting rest (*300 days Ind., applicable to the dead*).

MATRIMONY. *Jesus has promised to bless the house where the Image of His Sacred Heart is exposed and honored. Once a week, set a time, when the family gathers together, at meal time or at evening prayers and recite this*

CONSECRATION of FAMILY

O JESUS, behold our family prostrate before Thee. Once more do we consecrate ourselves to Thee — our trials and joys — that our home, like Thine, may ever be the shrine of peace, purity, love, labor and faith. Do Thou protect and bless all of us, absent and present, living and dead.

O MARY, loving Mother of Jesus — and our Mother — pray to Jesus for our family, for all the families of the world, to guard the cradle of the newborn, the schools of the young and their vocations.

O JOSEPH, Holy Guardian of Jesus and Mary, assist us by thy prayers in all the necessities of life. Ask of Jesus that special grace which He granted to thee, to watch over our home at the pillow of the sick and the dying, so that with Mary and with thee, Heaven may find our family unbroken in the Sacred Heart of Jesus. Amen.

OFFER SATURDAY for PRIESTS

HOLY ORDERS. *Priests are messengers of God's Truth, dispensers of His Sacraments, announcers of Divine Law. They are ordained for your sake. For their sake, in union with Mary, Mother of the High Priest, give all of Saturday to God for His priests.* *(See Catechism, page 252).*

DIVINE SAVIOR JESUS CHRIST, Who hast entrusted the whole work of Thy Redemption, the welfare and salvation of the world, to priests as Thy representatives, I offer Thee through the hands of Thy most holy Mother, all the prayers, works, sacrifices, joys and sorrows of this day for the sanctification of Thy priests. Give us truly holy priests who seek nothing but Thy greater glory and the salvation of our souls. Bless their words and prayers at the altar, in the confessional, in the pulpit, in all their work for the young, the sick and the aged. Do thou, O Mary, Mother of the High Priest, protect all priests from dangers to their holy vocation. Obtain for me a true spirit of faith and humble obedience so that I may ever behold the priest as the representative of God and willingly follow him in the Way, the Truth and the Life of Christ. Amen.

Preparation for CONFESSION

O MY GOD, grant me light to be truly sorry for my sins. To think that I have offended Thee after being forgiven so many times! I lay the rest of my life at Thy feet. How much more there is to come, I know not, but long or short, let it atone for my past. Mary, my Mother, help me to make a good confession.

CONFESSION—EXAMINE CONSCIENCE

In My DUTIES to GOD

Neglect morning or evening prayer . . . Superstitious practices . . . Consulting Fortune Tellers . . . Receiving Sacraments sacrilegiously . . . Against FAITH by wilful doubts concerning any article of the Creed or by reading or circulating irreligious books . . . Against HOPE by despair, murmuring or presuming on God's Mercy . . . Against CHARITY by wilfully rebellious thoughts against God, or His Law or by omitting good works through fear of others.

Irreverence towards God, His Name, His Church . . . Cursing or swearing . . . False, unlawful and unnecessary oaths . . . Breaking lawful vows . . . Neglecting Mass on Sundays and Holydays, or performing unrequired servile work.

In My DUTIES to My NEIGHBOR

Insulting or neglecting parents . . . Failing to send children to religious schools when possible . . . Bad example . . . Neglect of home, trade, professional, civil service duties . . . Ignoring the spiritual and corporal works of mercy . . . Any violent act . . . Causing hard feeling . . . Revenge . . . Refusing reconciliation . . . Inducing others to sin. Stealing (what value or damage) . . . Possession of illgotten goods . . . Cheating . . . Culpable delay in paying lawful debts . . . Lying . . . Perjury . . . Fraud . . . Slander or detraction or rash judgments . . . Failure to support my Church.

In RELATION to MYSELF

Obstinacy . . . Sloth . . . Desiring or yielding to sensuality, impurity, gluttony, drunkenness . . . Rage, envy, impatience, jealousy . . . Failure to fast or abstain . . . Failure to make my Easter Duty . . . Waste of time, monev or talents.

ACT of CONTRITION

O MY GOD! I am heartily sorry for having offended Thee, and I detest all my sins, because I dread the loss of heaven and the pains of hell, but most of all because I have offended Thee, my God, Who art all good and deserving of all my love. I firmly resolve, with the help of Thy grace, to confess my sins, to do penance, and to amend my life. Amen.

STUDY PERFECT CONTRITION

¶*Perfect Contrition washes away even mortal sin, but in such a case it is necessary to go to Confession before Holy Communion. It may save your soul at death if no priest is near for the Sacraments.*

¶*Perfect Contrition becomes easy by meditating on a Crucifix: "Who" is suffering? "What" is He suffering? "Why?"*

¶ *Teach this Act of Perfect Contrition to non-Catholics, especially to one near death.*

O MY GOD, I am heartily sorry and beg pardon for all my sins, NOT SO MUCH because these sins bring suffering and Hell to me, but because they have crucified my loving Saviour Jesus Christ and offended Thy Infinite Goodness. I firmly resolve, with the help of Thy grace, to confess my sins, to do penance and to amend my life. Amen.

or as Ejaculation say frequently

O MY GOD, I am sorry for having offended Thee, because I love Thee.

Holy Communion—Prepare—Give Thanks

The use of "My Sunday Missal" during Mass is the best way to "prepare." All the "Acts" are contained in the Mass prayers, which stress not only your privilege to "receive" Christ, but also to "give" yourself.

The Sacrament remains within you at least fifteen minutes—a time for communing with God, personally, intimately: you speaking to God; God speaking to you.

✚✚✚ PRAYER BEFORE A CRUCIFIX ✚✚✚

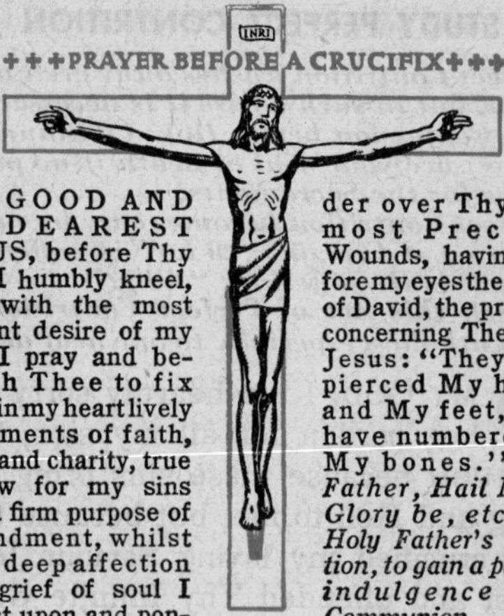

O GOOD AND DEAREST JESUS, before Thy face I humbly kneel, and with the most fervent desire of my soul I pray and beseech Thee to fix deep in my heart lively sentiments of faith, hope and charity, true sorrow for my sins and a firm purpose of amendment, whilst with deep affection and grief of soul I reflect upon and ponder over Thy five most Precious Wounds, having before my eyes the words of David, the prophet, concerning Thee, my Jesus: "They have pierced My hands and My feet, they have numbered all My bones." *Our Father, Hail Mary, Glory be, etc., for Holy Father's intention, to gain a plenary indulgence after Communion.*

WHAT SHALL I GIVE THEE?

I HAVE RECEIVED into my heart Jesus Christ, His Body and Blood, Soul and Divinity. I begin this day, as a day in Heaven. He is in my soul the Divine Infant in the crib, the growing Boy at Nazareth, the Apostle acclaimed by crowds on the roads of Galilee, the Miracle-Worker Who performed such prodigies, the Martyr Who completed His Sacrifice on Calvary.

And now, O good Master, what shall I give Thee in exchange for Thy visit . . .?

I would like to pray to Thee with the burning words of Thy Mother and her court of Heaven, but I feel riveted to earthly things . . . .

I would like to offer Thee courageous loyalty to my Baptismal Vows and Confirmation Graces but alas, I have so often been disloyal. . . .

I would like, at least, to have a desire for the Christian life, but I allow myself to be discouraged by my failures. . . .

O good Jesus, I have nothing to give Thee, and Thou hast given Everything; Thou hast given Thyself to me. I can only join my poor voice in the chorus of praise to Thee, rising out of all the works of Thy Creation here on earth. . . .

With fifteen hundred millions now living on earth, *I shall praise Thy Mercy!* May our voices unite with the billions of those who inhabited the earth before us, and out of whose dust the beauty of Nature perpetually rises to *praise Thy Glory!*

May an infinite concert of voices from cottages and palaces, from fields and forests, from towns and deserts, from workshops and cathedrals, from earth and from heaven, from time and from eternity, arise to give my thanks unto Thee! Amen.

12 PROMISES to ST. MARGARET MARY

1. Heart of Jesus, give us all the graces necessary for our state in life. *Thou hast promised it, O Jesus!*

2. Heart of Jesus, grant peace to our families. *Thou hast promised it, O Jesus!*

3. Heart of Jesus, console us in all our sorrows. *Thou hast promised it, O Jesus!*

4. Heart of Jesus, be our safe Refuge during life, and above all at the hour of our death. *Thou hast promised it, O Jesus!*

5. Heart of Jesus, pour abundant blessings on all our labors. *Thou hast promised it, O Jesus!*

6. Heart of Jesus, be for sinners the Source and Infinite Ocean of Mercy. *Thou hast, etc.*

7. Heart of Jesus, make indifferent souls fervent. *Thou hast promised it, O Jesus!*

8. Heart of Jesus, make fervent souls advance rapidly to perfection. *Thou hast promised, etc.*

9. Heart of Jesus, bless the houses where Thine Image is exposed and honored. *Thou, etc.*

10. Heart of Jesus, give to priests the power of touching the most hardened hearts. *Thou, etc.*

11. Heart of Jesus, engrave on Thy Heart forever the names of those who propagate this devotion. *Thou hast promised it, O Jesus!*

12. Heart of Jesus, give those who RECEIVE HOLY COMMUNION NINE CONSECUTIVE FIRST FRIDAYS, the grace of final repentance, that they may not die under Thy displeasure, but, strengthened by the reception of the Sacraments, may Thy Heart be their secure refuge at their last hour. *Thou hast promised it, O Jesus!*

MEDITATE on the ROSARY

IT IS the special prayer to Our Lady. The oftener we say it, the more we shall love it. It brings us the special blessing of God, particularly when the family recites it together. On Indulgenced Beads, it is powerful in relieving souls in Purgatory.

In each mystery, Mary shows us a picture of Christ. Meditate on it. Ask for the grace suggested by each mystery.

JOYFUL MYSTERIES — Monday, Thursday

1. ANNUNCIATION to obtain Humility.
2. VISITATION to obtain Love for neighbor.
3. BIRTH OF CHRIST to obtain Detachment from the World.
4. PRESENTATION OF JESUS to obtain Respect for Authority.
5. FINDING OF JESUS to obtain Love of Jesus.

SORROWFUL MYSTERIES — Tuesday, Friday

1. AGONY OF JESUS to obtain Resignation to God's Will.
2. SCOURGING to obtain Spirit of Purity.
3. CROWNING WITH THORNS to obtain Moral Courage.
4. CARRYING OF CROSS to obtain Patience in Adversity.
5. CRUCIFIXION to obtain Sorrow for Sin.

GLORIOUS MYSTERIES
Sunday, Wednesday, Saturday

1. RESURRECTION to obtain Increase of Faith.
2. ASCENSION to obtain Increase of Hope.
3. DESCENT OF HOLY GHOST to obtain Increase of Love.
4. ASSUMPTION to obtain Devotion to Mary.
5. CROWNING OF MARY to obtain Grace of Perseverance.

MY VOCATION IN LIFE

¶ ***Pray fervently to make the right choice of the married, single or "religious" life. On it depends the happiness of your own soul and other souls in this life and for all eternity.***

BEHOLD ME at thy feet, O Virgin most kind, seeking to obtain through thee, the most important grace of knowing what I ought to do. I desire nothing but to comply perfectly with the Will of thy Divine Son at every moment of my life. Mother of Good Counsel, let me hear thy voice. It will dispel every doubt that troubles my mind.

I trust in thee, being confident that, since thou art the Mother of my Redeemer, thou wilt also be the Mother of my salvation. If thou, O Mary, wilt not send me a ray of the Divine Sun, what light will enlighten me? Who will direct me if thou refusest, who art the Mother of the uncreated Wisdom?

Listen, then, to my humble prayers. Let me not be lost in my uncertainty and instability; lead me along the straight road that ends in life everlasting, thou who art my only hope, and whose hands are full of the riches of virtue and of life, and who dispensest the fruits of honor and holiness. *300 days Ind. once a day.*

FOR and TO the HOLY SOULS

ALL YOU ANGELS of Consolation, go and visit those patient sufferers, offer for them the merits of the Sacred Hearts of Jesus, Mary, and Joseph, and obtain their speedy union with Jesus, Whose vision is bliss, and Who yearns to have them with Him.

O sweet brethren, so mightily afflicted, knowing your fear and love of God and your charity for souls, pray for us that we may speedily obtain what we now ask for our urgent needs and also the grace of a good life and a holy death. Amen.

FOR OUR OWN BELOVED DEAD

GOOD JESUS, Whose loving Heart was ever troubled by the sorrows of others, look with pity on the souls of our dear ones in Purgatory. O You, Who "Loved Your Own," hear our cry for mercy, and grant that those whom You called from our homes and hearts, may soon enjoy everlasting rest in the home of Thy Love in Heaven. Amen.

Eternal rest grant unto them, O Lord. And let perpetual light shine on them. Amen.

May their souls and the souls of all the faithful departed, through the mercy of God, rest in peace. Amen.

7 BLOODSHEDDINGS: 1—*Circumcision.* 2—*Agony.* 3—*Scourging.* 4—*Crowning with thorns.* 5—*Carries Cross.* 6—*Crucifixion.* 7—*Heart pierced.*

NOVENA to the PRECIOUS BLOOD

O JESUS, Who hast said, "Ask, and it shall be given you; seek, and you shall find; knock, and it shall be opened to you," with Mary, Thy Most Holy Mother, and through the merits of Thy Most Precious Blood, I seek, I knock, and I ask that my prayers may be heard. *Glory, etc.*

O JESUS, Who hast said, "If you ask the Father in My Name, He will give it to you," with Mary, Thy Most Holy Mother, and through the merits of Thy Most Precious Blood, I humbly and earnestly ask that my prayers may be heard. *Glory be to the Father, etc.*

ETERNAL FATHER, I offer Thee the Most Precious Blood of Jesus Christ, the merits, love and sufferings of His Sacred Heart, the tears and sorrows of our Immaculate Mother, as the price of the favor I wish to obtain from Thine Infinite Goodness. Amen.

7 SORROWS: 1—*Simeon's prophecy.* 2—*Flight to Egypt.* 3—*Jesus lost.* 4—*Way to Calvary.* 5—*Jesus dies.* 6—*Descent from Cross.* 7—*Jesus buried.*

NOVENA to SORROWFUL MOTHER

O MARY, Mother of Sorrows, I beseech Thee, by the bitter agony thou didst endure at the foot of the Cross, offer to the Eternal Father, in my name, thy Beloved Son, Jesus, all covered with Blood and Wounds, in satisfaction for my sins, for the needs of Holy Church, the conversion of sinners, the relief of the Souls in Purgatory, and for the special grace I now implore. Amen. *Mention your request.*

The MIRACULOUS MEDAL

MAY thy special aid be granted to those who wear thy Medal. . . . May it be their strength in combat and their all powerful shield against their enemies. . . . May it bring consolation to those who weep, solace to the afflicted. . . . May it, at the hour of death, be the pledge of a glorious eternity. . . . Amen.

O Mary, conceived without sin, pray for us who have recourse to thee. *100 days Ind. once a day.*

TO JOSEPH

7 JOYS: **1**—*Told of Incarnation.* **2**—*Angels adore Infant.* **3**—*Gives name to Jesus.* **4**—*Adoration by wise men.* **5**—*Prophecy of salvation.* **6**—*Return to Nazareth.* **7**—*Jesus found in temple.*

NOVENA to ST. JOSEPH

O GLORIOUS ST. JOSEPH, appointed by the Eternal Father as the guardian and protector of the life of Jesus Christ, the comfort and support of His Holy Mother, and the instrument in His great design for the Redemption of mankind; thou who hadst the happiness of living with Jesus and Mary, and of dying in Their arms, be moved with the confidence we place in thee, and procure for us from the Almighty, the particular favors which we humbly ask through thine intercession.

Here ask the favors you wish to obtain.

PRAY for us, then, O great Saint Joseph, and by thy love for Jesus and Mary, and by Their love for thee, obtain for us the supreme happiness of living and dying in the love of Jesus and Mary. Amen.